STORM OVER
KOKODA

*Dedicated to the memory of Sergeant David Stuart Brown,
a pilot of 75 Squadron, Royal Australian Air Force,
executed while a prisoner of war,
on or about 4 November 1942,
aged 25 years.*

STORM OVER KOKODA

Australia's epic battle for the skies of New Guinea, 1942

PETER EWER

A combination of metric and Imperial measurements are used in this book. As the imperial system was officially used during the time of the Kokoda campaign any material (e.g., diary extracts) from that era uses the imperial system.

Imperial to metric
1 inch = 25.4 millimetres
1 foot = 30.5 centimetres
1 yard = 0.914 metres
1 mile = 1.61 kilometres
1 knot = 1.852 km/h
1 acre = 0.405 hectares
1 pound = 0.453 kilograms
1 ton (long, UK) = 1.016 tonnes
1 ton (short, US) = 0.907 184 74 tonne

Metric to imperial
1 centimetre = 0.394 inches
1 metre = 3.28 feet
1 metre = 1.09 yards
1 kilometre = 0.621 miles
1 km/h = 0.54 knots
1 hectare = 2.47 acres
1 kilogram = 2.204 pounds
1 tonne = 0.984 tons (long, UK)
1 tonne = 1.102 tons (long, US)

Published in 2011 by Pier 9, an imprint of Murdoch Books Pty Limited

Murdoch Books Australia
Pier 8/9
23 Hickson Road
Millers Point NSW 2000
Phone: +61 (0) 2 8220 2000
Fax: +61 (0) 2 8220 2558
www.murdochbooks.com.au

Murdoch Books UK Limited
Erico House, 6th Floor
93–99 Upper Richmond Road
Putney, London SW15 2TG
Phone: +44 (0) 20 8785 5995
Fax: +44 (0) 20 8785 5985
www.murdochbooks.co.uk

Publisher: Diana Hill
Designer: Simon Rattray
Editor: Janine Flew
Project Editor: Paul O'Beirne
Production: Joan Beal

Text copyright © Peter Ewer 2011
The moral right of the author has been asserted.
Design copyright © Murdoch Books Pty Limited 2011

Every reasonable effort has been made to trace the owners of copyright materials in this book, but in some instances this has proven impossible. The author(s) and publisher will be glad to receive information leading to more complete acknowledgments in subsequent printings of the book and in the meantime extend their apologies for any omissions.

All rights reserved. No part of this publication may be reproduced, stored in a retrieval system or transmitted in any form or by any means, electronic, mechanical, photocopying, recording or otherwise, without the prior written permission of the publisher.

National Library of Australia Cataloguing-in-Publication Data
Author: Ewer, Peter.
Title: Storm Over Kokoda : the air war for New Guinea, 1942 / Peter Ewer.
ISBN: 978-1-74266-095-0 (pbk.)
Notes: Includes index.
Subjects: Australia. Royal Australian Air Force. Fighter Squadron 75.
               World War, 1939–1945—Aerial operations, Australian.
               World War, 1939–1945—Campaigns—Papua New Guinea—Kokoda.
               World War, 1939–1945—Participation, Australian.
Dewey Number: 940.542651

A catalogue record for this book is available from the British Library.

Printed and bound in Australia by Griffin Press.

CONTENTS

CHAPTER ONE
'... a continuous lessening of the probability of an attack' **6**

CHAPTER TWO
'... Japanese fighting morale is excellent' **37**

CHAPTER THREE
'... we were content to let the enemy assume the initiative ...' **63**

CHAPTER FOUR
'We just got our beer ...' **80**

CHAPTER FIVE
'... a beautiful aeroplane to fly' **96**

CHAPTER SIX
'Step on it! Can't you drive any faster?' **121**

CHAPTER SEVEN
'Hey, Daddy, I want a diamond ring ...' **138**

CHAPTER EIGHT
'... shot my plane to bits' **162**

CHAPTER NINE
'... I've never been so scared in my life' **186**

CHAPTER TEN
'... our grief was overwhelming' **209**

References ... 241
Notes ... 244
Text credits ... 251
Acknowledgments ... 252
Image credits ... 252
Index ... 253

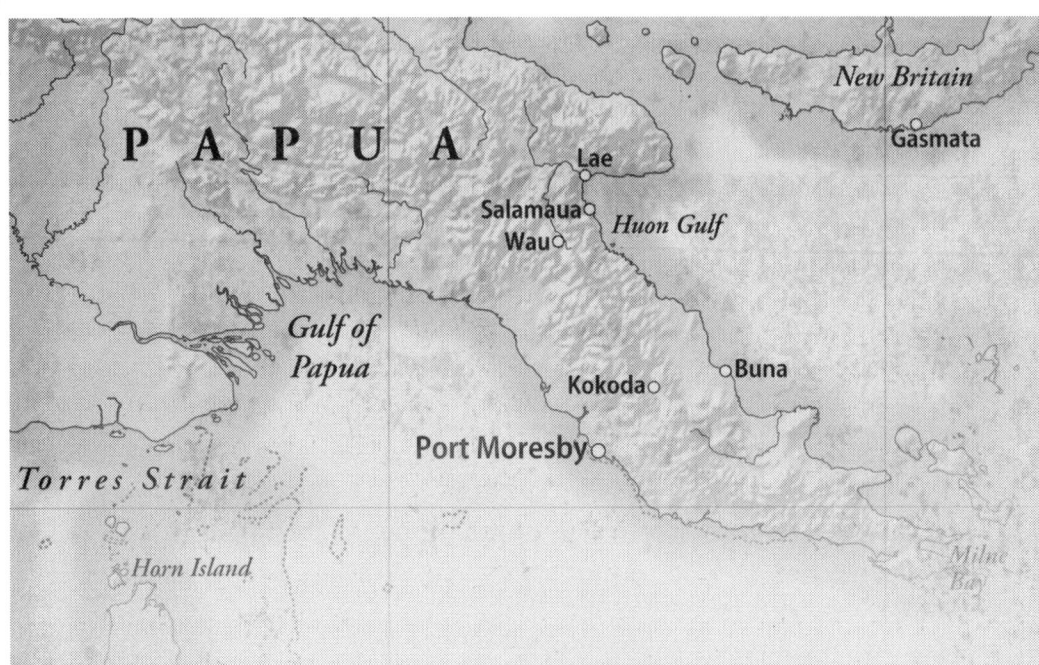

CHAPTER ONE
'... a continuous lessening of the probability of an attack'

Just 300 metres above the Bismarck Sea, Tom Keen, a twenty-five-year-old Queenslander from Townsville, scanned the horizon. The date: 21 January 1942. The mission: to find a Japanese task force that had devastated, just hours before, the Australian base at Rabaul, New Britain.

Keen was aboard a Catalina flying boat of 11 Squadron, Royal Australian Air Force (RAAF), one of the handful of combat aircraft operating out of Port Moresby. Key to the defence of New Guinea, Moresby formed the gateway to the Coral Sea, and thus served as an advance guard for the cities of Australia's east coast. Piloted by an American on exchange with the RAAF, Lieutenant G. Hutchinson, the big flying boat lifted off from Port Moresby harbour at 9.30 am.

The crew were no doubt anxious as they flew north, over Kokoda and across the rugged Owen Stanley Ranges that provide a mountainous spine to the island of New Guinea. The Japanese flotilla they sought had smashed with ease the modest defences of Rabaul. Opposed by a mere handful of Australian aircrews, flying low-performance Wirraway training planes, and by anti-aircraft gunners whose training consisted of tracking model planes stuck on the end of a bamboo pole, the elite Japanese pilots had blasted shipping, aerodromes and gun emplacements.

Having cast aside the defenders of Rabaul, which way would the Japanese now turn? West, to raid the rich gold-town of Lae on the north coast of New Guinea, or south, into the Coral Sea, to bombard the Australian garrison at Port Moresby, and perhaps keep going to sever its vital supply route running through Cooktown and Townsville in north Queensland?

Tom Keen found out soon enough. The shipping search required of him and his comrades meant the Catalina was down low, close to the unfriendly immensity of the tropical sea. The mighty flying boat got as far as 60 kilometres from Lae. Posted at the starboard observation blister, one of two 'glass-houses' on either side of the Catalina's fuselage, just before 1 pm Keen took in a sight to dry the throat and turn the stomach—twelve

Japanese fighter planes, the fabulous Mitsubishi Zeroes, flying parallel to the Australian crew, but headed in the opposite direction, towards Lae.

The odds were long, and Hutchinson needed to shorten them, and quickly. He yanked the big Cat into a climb, as steep as his straining Pratt & Whitney motors could manage, looking for the sanctuary of cloud cover at 2000 metres. Back at his observation post, Keen readied his guns; symbols of Australian defence preparedness, these were antique Lewis machine guns, of the sort that did battle with the Red Baron in the sky over Flanders in 1917.

The Japanese meanwhile let the Australians pass by, only to swing around to make their firing passes from astern. Five Zeroes were detached from the larger formation to deal with the Catalina. To co-ordinate the defence, co-pilot Tom Rowe left the flight-deck and made his way to the rear of the aircraft. Tall, athletic and just twenty-two, Rowe had been studying hard only a few months before, looking to graduate as an engineer from the University of Melbourne. Rowe's service record bore witness to his age: it describes his complexion as 'fresh'.

Still, this young man did his best, standing in the middle of the fuselage, between Keen and John Craigie, who crewed the port blister. An older man at twenty-nine, Craigie was not even trained as an air-gunner, but served as a fitter–armourer. The Australian flying crews, often called to remote locations throughout New Guinea and the Solomon Islands, invariably performed their own maintenance work away from base, and doubtless, with little combat training, Craigie was pressed into service as a gunner to supplement his principal role.

With the Japanese about to make their deadly firing passes, Rowe directed the reply of his gunners, and called out evasive manoeuvres to Hutchinson on the flight-deck. But the Japanese knew their quarry well enough. To break up Rowe's defensive fire, the Japanese pilots fanned out. Keen saw a puff of smoke appear in front of one—immediately, his Perspex bubble blew to pieces, as shells raked the Catalina's fuselage.

A Catalina of 11 Squadron on patrol near Port Moresby before the war; the fuselage blisters in which the likes of Tom Keen fought back with antique machine guns are clearly visible.

The long-range cannon of the Japanese fighters meant they scored the first hits, and only when the Zeroes closed in did they come within reach of the feeble guns used by the Australians. Keen opened up, and Rowe exclaimed, 'You've got him', as the Japanese pilot dived away. But the flying boat was still taking hits. As Craigie opened fire from the port hatch, Keen felt the fuselage shudder from a cannon strike.

The Zeroes were now swarming over the hapless Catalina. For Keen, events became a blur. Craigie slumped over his guns, holding his shoulder. A fire broke out somewhere in the cabin. Through the intercom, Keen heard Hutchinson announce that he was trying to jettison the bomb load, but communications then went dead. Back at the Port Moresby base, radio operators heard the Catalina report 'on fire', suggesting that wireless operator Sergeant Doug Coote, a twenty-nine-year-old South

Australian from Port Elliot, was still manning his set in the cabin behind the cockpit, even as the plane went down in flames.

Back in the hull compartment, the fabric partitions around Keen's blister were ablaze. The sights on his Lewis guns were shot away. Although still in a climbing attitude, the flying boat was actually losing height, sinking through the air with its nose high. Craigie was seemingly dead, and Rowe nowhere to be seen amid the smoke and flames. Within seconds, the aircraft slipped into a dive, albeit with wings level, and Keen decided it was time to get out. He scrambled around the compartment looking for his parachute harness, and noticed the bombs still aboard, a sign that Hutchinson on the flight-deck was probably dead, having failed to jettison the load. Alarmed that the blaze might detonate the explosives, and without his harness properly fitted, Keen bailed out. In mid-air, he forced the pack down in front of him, held it with one hand and pulled on the rip cord with the other.

When the chute opened, the jolt split open Keen's mouth, but this injury soon paled in comparison to the fate intended for him by one Japanese pilot. Not satisfied with crippling the Catalina, as Keen drifted helplessly a Zero pilot set out to kill him. Turning towards the dangling Australian, the Japanese fighter began a firing pass. The pilot missed, but so close was the stream of lead that Keen thought he felt the shells go past his left leg. To deter another attack, Keen lolled in his harness, feigning death. Soon an explosion rocked him back and forth across the sky. The Catalina had crashed to earth, having got as far as the coast, hitting a ridge in a fireball that consumed the wreckage and those still aboard. Keen dropped into the trees nearly two kilometres away, and came to rest three metres from the ground, his silk canopy snarled on that of the green jungle.

Keen was the sole survivor of this vicious combat. Shocked, and driven near-mad by thirst, made worse by licking the blood from his injured mouth, he was rescued by villagers and delivered safely to a nearby

Christian mission. (The RAAF Official History later blandly described Keen as landing 'unhurt'.) The missionaries inspected the crash site, but the only trace they could find of the crew were two revolvers, so badly damaged that the wooden stocks had burnt away. While Keen endured a trek through the jungle to Lae, the Japanese aircraft that had shot him down had already attacked the town, and nearby Salamaua, in softening-up raids for a later invasion.

The air war for New Guinea had begun, and the Japanese looked to hold every advantage.

Winston Churchill made famous 'The Few', the thousand-plus fighter pilots who in the service of the RAF's Fighter Command won the Battle of Britain and thereby changed the course of world history. In early 1942, Australia had its own 'Few', and they too changed the course of the conflict. In the key weeks between January and May 1942, a handful of Australian aircrew 'held the line' in New Guinea. Their resistance forced the Japanese into ever-larger operations to take Port Moresby, first by direct assault, a plan blocked by the US Navy at the Battle of the Coral Sea, and second by an overland march from the north coast of New Guinea, a venture halted by Australian troops on the bloody Kokoda Track.

Success greeted the Allies in these later campaigns, but none of them would have been possible without Australia's 'Few'. This is their story. They were even smaller in number than the pilots of Fighter Command, numbering only in the dozens, and very poorly equipped in contrast to the young men who prevailed in the skies of Kent and Surrey. At exactly the same time that Keen was attempting to deal with modern fighter aircraft equipped only with World War I machine guns, others from his unit were conducting combat missions aboard civilian aircraft. These were Empire flying boats requisitioned from QANTAS, and although fitted with bomb racks, they had no defensive weapons of any kind, leaving them at the mercy of any Japanese machine they came across.

How had it come to this? In 1918, Australian airmen left the skies of France and Palestine among the foremost practitioners of airpower, a new science of war. They immediately made an impact on international civil aviation, thanks to the trailblazing flights of Ross and Keith Smith, and of course the immortal Charles Kingsford Smith. Australians also pioneered an airborne medical service, the Royal Flying Doctor Service, and although this is largely unknown today, they led the world in private air-freight, ironically thanks to operations in New Guinea skies.

Talent was clearly not the issue, and nor was good planning. Head of the RAAF between the wars, Richard 'Dickie' Williams made his reputation on the back of outstanding innovations in airpower tactics, fighting the Turks in Palestine in 1918. Looking at the defence problem facing Australia in the 1920s, Williams grasped the strategic problem facing the country in a way that escaped most politicians. At the time, Australia's national 'assets'—in terms of heavy industry and munitions plants — were in the south-east corner of the continent, in the big population centres of Sydney and Melbourne, and the steel towns of Newcastle and Wollongong. On any commonsense geo-strategic assessment, protecting these needed to be the bedrock of national defence planning.

Considering the problem in this light, Williams saw that a potential enemy could only approach Australia's vital interests by one of three routes—south to Darwin, then east through the Torres Strait and down the Queensland coast; south along the Western Australian coast and then east across the Great Australian Bight; or east of New Guinea, through the Solomon Islands, into the Coral Sea.

From an air defence perspective, the first and second scenarios were easy enough to counter. Defensive forces at Darwin and Perth could serve as advance guards, and mount reconnaissance operations to track the enemy as he approached the strategically decisive south-east corner.

But the problem in New Guinea was much more difficult. The numerous islands provided an enemy with any number of opportunities to hide and to prepare bases for further operations.

Thanks to the territorial carve-up of the German Empire after World War I, the geographic challenges of the New Guinea theatre were compounded by the looming presence of Australia's most likely enemy. At the peace negotiations that followed the 1918 armistice, Billy Hughes, the bellicose 'Little Digger' who served as Australia's Prime Minister from 1916 to 1923, set out to construct a Pacific empire all of our own. In his mind, Australia's 60,000 war dead demanded as much. In 1914, it had been the Australian Navy that seized Germany's colonies to the near north, in New Guinea and New Britain, and Hughes was adamant Australia would keep them.

Public opinion everywhere was horrified by the loss of life in the great clash of empires, and this prevented the subsequent peace negotiations from being converted into an outright auction of the spoils of war, so Hughes' territorial demands, and those of other allies, needed a diplomatic fig-leaf. The politicians found a suitable sleight of hand. Rather than allow the allied empires to merely annex Germany's former colonies, the League of Nations, ancestor of the United Nations, agreed that these could be administered by the victorious powers under international 'mandates'.

Australia, originally a colony itself, thereby gained a mini-colonial empire all of her own. However, the problem with empires is that they bring a certain international rivalry and competition with them, and so it proved in New Guinea and the neighbouring islands. Australia was not the only beneficiary from the dissolution of the German Empire. So too was Japan. Having entered the war as a British ally in 1914, Japan also looked to Germany's Pacific holdings as an opportunity for expansion, and from among the Kaiser's island chains, quickly seized the Caroline Islands in the early months of World War I. This mid-Pacific paradise included a magnificent natural harbour at Truk, easily capable of development into a large fleet base. Problematically, this potential base lay not much more than 1000 kilometres north, as a seagull flies, from Australia's own recently acquired 'mandate'. Prime Minister Billy Hughes did little to lessen possible tensions, offending the Japanese in post-war negotiations by refusing Tokyo's proposal that the League of Nations formally recognise the principle of racial equality.

As a competent strategist, it did not take Dickie Williams long to draw the obvious conclusions from this collision between Australian and Japanese spheres of influence. As early as 1926, Williams concluded that New Guinea would be Australia's key theatre of operations in any future war. For that reason, he clambered aboard a fragile single-engined floatplane, and went to look at what he was convinced would be the country's region of destiny. At a time when over-water flying was still a pioneering event, Williams surveyed New Guinea and the islands to the east by air, and drew from his inspection far-reaching and prescient conclusions about the type of aircraft the RAAF needed. This technical assessment would stand the test of time, but tragically, not meet with any political favour.

Ten years later, as the world hurtled towards a new global conflict, Williams began putting all of his career wisdom into action, playing a key role in the establishment of an Australian aircraft manufacturing industry, and planning for the design and manufacture of a local fighter aircraft, purpose built to oppose Japanese carrier aircraft. But in a series of events that cost Australia its best military mind at its greatest hour of need, Williams was pushed from office just as his careful professional plans were coming to fruition. For the government of the day, Australia could only be safe while Britain ruled the waves. In particular, this meant 'Fortress Singapore' had to hold out as a base for the Royal Navy in the 'Far East'.

What was the distant east for London was Australia's back door, a point Williams understood—too well, as it proved, because his proposals for a national defence plan, as distinct from slavish adherence to 'imperial defence', cost him his job. In a succession of bewildering decisions over the course of 1939, the government removed the troublesome Williams by posting him away to London on secondment; restructured the Australian aircraft manufacturing industry to marginalise the expert local company set up by BHP to produce machines for the RAAF (the government preferred to build a poor British bomber in railway workshops!); converted the greater part of the RAAF into a training school for the British; and capped the whole sorry mess by recalling a mediocre British officer, Charles Burnett, from a well-merited retirement to replace Williams as Chief of Air Staff.

The latter appointment proved particularly disastrous. Some sense of Burnett's thinking (and ability) can be gauged from his conclusion in April 1940 that 'the development of the war indicates a continuous lessening of the probability of an attack on Australian territory by Japan and therefore the possibility of carrier borne aircraft operating against this country is remote'. On the back of this bizarre and naïve appreciation, the RAAF cancelled its plans for a local fighter force, and Burnett instead ploughed resources into training crews for the British.

Unfortunately, although dark clouds gathered, no amount of intelligence about the looming storm to the north would convince Burnett to adjust his plans. The RAAF (and the War Cabinet) were first aware of the capabilities of the Japanese Zero fighter in December 1940, and during the following year, the RAAF received a stream of more technical details about what the Zero could do. Still no fundamental review of RAAF plans followed, even though in June 1941, Japanese potentialities and actual combat performance were clearly demonstrated to the RAAF when a Japanese reconnaissance flight flew over Rabaul, a mission duly recorded and analysed by RAAF Intelligence. Under international law, this was an act of war, but Burnett didn't even bother to inform the government of the incident. With this sort of maladministration, by December 1941 the RAAF squadrons that remained in Australia had no modern fighters to fly, no long-range strike bombers, and only half the trained pilots they required.

As soon as war came to the Pacific, the pressure quickly told on an over-stretched air force. On the night of 8 December 1941, a Catalina from 11 Squadron flown by Flying Officer Lincoln Sloan crashed into a hillside near Port Moresby, killing all eight men on board. The official investigation that followed concluded glumly that although Sloan's errors of judgment were the immediate cause of the crash, the underlying reasons were more fundamental and distressing. Sloan had been with 11 Squadron for four months prior to the crash, but throughout that time his commanding officer had been unable to find the time to properly assess his flying skills. The reason for this 'most unsatisfactory' state of affairs was that the RAAF's chronic shortage of trained crews had forced the commanding officers of the flying boat squadrons to spend too much of their own time in the air, with the result that they were unable to adequately supervise the training of their units.

Thus it fell to men like Tom Keen to fill the gaps left in Australia's defences by nostalgia and armchair strategy. As Keen scrambled through the jungle looking for help on the north coast of New Guinea, another Catalina crew—this time from 20 Squadron, the second flying boat unit based at Moresby—was confronting the realities of Japanese carrier strength, which Charles Burnett had so glibly dismissed not two years earlier.

At about the same time Keen's crew were leaving Port Moresby on the morning of 21 January, Flight Lieutenant Bob Thompson lifted Catalina A24-8 off the water near Gizo Island, a tiny piece of land in the Solomon Islands. This was one of the refuelling bases used by the RAAF to lengthen patrol flights from the main base at Moresby. Thompson was assisted by co-pilot Flight Lieutenant Paul Metzler, a twenty-eight-year-old Sydneysider who joined the RAAF in 1938.

The two men set course, knowing they had a long way to go to reach their designated patrol zone, over New Britain to the northern approaches of Rabaul, near the village of Kavieng. This was an extraordinarily dangerous mission. The waters they searched were the most likely area in which to find the Japanese carriers, because a strike on Rabaul could only be undertaken within a (roughly) 250 to 300 kilometre radius, and it was into this sector the Australians now ventured.

Arriving west of New Ireland, Thompson and his crew soon found what they were looking for, and reported to Port Moresby that four Japanese warships were in sight, a report that provided the first evidence of the invasion fleet headed towards Rabaul. The Australians could not savour their success for long. They were immediately brought under heavy anti-aircraft fire, and reported this to base. Thompson and his men had chanced upon the Japanese Navy's 6th Squadron, commanded by Rear Admiral Goto Aritomo, made up by the heavy cruisers *Aoba*, *Kinugasa*, *Kako* and *Furutaka*, 9000-tonne monsters bristling with 20-centimetre guns. With so much at stake, and despite the obvious dangers, Port Moresby ordered Thompson to shadow the Japanese.

This was a mistake. Thompson and Metzler had found not an isolated flotilla of cruisers, but the flank guard of a Japanese carrier force. Zero fighters were quickly in the air to deal with the persistent Australian patrol plane, and soon Port Moresby received a brief but horrifying message: 'Rudder gone'. For many years, the earlier report of anti-aircraft fire was thought to have accounted for A24-8. In fact, like Hutchinson near Lae, Thompson fell foul of the dreaded Zeroes flying off the big fleet carriers *Akagi* and *Kaga*, ships that formed the premier division of the Japanese carrier fleet, recently victorious at Pearl Harbor. The Catalina was quickly shot down into the sea.

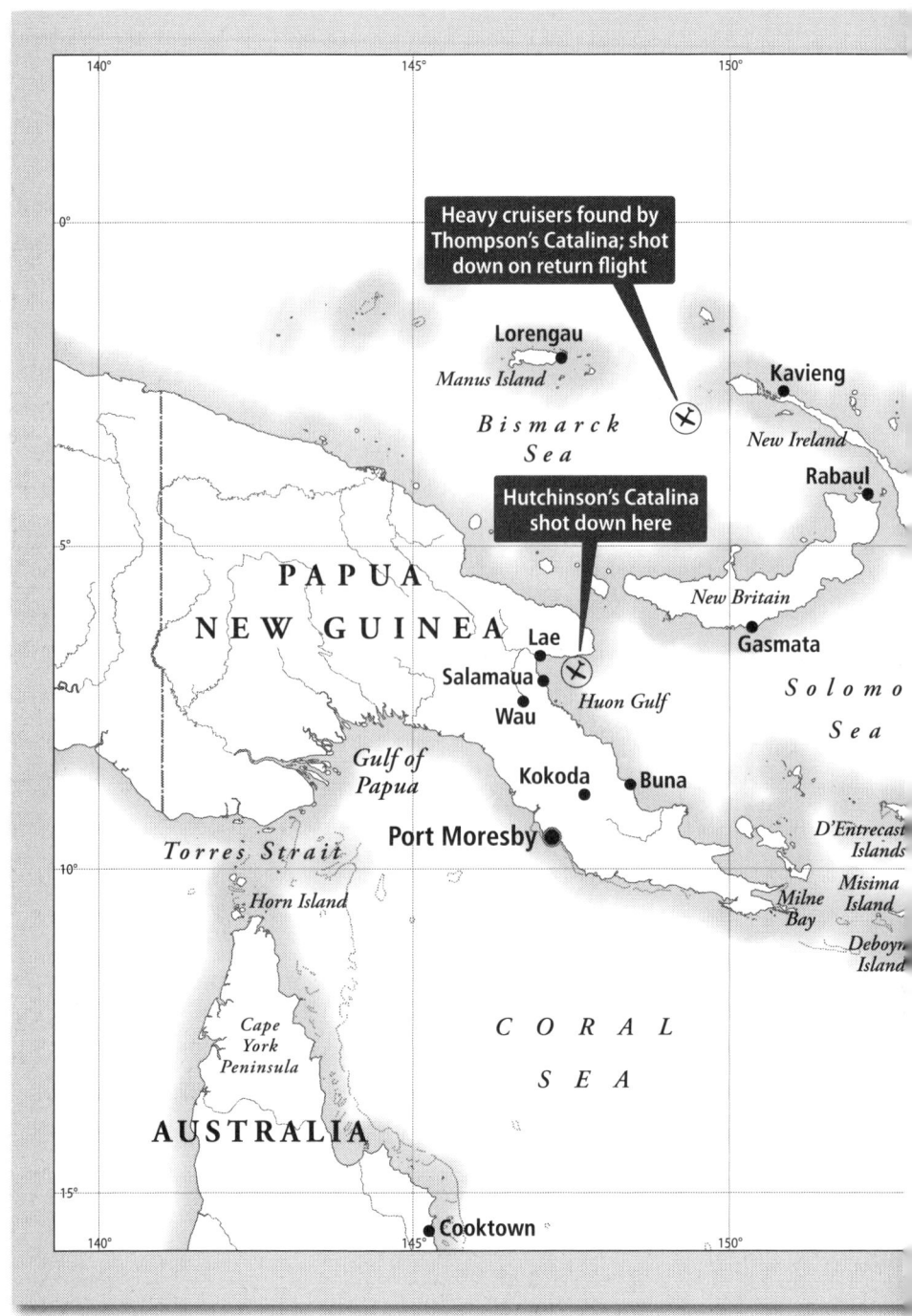

Eve of the battle: the struggle for mainland New Guinea began on 21 January 1942, with shocking losses for RAAF Catalina crews.

The Catalinas were not the only Australian aircraft lost that day. Lae and Salamaua may have been remote outposts in the early 1940s, but they were also home to some of the most advanced civil aviation operations in the world. It was these that the Japanese targeted on 21 January 1942, thinking the busy commercial airports on the shores of the Huon Gulf were home to RAAF combat machines.

The story of aviation in these remote parts is worth telling, because it confirms the technical acumen of Australian aviators when they were free of political interference. By the early 1920s, Bill 'Sharkeye' Park had spent twenty years of his life prospecting for gold in New Guinea. In 1922, he found what he was looking for, in the rivers of northern New Guinea. There really was gold in the hills, but how to get it out was more challenging: driving roads into the monsoonal wilderness was obviously a hopeless proposition.

The aeroplane seemed the only alternative, and Cecil Levien, a district officer in the government administration, took the opportunity to change careers. He formed a company to use a de Havilland DH 37 biplane to fly between Lae and Wau to support mining operations. The machine was unsuited to the task, since its wooden structure warped in the tropical heat and moisture, but the commercial prospects were uniquely suitable. The commercial returns available through gold mining completely transformed the economics of air transport, because those seeking to exploit the riches of the hinterland faced either a ten-day march through the jungle, or paying £25 (equivalent to about $1760 today) for an air ticket. This sort of profit margin immediately liberated air transport from the need for a government subsidy, which was a fundamental precondition to air transports in less exotic climes. Thus, without the need to jostle politicians and bureaucrats for a subsidy, all that remained was to find equipment that could withstand the daunting physical environment. Apart from the enervating heat, humidity and storms of the tropics, the Wau landing field was a test in itself, being located on the

'... A CONTINUOUS LESSENING OF THE PROBABILITY OF AN ATTACK'

edge of a mountain at a height of 1250 metres, and comprising a slope with a four-degree fall. That might not seem much, but it meant aircraft landing at Wau had to have their wheels chocked immediately they came to a halt, otherwise they would suffer the indignity of rolling backwards down the hill and into the long grass that encircled the strip.

Clearly a tough all-metal aircraft was needed for these merciless conditions. When Levien's original company was re-formed as Guinea Airways at the end of 1927, the fledgling operator cast about for an alternative to outmoded wooden British biplanes, and went in search of an aeroplane that could survive the climatic challenges of the tropics.

This was a process that left no room for sentiment—either the available aircraft, and their ancillary technologies like radio, could conquer the distances, weather and topography of New Guinea, or the gold would stay in the riverbeds. At the time, German aviation firms led the world in all-metal construction techniques, courtesy of their experience with Zeppelin airships. These gargantuan gasbags had a skeleton crafted from an aluminium alloy known as duralumin, and German aircraft constructors saw the merits of the material and began to fashion aeroplanes from it. Professor Hugo Junkers was one such designer, and by 1918 he had combined a construction technique comprising a metal framework covered by corrugated duralumin sheets, with a monoplane layout, to produce the world's most advanced and rugged airframes.

This technology was just what Guinea Airways needed. In March 1928, the airline took delivery of its first Junkers, a single-engined model W33. Guinea Airways fitted floats to its new aircraft, which was assembled on the beach at Rabaul, pushed it out onto Simpson Harbour, and flew it to Lae; the Junkers then made its first revenue flight on 14 April 1928. A second aircraft was delivered to Melbourne for assembly in November 1928. When they assembled it at RAAF Point Cook, Australian air force pilots, accustomed to stick-and-string British biplanes, thought with good reason that the Junkers was a machine from a different age. Even so, Guinea Airways found Australian officialdom largely uninterested in what developments in New Guinea might mean for the wider aviation scene. They wrote repeatedly to the Australian authorities in the early 1930s drawing attention to their achievements and inviting official inspection, without success.

Guinea Airways had found the machines it needed. When the Canadian mining company Placer bought into the New Guinea goldfields in 1928, it formed Bulolo Gold Dredging (BGD) for the purpose. BGD was initially sceptical that aircraft, even the durable Junkers, would provide a feasible alternative to hacking a way on foot through kilometres of mountainous jungle. The initial operations of the first W33 provided enough evidence to confound the cynics. Having just completed lifting enough structural material to build a hangar at Wau aerodrome, the W33 carried a 118-kilogram casting needed for the mining dredges into the new base on a proving flight in February 1930.

The miners were convinced by this, and by a scale model of a new Junkers type, demonstrated to them in Melbourne. This was the G31, the immediate ancestor of the famous Ju 52, which would acquire its greatest notoriety in the service of Hitler's Luftwaffe. The G31 was a tri-motor, using German-built American radial engines to give unprecedented reliability and weight-carrying capability. Specially for Guinea Airways, Junkers engineers modified the G31, fitting a 3.5 by 1.7 metre loading hatch in the fuselage roof, which gave access to a 7.3-metre-long cargo bay, a cavernous expanse inside any aeroplane of the day. To cope with the change this caused to the aircraft's centre of gravity, Junkers then had to extend the central engine mount and install a ballast weight of 454 kilograms in the tail, but even so the modified G31 boasted a lifting capacity of 3175 kilograms, an extraordinary achievement for its time.

With the bountiful promise of a virgin goldfield luring them on, the directors of BGD needed no second bidding, and ordered two G31 machines from Junkers, sub-contracting their operation to Guinea

Airways; the airline then ordered a third machine, for its own use. The first of this fleet—christened 'Peter'—arrived at Lae in December 1930, and performed its first revenue flight the following April. A second, 'Pat', followed in May 1931, and the third, 'Paul', shortly after. By breaking down the mining equipment into component parts, the big Junkers flew a complete mining dredge into the wild New Guinea highlands. In November 1931 alone, the three aircraft shifted nearly 400 tonnes of machinery and equipment, allowing the first dredge to become operational at Bulolo in March 1932. These dredges were mighty pieces of engineering. The first weighed 1000 tonnes when assembled, and by the time Dredge No. 7 sucked up its first load of New Guinea mud, it topped the scales at a whopping 4000 tonnes.

In the five years to 1933, Guinea Airways shifted freight totalling 9.2 million kilograms, and found the trade fabulously profitable—in the twelve months to February 1933, the airline turned a profit of £13,053 (equivalent to $1,128,000 today), on turnover of £77,694 ($6,715,000 today)—more than a small fortune for the time. The environmental consequences were less bountiful, however. The Bulolo operations rehearsed what BHP later inflicted on the Fly River from its Ok Tedi mine in the 1990s. At Bulolo, within months of the dredges coming on stream, the result was a moonscape, in which seven kilometres of pristine jungle were converted into a mass of 'bare boulders, stones and slags that covered every square centimetre and smothered any form of vegetation'.

As with any goldrush, the riches of Bulolo attracted thousands, eager to make their fortunes. Chinese traders flocked to the districts, opening stores that stocked the exotic goods of the east, 'camphorwood boxes, satin and silk kimonos'. Labour was naturally in high demand. Jim Huxley, a young man whose father found work with BGD, took a job himself in the highlands as a dredge hand.

Arriving at Salamaua en route to the goldfields, Huxley found the rhythms of frontier life already established. Salamaua township was a

Aussie know-how: Junkers G31 'Paul' of Guinea Airways on the strip at Salamaua in the 1930s.

tropical paradise, its neat bungalows laid elegantly along a sand isthmus that linked a headland jutting out into the Huon Gulf to the mainland. A shark-proof swimming pool was soon built so the townsfolk could enjoy the tropical waters, but the principal form of entertainment came in the form of other liquids. The pub was the centre of social life, and although young Huxley found beers like Foster's and Victoria Bitter popular, the drink of choice had a sharper edge—it was rum, and plenty of it.

Huxley left the delights of Salamaua for Bulolo, where his father had already warned him that he could expect to find himself in the company of hardened drinkers. Invited to pre-dinner drinks by the town's only doctor, Carl Gunther, Huxley took the gin and tonic proffered by his host, but hoping to pace himself through the night, put the drink on the floor next to his foot. Bending down a few minutes later to resume his tipple, Huxley found the glass completely empty—Gunther's eight-year-old son, hiding with some cunning under a nearby table, had downed the lot, apparently without ill effect. Huxley could only agree with his father that Bulolo did indeed boast hardened drinkers.

Whether men were pickled by liquor or toughened by the climate, when war came the mining camps of Bulolo and Wau, and the administrative bases at Lae and Salamaua, provided a valuable source of recruitment for the Australian Army. The New Guinea Volunteer Rifles (NGVR) was quickly formed as a local reserve force, and the miners, already acclimatised and relatively accustomed to the jungle, would prove invaluable in the campaigns to come.

Huxley himself joined up, and had a ringside seat when war arrived in New Guinea on 21 January 1942. Having blasted Rabaul, the Japanese carriers sent waves of aircraft against Lae and Salamaua and into the highlands, hunting for Australian transport aircraft, just as they had tracked down Tom Keen and his mates aboard the ill-fated Catalina out to sea.

At Bulolo strip, the now elderly Junkers 'Paul' was on final approach. Skippered by veteran bush-pilot Bert Heath, the big transport had aboard a vital cargo—26-ounce bottles of Foster's beer, bundled up in bags—but no radio. Thus there was no way Heath could receive a warning message, and he duly landed and pulled up next to the other two Junkers that had formed the mainstay of the aircraft fleet over the previous decade.

The NGVR men around the airfield did at least get some warning. Power to the mining dredges was cut, as a pre-arranged warning to the crews, and on the airfield, the guard of six men under Sergeant Richard 'Van' Vandenberg went to their weapon, a World War I Vickers machine gun.

Five Zero fighters followed Heath in. Pulling up in an understandable hurry, the Australian pilot and his teenaged sidekick, Malcolm Goad, leapt from the Junkers and took shelter in a slit trench. Van and his men put up what fire they could, but it proved insufficient to deter the Japanese, who went over the base like a 'swarm of wasps'. Amid 'ear shattering noise', the three Junkers were soon in flames, and the NGVR men seemed to be suffering too. Vandenberg fell to the bottom of the gun pit, calling out gamely, 'I've been hit, boys—carry on without me'. Searching about for what he thought to be the wound on the side of his head, Van found no blood—he had been struck there by clods of earth, flung up by the Japanese strafing, and assumed these were bullets. Rising to his feet, somewhat embarrassed, Vandenberg went back into battle, even more determined: 'No, I haven't been bloody well hit, boys—give it to the bastards!' The doughty sergeant might as well have saved his breath. After fifteen minutes of mayhem, the Japanese departed as swiftly as they had come, leaving the defenders to scratch their way through the wreckage. Australian salvage priorities took an understandable form. In the shattered remains of 'Paul', most of the Foster's bottles on the top layer of the cargo had burst from the heat of fire, but happily a 'good supply from the bottom of the pile was still drinkable'. While preparations began at NGVR headquarters to permanently mobilise a company of reservists and deploy it to Lae for coastwatching, men 'who could smell the cap being removed from a beer bottle from a long way off' gathered around the burnt-out wreck of 'Paul', to take the consolation of a salvaged ale, and await the next phase of the war.

In dealing with the Australian transport planes, the Japanese probably thought they wiped out a force of multi-engined bombers. With their operations now free of any threat from northern New Guinea, the Japanese landed at Rabaul in the early hours of 23 January.

The invaders soon drove the Australian garrison, principally men of the 2/22 Infantry Battalion and air and ground crews of 24 Squadron, RAAF, from Rabaul township and the surrounding airfields, severing communications with Port Moresby. Something had to be done to find out what was going on, and the task fell to one of the most remarkable combat pilots in the south-west Pacific.

Bob Yeowart, aged twenty-six, another resourceful Queenslander, had already distinguished himself in the first weeks of the war. In the days after Pearl Harbor, as Australian military chiefs looked anxiously to the north, they saw the advancing Japanese moving on all fronts—in Malaya, towards the 'impregnable' Fortress Singapore, and through the Philippines to the Netherlands East Indies (now Indonesia). And from Truk, in December 1941 and January 1942, came air attacks on the Rabaul garrison, surely a prelude to another offensive. But when would the blow fall, and in what strength?

Yeowart got the job to find out. Flying a specially prepared Lockheed Hudson twin-engined bomber, on 9 January 1942 Yeowart and his crew flew a 2000-kilometre round-trip reconnaissance from Kavieng, the northernmost airfield in Australian hands, to Truk and back. Flying into the airspace over a Japanese fleet base took more than a little gumption, but Yeowart skilfully evaded intercepting Japanese fighters and brought his precious photographic plates back to Australia, where they were developed to show the build-up of Japanese forces that would eventually overwhelm the garrison of Rabaul.

Further daring reconnaissance missions followed to other, more isolated, Japanese bases, before Yeowart flew his weary Hudson back to Richmond airbase, near Sydney, for maintenance on 17 January. Having more than earned a period of leave, Yeowart took the train north to his hometown, Brisbane. He did not get far. At Coffs Harbour on the mid-north coast of New South Wales, Yeowart was bundled off the train and told to return to Richmond. He was going back into combat, now to over-fly Rabaul and find out what forces the Japanese had in the area, and whether the beleaguered Australian garrison was holding out against them.

Yeowart reported to the Richmond operations room at 7 pm on 21 January. By 2 am the next morning, he was in the air again, heading north through drizzling rain, landing at Port Moresby's Seven Mile airbase at 3 pm on 22 January. Despite Seven Mile's role as the RAAF's major facility for landplanes in New Guinea, conditions there were haphazard to say the least. To get shelter for the night, Yeowart persuaded construction workers at the base to put sheets of iron over a half-finished hut. Undeterred by a fitful rest, Yeowart was airborne once more at 2 pm on 23 January, arriving over Rabaul two hours later.

Coming in over the target at 5000 metres, all seemed in order, but at this delicate moment, Yeowart lost engine power, his flight engineer having allowed one of the bomber's fuel tanks to run dry before switching over to the next tank. As he glided down to just 1500 metres while waiting for the fuel supply to resume, Yeowart was not unduly concerned by the fourteen transport ships in Rabaul harbour, busily unloading supplies. Plans had been under discussion for some months between the Australian and US navies. Before leaving Port Moresby, Yeowart had been assured that Rabaul would be held 'at all costs', and he convinced himself now that the shipping in view heralded the arrival of the Americans.

As engine power returned to the Hudson, Yeowart noticed something that did not quite tally with the apparent facts. There, beneath a nearby cloud, was a large aircraft carrier, in the act of launching its planes. With the US Navy still licking its wounds after Pearl Harbor, this ship could hardly be friendly, and Yeowart summed up the situation promptly and with some understatement: 'the Japs were here ... and no time was lost in opening the throttles wide and streaking across the harbour for the safety of the clouds'.

Making use of storm fronts, Yeowart headed south, and when things had 'just settled down', he began preparing to contact Port Moresby with his dramatic news. This report was interrupted by a warning cry from his crew—six Zeroes were closing on the Hudson. 'I could hardly believe it', Yeowart wrote later. He responded quickly again, plunging the Hudson back into the storm clouds. With the 'instruments ... a maze', the bomber 'shot madly out of the cloud ... and continued on to the tree tops'.

Like all good reconnaissance pilots, Yeowart preferred discretion to valour. He circled for half an hour under the darkest cloud he could find, before venturing out again. Now low on fuel, Yeowart made for Salamaua, to find the base ablaze from Japanese bombing, with wrecked aircraft littering the airfield.

Refuelling the Hudson as quickly as he could, Yeowart aimed to get away at once, but by the time preparations were complete, night had fallen and it was pouring rain. Taking shelter in the deserted township, Yeowart and his crew were awoken at 1 am on 24 January with news that the Japanese had landed. Rifle shots broke the night.

The pandemonium was a false alarm. At Lae, after the Japanese raid, Major Bill 'Mudguts' Edwards, NGVR commander, received laughable orders to 'prevent the enemy crossing the mountains'. What with, Edwards knew not, and he took the more sensible step of organising the evacuation of those final civilians who had not already left. Taking charge of a motor boat, and heading off across the Huon Gulf to Salamaua, the Lae evacuees served only to convince the townsfolk there that the Japanese were about to land.

In the chaos that ensued, Yeowart resolved to get out, and fast. Taking the most rugged-looking car available, the Australian aircrew made for the airfield, but ran off the darkened road and bogged the vehicle. Making their way on foot, they arrived to find their machine being warmed up, ready for a hasty departure. Only then were they informed that the 'invasion' comprised a group of civilians aboard a motor launch. At first light Yeowart took off, and regained Port Moresby at 7 am on 24 January. As his crew staggered from the overworked bomber, Yeowart recorded simply that they were 'worn out'.

Yeowart and his men might have been tired, but many of those scrambling to get away from Salamaua would have happily taken a flight to Moresby over the trek now facing them. While Yeowart got his plane ready on the Salamaua strip, the townsfolk gathered and resolved to follow the example at Lae, and evacuate immediately. One hundred able-bodied men elected to walk overland to the hilltop mining outpost of Wau, where they could be evacuated by air, a trek of more than 80 kilometres into a jungle-clad mountain range more than 2000 metres high.

Although the trek was trial enough, this group had it easy in comparison to the thirty-one elderly or injured men who were forced to make their way around the coast, tended by the sole Australian woman then resident at Salamaua, Esther Stock, an experienced Victorian nurse from Portland. Thirty-two years old, Stock was short—not much more than five feet tall—but no nonsense, with her 'straight black hair, uncompromisingly parted in the middle, clipped back with bobby pins'. She first went to New Guinea in 1938, initially on a two-year posting, at the princely wage of £170 per annum (equivalent to $13,000 today), with travel costs thrown in.

Stock was a model product of Victorian nurse education, having worked on 'day and night duty in the various men's and women's medical, surgical, gynaecological, eye, ear, nose and throat, isolation and refractory wards' of Melbourne Hospital. In the dark hours of late January 1942, she would need all that training, and more.

Stuffing some underwear, a blanket, a pillow and a mosquito net into an old mailbag, Stock set out with her patients. A newspaper report later commended Stock for bearing a 'man's part in the adventure', which seems a modest tribute given that she spent most of her time caring for male infirmity. Among her charges was the civilian Governor of Lae, Sir Walter McNicol, whose strength faded so quickly that he was carried throughout the journey on a litter borne by a team of Papuan men.

Stock and her party originally planned to make their way along the north coast of Papua New Guinea, sustained by supplies carried aboard a motor pinnace, itself towing another broken-down launch which bore the most seriously injured and sick. Propelling the Australians was fear. Jack Rigby, a police officer in the government administration, observed later, 'We made all speed, thinking the Japanese were on our tails'. Disaster of another variety soon intervened, when the supply launch capsized, still 200 kilometres short of Buna, on the mid-north coast. Forced into the canoes of local villagers, the party proceeded through 'swamps, mosquito-infested jungle, crocodile rivers and heavy seas'. The canoes frequently overturned, but throughout young Stock 'never complained once', and Rigby ruefully concluded 'she had more guts than all of us put together'. Esther, with the common sense of her profession, later explained humbly that she was only doing her job, and well, 'grumbling would have been silly'.

For three weeks Stock kept going in these circumstances, hauling herself around the New Guinea coast and tending as best she could to the ill and the injured. The group made Port Moresby on 14 February, to be met by the applause of the press, and transport south to the hospitals of

'... A CONTINUOUS LESSENING OF THE PROBABILITY OF AN ATTACK'

Bred from tough stock: Nurse Esther Stock (*left*) talks to the press after her New Guinea ordeal.

Australia. Interviewed on Sydney's Central Station after the long train trip from Cairns, Stock found herself the darling of the women's magazines, who thought her 'orange linen dress and stitched brown georgette hat' a very 'efficient style for girls who wade through crocodile-infested jungle rivers'. She promptly announced her determination to return to New Guinea, and once the war was over, made good her promise.

For the RAAF, the fall of Rabaul and the accompanying raids on Lae and Salamaua were a shock indeed. It appeared that the Australian high command could scarcely comprehend the news brought back from Rabaul by Yeowart and his brave crew. Even while the Japanese were surging through the coconut plantations of New Britain, hunting down the Rabaul garrison as it fled in small parties into the jungle and putting to death the Australians they captured, in shocking acts of summary execution, RAAF Chief of Staff Charles Burnett was assuming he still had time to prepare a 'reconnaissance screen through the islands from New Caledonia to New Guinea, supported by a striking force in the islands with the main reserve on the mainland'. He even put a proposal to that effect to the Australian War Cabinet, nearly a fortnight after Rabaul fell. This was a defence line that should have been in place four years before, and might have been had not Burnett himself overturned local plans in favour of converting the RAAF into a training school for Britain. Now it was much too late for independent action. Without coherent plans, or aeroplanes to implement them, the RAAF was reduced to begging for equipment from Australia's new ally, the United States. Burnett requested some Curtiss P40 Kittyhawk fighters to defend the cornerstone of his proposed defence line at Port Moresby, but their delivery was a hostage to wider developments in the war. In late January 1942, Australian technicians were assembling 18 Kittyhawks at the Amberley base west of

Brisbane, and Burnett had the temerity to order these to be transferred to Moresby for the defence of New Guinea. Three days after the Australian high command issued that order, it was countermanded on 26 January by the American General Lewis Brereton, then deputy commander of the allied air forces in Java. Whatever Australia's requirements in New Guinea, sustaining Dutch resistance in the Netherlands East Indies came first. As a result, the Kittyhawks went to Java, and the RAAF would have to continue its fight with the Japanese through New Britain and New Guinea without modern fighter aircraft.

The early exchanges in the air war for New Guinea showed the best, and worst, of the Australian defence effort. In their flight over Rabaul, Yeowart and his crew amply demonstrated the skill and valour of Australian aircrews, but otherwise, the bankruptcy of planning on the part of the Australian government and RAAF high command was everywhere on show. The question now was whether, having prised open the door to the Australian east coast at Rabaul, the Japanese could kick it down by moving on to take Port Moresby.

On 30 January 1942, the Reverend William Hardie wrote the kind of letter that the family of a serving soldier might find consoling, or equally, the most unwanted correspondence imaginable. Hardie was the RAAF Chaplain at Port Moresby, and to him fell the responsibility of writing to those bereaved by the loss of life aboard the reconnaissance Catalina A24-8 piloted by Bob Thompson and Paul Metzler, shot down near Kavieng on 21 January. As was air force practice, with the fate of the men still unknown, the families had already received a telegram advising them that their loved ones were missing in action. Now their anxiety over the final fate of the men aboard could be put to rest, as Hardie confirmed their worst fears. The men were dead.

To Mrs 'Kit' Metzler, Hardie extended 'very readily and sincerely' his sympathies on the death of her husband Paul. Hardie encouraged the new widow to take solace from his belief that Paul was finding 'fulfilment and reward in the great providence of God, at present so mysterious to us, but some day to be revealed'.

Whether Kit Metzler took much consolation from these words we will probably never know. What we do know is that, well intentioned though Reverend Hardie might have been, he was also completely, dreadfully wrong. As Kit opened Hardie's letter of condolence and took in the dreadful news of her husband's loss, Paul Metzler was alive and well, aboard the Japanese warship that had plucked him and five of his comrades from the sea.

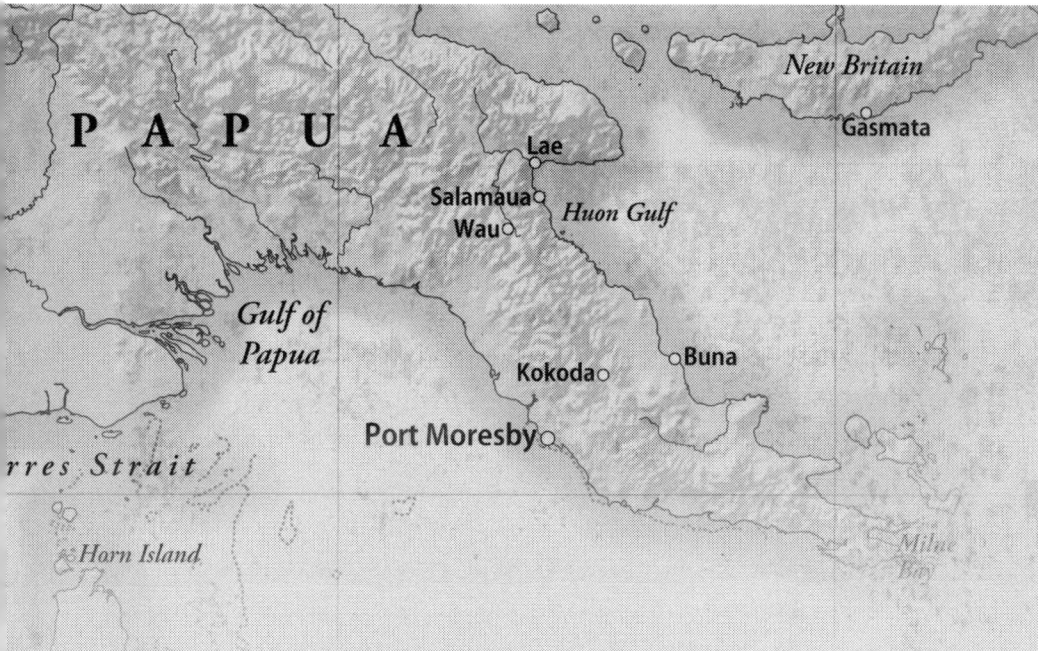

CHAPTER TWO
'... Japanese fighting morale is excellent'

Before midnight on 3 February 1942, nineteen-year-old Doug Dick stared into the darkness over Simpson Harbour, Rabaul, as his Catalina made a bomb run on the Japanese shipping at anchor below. Dick's air force service totalled barely ten months. He joined up as an engineering fitter, only to find himself pressed into service with scant training as a gunner. Coming into the target at 2500 metres on his first combat mission, Dick reassuringly found 'everything was quiet'.

The silence ended abruptly. Hunched over his twin Lewis guns in the flying boat's port blister, Dick's first intimation of trouble was what he took to be an anti-aircraft shell whistling by. He reported the near miss to his captain, Godfrey 'Goff' Hemsworth, who sent his crew to heightened alert with an instruction to 'keep a sharp look out for fighters'.

The warning was justified. Nearby, another Australian Catalina was fighting for life. At the controls of this machine was twenty-seven-year-old Brian Higgins, until recently a journalist from the Victorian country town of Wangaratta. Suddenly his Catalina was under fire. Heeding the lessons the Australian flying boat crews had recently learnt at the hands of Japanese fighters, Higgins did not seek to fight it out, but instead dumped his bomb load and looked for an escape route.

Ordinarily, a plume of volcanic ash is an object of dread, foreshadowing as it does a natural event beyond the control of humankind. Higgins now had reason to think otherwise. Spying the cloud of pumice and dust spewing up from the Matupi volcano on the shores of Simpson Harbour, Higgins plunged his big boat into the smoke and grit, shaking off his pursuers.

Foiled by Higgins' risky manoeuvre, the Japanese interceptors looked for other quarry. In Hemsworth's Catalina, Doug Dick suddenly saw a fighter come up at an angle of 15 degrees. At once the Japanese pilot opened fire, raking the Catalina's port wing and motor. Hemsworth ordered his gunners to reply—at that time, only when instructed by the aircraft captain could the likes of Dick return fire. The Japanese fighter was boring in again, approaching from astern, and slightly to starboard. In this dead spot behind the flying boat, Dick had to endure the fighter's firing pass before he could let fly. With bullets exploding in the blister around him, Dick could only track the Japanese machine from the flash of its guns, but when at last it came into his field of fire, Dick opened up. He thought the fighter passed through his stream of bullets as it climbed up above the flying boat, until it flicked over and spun away. Dick kept up his fire, believing that his rounds 'hit the enemy aircraft right in the belly'.

Dick was game, and had he done as much damage as he thought, he might have spared the lives of many allied aircrew in the months to come. He could not have known it, but his opponent that night was one of the rising stars of the Japanese Naval Air Force, Lieutenant Hiroyoshi Nishizawa. Born in 1920 in a mountain village in Nagano Prefecture, son of a brewer manager, Nishizawa—like boys the world over—was driven by the desire to fly. Chancing upon a naval recruiting poster as a sixteen-year-old, Nishizawa compared the glamour of flight training with his then job as a mill hand in a textile factory, and not surprisingly landed on the side of adventure.

In June 1936, Nishizawa joined the *Yokaren*, the Japanese Navy's flight training program, and by doing so entered one of the most demanding military academies anywhere in the world. It owed much to the Japanese samurai tradition, emphasising uncompromising quality over quantity. Each year's intake was limited to a handful of places, and cadets were constantly required to demonstrate their prowess, in the air, in the classroom and in the gymnasium. Wrestling bouts were a favoured means of weeding out the weak. These were arranged so that any cadet losing a bout was then required to fight again, until such time as he either won a contest, or was struck from the course.

Nishizawa survived this gruelling program to earn his wings in 1939. Of men like him the RAAF was surprisingly well aware, even before the outbreak of hostilities. In July 1941, RAAF Intelligence concluded that the pilots it would meet in combat if war came to the Pacific were high-

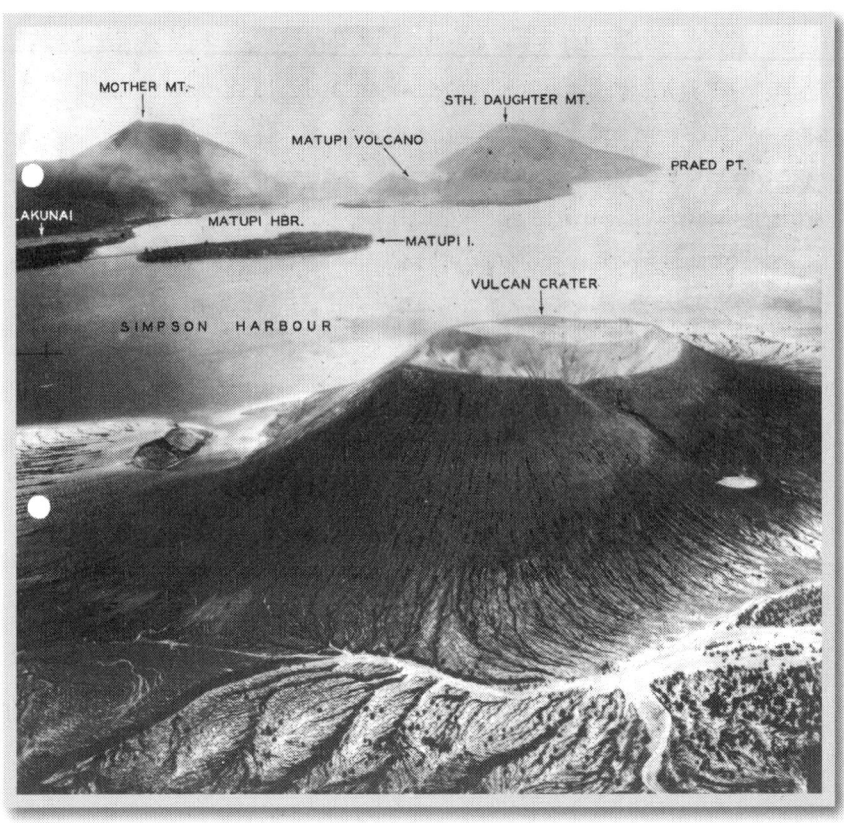

The lunar landscape of Simpson Harbour, seen here before the war, but showing in the mid-distance the type of cloud spewing from Matupi Volcano that saved the lives of Brian Higgins and his men.

quality and fearless individuals. A report circulated among the air force top brass that month concluded:

> *On one point we are left in little doubt, and that is that Japanese fighting morale is excellent. There will be no question of Japanese pilots retiring before superior forces and once in an engagement the Japanese pilot will not break contact until he is either forced down or has destroyed his opponent; if he is outclassed he will ram rather than run.*

In the darkness over Simpson Harbour that February night, Nishizawa soon validated the RAAF's assessment of the fighting prowess of Japanese pilots. Having wracked the flying boat with bullets, he was so certain of his work that Japanese records mark Hemsworth's machine as Nishizawa's first combat success.

Given the damage he inflicted, Nishizawa's confidence was understandable, but Hemsworth himself was a notably experienced pilot, having flown in the 1934 London to Melbourne air race and then civilian Empire flying boats for QANTAS before the war. He needed all of that accumulated flying skill now. Nishizawa scored many hits, holing the Catalina's petrol tanks. To throw off his attackers, Hemsworth pitched his Catalina into a fearsome dive. Along the way, he stopped his stricken port motor, and 'feathered' the airscrew (this involved disengaging the propeller from the now dead engine, so that it did not continue to windmill in the slipstream and thereby shake the wing to pieces).

Down to 60 metres, the flying boat was still in trouble. Back in the hull, Dick and the rest of the crew jettisoned equipment—ammunition, guns, flares, anything that could be moved to lighten the big boat. By these desperate means, with petrol sloshing though the interior of the aircraft and one engine knocked out, Hemsworth succeeded in keeping the Catalina airborne for five hours. After alighting at Salamaua for running repairs, Hemsworth took off again, but without the power needed to climb over the Owen Stanley mountain range, he flew back to base around the coast at just 15 metres, a one-engine marathon that dragged on for fourteen and a half long, weary hours. When the Australians got back to Port Moresby, Dick and his mates counted 100 bullet holes in their machine. Understandably, Dick was grateful to survive his first mission.

Despite Hemsworth's outstanding achievement in bringing his crew and aircraft home in the most challenging circumstances, he was thought by his superiors to be too cautious a pilot, and some even questioned his motives. Like Hemsworth, the commander of RAAF forces in New Guinea, Charles Pearce, was a flying boat skipper, having survived a tour in Europe as the captain of a Short Sunderland on anti-U-boat operations with 10 Squadron, the only regular RAAF unit to see service in England during the dark days of 1940. When he first met Hemsworth, Pearce was not altogether impressed. He acknowledged thirty-one-year-old Hemsworth to be an 'efficient flyer' and a 'good pilot', but one inclined to be 'argumentative with his seniors'. Worse, Pearce thought Hemsworth valued his career over winning the war. Pearce wrote in an official report in November 1941 that Hemsworth, a 'QANTAS man', refused to take any undue risk 'in case it will jeopardise his position with QANTAS Airways after the war'.

This would not be the last unkind thing Pearce would have to say of the men under his command. But later and more public remarks about the bravery of his aircrew, or the lack of it, would have more tragic consequences than the uncharitable stain left on the service record of Goff Hemsworth.

The work of Higgins and Hemsworth over Rabaul on that tumultuous night was but one episode in the Australian bombing campaign against the new Japanese base. This began within hours of Yeowart's return to Port Moresby early on the morning of 24 January. The very next evening, Catalinas counter-attacked the invasion fleet now anchored in Simpson Harbour, with some success; Japanese records reveal an army transport ship was hit and damaged.

This first raid was led by the commander of 11 Squadron, Julius Cohen. Tall, with 'reflective and gentle' brown eyes, Cohen was already a decorated veteran following his service with 10 Squadron in 1940, but he won his Distinguished Flying Cross not for valour in combat with the Luftwaffe, but for a diplomatic cloak-and-dagger adventure in

'... JAPANESE FIGHTING MORALE IS EXCELLENT'

'Reflective and gentle': Julius Cohen about the time of his adventures in Morocco.

French Morocco that would have done Humphrey Bogart proud in the Hollywood classic *Casablanca*. As the captain of a Sunderland flying boat, Cohen was called on in July 1940 to take the British diplomat Duff Cooper and General Lord Gort from Gibraltar to the Moroccan city of Rabat, as Britain looked to test out the opinion of French military and political leaders in the French colonies in the hope of drawing them away from the puppet Vichy government, installed by Hitler to govern the rump of metropolitan France that remained unoccupied by the Germans.

However, the British delegation found the French leadership in Rabat in no mood to desert Vichy. Among many French, antipathy to Britain was high, especially after the Royal Navy destroyed much of the French war fleet at anchorages in Algeria to prevent it from falling into German hands. After Cooper and Gort disembarked and went into Rabat to parlay, Cohen received a coded message from London to break off negotiations, and for good reason. When Cohen asked for a boat to go ashore, French harbour authorities refused, and it appeared that the British delegation might be interned. Undeterred, Cohen rowed ashore with his co-pilot in the Sunderland's rubber dinghy, a flimsy vessel more usually employed as a life-raft, and proceeded into town, revolver in hand. The French then threatened to seize the Sunderland unless the aircraft's captain returned to it. To appease this demand, Cohen pretended his co-pilot was in charge, and sent him back to the flying boat, while Cohen himself pressed on to the hotel where Cooper and Gort were being detained. Furious arguments with the French authorities then went on into the small hours of the night, before Cohen's determined performance and the prospect of a full-scale diplomatic incident prompted the French to relent and allow the Australian to remove his party and depart. In a heavy swell, Cohen got his dignitaries aboard, and away into the safety of the dawn sky.

After these adventures, Cohen spent the rest of 1940 on long and arduous anti-submarine patrols over the North Atlantic. The Nazi occupation of the French ports along the Bay of Biscay gave the German

U-boats newfound advantages in their attempts to sever Britain's Atlantic supply line, and 10 Squadron, RAAF was in the thick of attempts to stop them. Indeed, the Australian flyers were among the first to sink a U-boat from the air in World War II, when on 1 July 1940 a Sunderland captained by Flight Lieutenant Bill Gibson helped a British destroyer sink the German submarine *U26* in the North Atlantic.

Gibson and Cohen then went on to play important roles in the New Guinea air war, Gibson as the commander of the RAAF base at Moresby, and Cohen as commanding officer, 11 Squadron. To keep track of Japanese preparations at Rabaul, Gibson needed more than night raids by Catalinas. Only daylight photo reconnaissance could provide up-to-date intelligence on Japanese intentions, and the only machines capable of the task were a handful of Hudson bombers.

On 6 February, twenty-six-year-old David Campbell was ordered to undertake this critical mission, but unlike Yeowart's flight to the same target a fortnight earlier, there was no longer any doubt that high-performance fighters would be on hand to bar his progress. Campbell got as far as the beginning of his photo run over Simpson Harbour before his crew reported a Japanese interceptor taking off from Lakunai airfield. Just four minutes later, battle commenced. Campbell successfully sought cloud cover, but not before the Japanese pilot raked the Hudson with gunfire. A bullet smashed Campbell's left-hand and wrist. His crew fared no better. Co-pilot John Lauder's left arm was fractured, and another round found its mark in his right-hand. Gunner Geoff O'Hea, gamely trading fire with the Japanese fighter, was hit with a bullet in the left thigh. The Hudson itself was a shambles. Campbell watched as his instrument panel disintegrated from a succession of hits. The starboard undercarriage wheel was punctured and the petrol tanks holed. In a final dramatic flourish, Japanese shells smashed open the bomber's sea markers. These were stored in a fuselage rack and dropped near an object in the water, to reveal its presence to searching ships and aircraft. To stain the water, such markers were filled with fine aluminium powder, and with the canisters now shot to pieces, their contents coated everything in the interior of the Hudson with a ghastly silver pallor.

In this condition, Campbell flew his battered bomber 800 kilometres back to base with one hand, then landed safely on one tyre, and before medical treatment, gave a coherent verbal report of his mission. The reconnaissance photos safely recovered from the Hudson's camera subsequently corroborated the details of Campbell's report. Never was a Distinguished Flying Cross better merited than the one awarded to David Campbell for his valour that day.

The Australians were not the only ones working hard on reconnaissance operations. On 27 January, a Japanese Kawanishi flying boat exploring the south coast of New Britain came across the now deserted Australian landing strip at Gasmata, hitherto used as a staging post for crews transiting from Port Moresby to Rabaul. The Japanese moved quickly to secure this new stepping stone on the route to the Coral Sea. Within days, a powerful invasion force was assembled, built around a formation of Japanese marines, the Maizuru 2nd Special Naval Landing Force, escorted by the 6th Torpedo Squadron, and the 18th Squadron, comprising the cruisers *Tenryu* and *Tatsuta*, and three destroyers. This formidable flotilla arrived off Gasmata on 9 February, went ashore with great efficiency and secured the airfield within hours.

Back in Moresby, Gibson and his fellow commanders looked at this latest development and could see immediately that the threat to Moresby was intensifying, and quickly. With an invasion fleet most vulnerable when key supplies are still on board, an Australian air strike might yet do heavy damage, but there was little point in sending Catalinas by night, as the required precision bombing was beyond them.

A daylight raid was needed, but the resources to mount it were desperately thin. Just three Hudson bombers could be readied in time. The Australian strike force certainly lacked numbers, but it did not want for skill and bravery. It was led by one of the most dashing combat pilots from the first months of the Pacific war, John Maynard Lerew.

Twenty-nine-year-old Lerew used the advantages of an elite education to seek achievement and distinction from an early age. As an eleven-year-old, he won athletics prizes at the prestigious Scots College in Melbourne. Taking up car racing as soon as he was able, Lerew took third place in the Australian Grand Prix aged just eighteen. After graduating from the University of Melbourne with a civil engineering degree, he joined the regular RAAF in the early 1930s.

As with most professional airmen, the war accelerated Lerew's career. Quickly promoted to Squadron Commander to take charge of 24 Squadron, he assumed responsibility for the air defence of Rabaul, something of a poisoned chalice given the lack of modern aircraft available for the task. Nevertheless, it was during the fighting there in December 1941 and January 1942 that Lerew distinguished himself on two counts, first as a combat pilot, and second as a nettlesome subordinate. Before the Japanese invasion, Lerew flew several bombing sorties against outlying Japanese bases. Back in Melbourne, RAAF chief Charles Burnett expressed disappointment with the results achieved by these raids, to which Lerew bluntly but accurately replied that the fault lay with the 'lack of assistance rendered by the Almighty'. On the eve of the Japanese landing, Burnett persisted with exhortations for the airmen in Rabaul to do more with the few and inadequate machines they possessed. When told to attack the Japanese at all costs, Lerew replied with the declaration used by the Roman gladiators before a bout in the Colosseum—*Nos morituri te sautamus*, or 'We who are about to die salute you!' (Although Lerew studied Latin at school, he later admitted he referred his cheeky riposte to an army padre to check on the accuracy of his grammar.)

With exchanges like these, relations between Lerew and his superiors were prickly to say the least, but with experienced leaders in short supply thanks to the pre-war mismanagement of the RAAF, Lerew had to stay. Falling back to Moresby, Lerew was given command of a 'composite' squadron, a makeshift affair in which planes and men from a number of units were scraped together while something better was organised.

Equipped with Hudson bombers, Lerew's ad hoc squadron was the only long-range, daytime strike force available to attack the Japanese fleet off Gasmata. Never one to shirk the issue, Lerew took command of the mission himself. Experienced captains were also at the controls of the other two Hudsons. Bill Pedrina, an engineer's assistant from Hamilton, Victoria, joined the RAAF aged just eighteen in 1938, married the following year and celebrated the birth of his son Jeff—who later became a renowned RAAF pilot himself—in March 1940. Graham Gibson was initially rejected for RAAF service on medical grounds, but persevered and began flight training in early 1940. One of his first commanding officers described the Perth native as 'quiet and unassuming' and 'level-headed, keen and hardworking'.

As Lerew contemplated the task ahead, he did not have much going for him, and the one advantage he did hold owed little to any preparations made by his government since the war began. Instead, Lerew and his men could thank Richard 'Dickie' Williams, the air force chief driven from office through political interference in early 1939, for the high performance of their Hudson bombers. As the world drifted to war, Williams realised that British manufacturers, on whom the RAAF had traditionally relied for its equipment, would not be able to maintain the supply of high-performance aircraft. Williams watched as the promised delivery of new machines from Britain was repeatedly delayed, until the Munich crisis of September 1938 threatened to plunge the world into a new war, into which the RAAF would have to fly aboard antique biplanes. Seizing his opportunity to prise a nostalgic government away from British traditionalism, Williams ordered Lockheed Hudsons from the United States to give the RAAF its first modern aeroplanes.

Not only was this a first-class political achievement on Williams' part, it was an outstanding technical success. The Hudson was a hurriedly militarised version of an airliner, ironically first put into production earlier in 1938 to meet a British order for the RAF, itself short on modern equipment. To power their fleet, the British chose a reliable but low-powered engine, whereas Williams was out to get the very best aeroplane he could. Thus for the RAAF, Lockheed installed more powerful Pratt & Whitney engines.

This family of engine was already in use by the RAAF, installed on the Wirraway training aircraft being built in Victoria by BHP's subsidiary, the Commonwealth Aircraft Corporation. By 'standardising' RAAF equipment on the one family of engine, Williams gave the RAAF a great advantage in economy, since 'training of airmen will be simplified if the engine installed in the Lockheeds is of the same basic type'.

More importantly for Australian aircrew flying a handful of bombers into the face of Japanese air defences in February 1942, Williams also ensured Australia got a better aeroplane than those first delivered to the British. With their bigger engines, the Australian machines were 60 kilometres an hour faster than the type used by the RAF, and boasted more than 300 kilometres extra range as well. Many young Australians would be grateful to Williams' technical acumen and political courage, and the tragedy is that the RAAF did not fight its most important battles under his outstanding leadership.

Even with good-quality machines, Lerew's force was puny in number. Knowing the odds facing him and his men, he planned accordingly.

Hoping to catch the Japanese by surprise at dawn, Lerew led his flight into the target at 4.30 am on 11 February. The maelstrom he feared did not take long to develop.

Skimming over the waves at 'zero feet', the Australians met a patrol of Japanese fighters, already flying cover for the shipping anchored just off shore. These were not the magical Zeroes, but an earlier machine with an open cockpit and old-fashioned fixed undercarriage—the Mitsubishi Type 96, code-named 'Claude' by the Allies.

At the controls of one of these fighters was Ensign Satoshi Yoshino. Born in Chiba Prefecture near Tokyo, Yoshino entered flight training in 1934, aged just sixteen. Having graduated from the elite Japanese flying academies, Yoshino had the skill to make best use of the elderly technology he was flying, and quickly latched onto the Australian Hudsons as they began their mast-top bombing runs.

First into action were the aircraft of Lerew and Gibson, and these attracted most of the attention from the Japanese fighters. Lerew was over his target, a merchant ship, when the Hudson's co-pilot reported they were on fire. Such was the chaos of the combat that the Australians were unaware whether they had been hit by fighters or anti-aircraft fire, but following up behind, Pedrina reported that he could see up to six Japanese fighters swarming over the stricken bomber. In fact, there were only four, not that it mattered to Lerew and his men. In one last desperate attempt to avoid disaster, Lerew's co-pilot smashed the cockpit window, and played a hand-held fire extinguisher onto the Hudson's blazing engine. As the extinguisher needed to first overcome a 370-kilometre-per-hour slipstream before it could make an impression on a high-octane petrol fire, the results were predictably unimpressive. Conceding the inevitable, Lerew gave orders to bail out, and pulled the stricken bomber up into a climb to give his men some chance of descending safely. Having lost sight of his crew as they made their way to the rear hatch, Lerew attempted to force himself through the narrow pilot's window, but found

'... JAPANESE FIGHTING MORALE IS EXCELLENT'

Hudson bombers of the sort used by Lerew's composite squadron, close to a typical New Guinea shoreline.

himself stuck. Blinded now by smoke, he hooked one leg around the control column, and in this way lifted the nose of the blazing bomber long enough to shove himself out. He tumbled to the ground scarcely 150 metres below, his chute barely opening in time before he crashed into the jungle trees, at which point Lerew was all but strangled by his life-vest as it caught on the foliage.

As he was coming down, Lerew caught a glimpse of a Hudson hurtling past, pursued by three Japanese fighters. This was Gibson's machine, and Lerew's fleeting sight of it was the last any Australian saw of the plane. Despite lengthy post-war searches, the wreckage of Gibson's Hudson was

51

never found, nor were the bodies of the four men aboard recovered. Thus, it was not until July 1946 that the authorities finally confirmed with his long-suffering widow that Gibson had been killed in action.

Having seen the fate of his commander, Pedrina nevertheless stayed in the fight long enough to bomb the target, before making off at low altitude. Deservedly, the action at Gasmata was later cited in Pedrina's commendation for a Distinguished Flying Cross.

As Lerew's bomber burnt in the jungle, Satoshi Yoshino climbed away from the battle, having secured his first combat success. Down below, battered and bruised, Lerew faced another battle for survival, one that would daunt most men. Lerew wrote later that he was 'determined to make a big effort to avoid capture', and he was nothing if not true to his word.

Lerew's first, sizable challenge was to complete his journey to mother earth. Caught in the branches, Lerew scrambled and fell 30 metres to the ground, losing in the process 'lots of skin'. No sooner had he descended than the sound of a cracking twig set his mind racing about the prospects of meeting a Japanese patrol. The alarm proved to be a wild pig, the first of several occasions when snuffling hogs put Lerew's heart in his mouth.

False alarm over, Lerew now struck out for the sea, somewhere to the south. Drinking dirty water from puddles, or sucking raindrops from leaves, he was soon exhausted, confronted by impenetrable sword grass and high, rugged hills. He tramped on as best he could, tormented by mosquitoes and steadily consumed by fever. On the afternoon of Thursday 14 February, he finally reached the sea, and disrobing, lay in the water to recover some strength, a moment he described as 'perfect'. That evening local villagers, although scared to help him, nevertheless provided some fruit, but this only caused him to vomit. Next day, he came across a European plantation owner. Many of these men went on to serve as 'coastwatchers', remaining behind on the islands to report on the movement of Japanese ships and aircraft. With the Japanese hunting such men down, Lerew named his helper only as 'Bill', to preserve his identity.

From him, Lerew got coffee and a 'marvellous soup'. Despite Japanese patrols coming ashore in the vicinity, Bill was determined to stay behind, so Lerew was still looking for a companion on his journey to safety.

Lerew found one in 'Harold', but thanks to the memoirs of Eric Feldt, the Director of Naval Intelligence who set up the coastwatch organisation, we know something about this man. 'Harold' was Harold Koch, a veteran of World War I. By then in his mid-fifties, Koch was determined to do his bit, first by getting Lerew to safety, and then by re-enlisting as a coastwatcher.

In Koch, Lerew found a fellow-traveller every bit as indomitable as he was himself. Koch had been twice wounded in World War I. Shot through the buttocks at Gallipoli, he lay dangerously ill in hospital for months, but recovered only to be severely injured by the accidental detonation of a hand grenade in training. He wore a Military Cross as evidence of his bravery.

With his spirit of adventure still intact, Koch took up coconut planting near Gasmata in the mid-1930s, and to sustain his operation, bought a small ketch. This now proved Lerew's deliverance. Setting out, the duo went south-west along the coast. Coming to another plantation, they enjoyed a 'sumptuous meal', and a prize above all others, the plantation owner's last bottle of beer. The sustenance was needed, as Lerew and Koch were determined to cross the unfriendly Bismarck Sea to New Guinea, albeit on a slighter larger boat. They set sail in this a week after Lerew was shot down, but the dauntless pair found the wind blowing hard, promising a crossing that looked from the start to be 'hazardous'. So it proved. A heavy sea began crashing over them, and Lerew found it 'difficult to hang on'. Water was sloshing into the 'black hole of Calcutta we called the engine room', and to keep them going, Lerew took on the role of chief engineer, in which capacity he was soon 'black with oil'. When the pumps failed, the men took to bailing out the boat with buckets.

After fighting for their lives through that dark night, Friday 22 February found them still far from land, but shortly after 1 pm, a motor patrol boat hove into sight. Lerew feared the Japanese had caught them after all, until he realised with gusto, 'No, whacko, I can see Aussie hats!' When the boat came alongside, her crew gave them a suitable Aussie welcome, asking the desperate refugees, 'What about a long, cold one?' As Lerew headed into a short convalescence, he agreed wholeheartedly that a cold beer was indeed the best tonic—'Oh boy, what about one!'

Lerew deserved his cleansing ale, but he might have asked for a stiffer drink had he been able to read the official interpretations of the disastrous Gasmata raid. One was intended for public consumption, in the shape of a press statement that distorted the facts in a way that could only have been designed to delude the public into thinking the Port Moresby defences were infinitely stronger than they really were. The other was a command appreciation of the action. In this, a visiting staff officer concluded glibly that Lerew's unit was 'suffering a definite inferiority complex as regards enemy fighters; aircraft would not press home the attack'.

As he staggered through the jungle, Lerew might have been offended by each of these fairytales. In the press coverage, Lerew's tiny flight was converted into a 'squadron', which was so strong it left Japanese shipping ablaze with 'many hits', albeit that 'two of our planes did not return to base'.

Given the understandable climate of trepidation in Australia, the true nature of the raid had to be kept from the public for fear of the consequences. To take just one example, public schools were already closed in Queensland until air raid shelters could be dug. Up and down the Queensland coast, parental working bees were quickly organised to dig slit trenches—Brisbane's *Courier Mail* reported that those attending should preferably bring their own tools, but those without would still be found productive work. Even when shelters were ready, state Cabinet soon decreed that children would only attend at the discretion of parents, and no new children would be enrolled for the 1942 year. One can only imagine what the public might have made of the raid on Gasmata, had they known the Australian 'squadron' comprised just three aeroplanes, and these suffered a loss rate of two-thirds.

At 2 pm on 13 February 1942, journalist Osmar White stepped from the cabin of the last commercial airliner to land at Port Moresby for the duration of the war, and 'stood blinking' in the savage heat. Having cut his literary teeth on the sedate rounds of the *Wagga Wagga Advertiser*, White now had a more dashing appointment as a war correspondent for the *Courier Mail*.

White joined a growing band of journalists at Port Moresby. As the national crisis deepened, the Australian press cottoned on to the fact that the immediate fate of the country turned on the events unfolding in New Guinea. Through January and February 1942, Australian newspapers were routinely illustrated with large-scale maps of the Japanese advance through Rabaul and the Solomon Islands. Showing better strategic judgment than pre-war governments, these were sometimes embellished with circles drawn around Port Moresby, to show the radius of action available to the Japanese should they succeed in taking the base. As White's own *Courier Mail* rightly concluded, the Japanese assault on New Guinea was designed to 'cut American and Australian communications' and 'immobilise Australia as a base'.

Like the service personnel around him, White found life in New Guinea a trial, with or without the violence of war. Starting the day 'by putting on a dry shirt' at 5.30 am, by the time White walked 30 metres to breakfast, he was 'drenched' in sweat, the shirt sticking to his back in dark patches. The unsanitary conditions were worse than, but obviously related to, the heat. Of the latrines, White recommended that those with a delicate stomach approach them only when equipped with a gas mask. Despite the primitive conditions, White nevertheless went on to record a remarkable first-hand account of the fighting, and to him we owe several intimate pen-portraits of the Australian aircrew involved in the 'Battle of Moresby'.

With John Lerew incapacitated by his ordeals, the embattled Australian Hudson squadron at Moresby needed reorganisation. To put the 'composite' squadron on a more permanent footing, a new unit, 32 Squadron, was formed on 24 February, bringing together what was left of Lerew's command, with separate flights from three other squadrons, and also the remnants of 24 Squadron. Squadron Leader Deryck Kingwell took command, replacing Lerew as the senior strike-commander at Moresby.

Kingwell was exceptionally well qualified for the daunting task he now faced. He was only the third Australian to complete the RAF's prestigious specialist navigation course in the United Kingdom. To pass on this knowledge, he spent twelve months at Point Cook as the RAAF's chief navigation instructor. If any man could keep his bearings in the tropical storms of New Guinea, it was Kingwell, and he would prove every bit as courageous as his blunt but heroic predecessor. Whatever helpful hints staff officers gave Lerew on how to turn back the enemy tide, Kingwell showed he understood the realities of Japanese airpower from the start. When his men went into battle, they donned the standard steel helmet used by infantry soldiers, unheard-of attire for aircrew, but a piece of equipment that was at least more practical than any advice coming out of RAAF headquarters.

Unknown to any of the Australians fighting to hold New Guinea at the time, the Japanese had already worked their way far to the south, reconnoitring Australian mainland targets. These reconnaissance missions were the work of Nobuo Fujita, arguably the most remarkable career scout pilot of any of the combatants in World War II. As Lerew struggled to keep afloat on the Bismarck Sea, Fujita got ready for his own adventure, 3000 kilometres to the south. To increase the reconnaissance reach of their navy, the Japanese had perfected a floatplane that could be carried aboard and launched from a submarine and which had a top speed of 246 kilometres an hour and a maximum range of 880 kilometres. It was this machine that Fujita now used to startling effect. In the pre-dawn gloom on 17 February 1942, Fujita's team of mechanics expertly put his little Yokosuka floatplane together on the deck of the submarine I-25. With flight checks complete, Fujita and his observer were shot into the sky by a charge of compressed air, and set course to the west.

As Fujita readied his floatplane, Sydneysiders were digesting with their breakfast the news that the Japanese had taken Singapore. For days, Australians had followed the course of the last-ditch stand to hold Britain's 'fortress' in the east. The shock to the national system was profound. Not only were the lives of thousands of Australian soldiers serving in Malaya at stake, but for a generation, Australians had been told their country would be safe while Singapore held out as a base for the Royal Navy.

Singapore proved unable to live up to this publicity. With the sad headline 'Fallen Bastion', the editor of the *Sydney Morning Herald* correctly observed that the myth peddled to Australia for all those years came in two parts. Not only had the fortress now capitulated, but even while it remained in British hands, it had failed Australian defence interests: 'the Japanese have shown that it was perfectly feasible, with Singapore still intact, for them to strike heavily in all direction from Sumatra to Wake Island and from the Philippines to the Solomons and the Gilberts'. Richard Williams knew as much in 1926, but only now did an Australian government acknowledge strategic reality, Prime Minister John Curtin declaring it would be a 'very dull person who could not discard his pre-conceived ideas of strategy and war, and who does not accept that the fall of Singapore as involving a completely new situation'. Curtin drew a parallel from events in Europe in 1940, declaring that just as defeat in France marked the opening of the Battle of Britain, so the loss of Singapore opened the 'Battle for Australia'.

All that could be done now was to brace for the national ordeal to follow. While parents in Brisbane organised working bees to dig slit trenches to protect their children at school, further south, preparations began for a 'scorched earth' policy to meet any Japanese invasion. The government canvassed plans to suspend all organised sport, which the *Sydney Morning Herald* warmly welcomed. The paper also offered optimistic tips on air raid precautions, asking citizens to stack 'heavy furniture or tightly packed books ... on a stoutly built table' in the hope that such a ramshackle arrangement would provide 'some measure of protection ... against blast and splinters striking through the window'.

The home handyman approach to civil defence was warranted given the state of air raid planning. Around this time, the federal censor prevented the Sydney *Sun* from publishing an exposé of shortages of critical equipment among the city's air raid wardens. The list of deficiencies ran from the prosaic—insufficient whistles with which to signal danger—to essential life-saving gear such as anti-gas respirators and tin helmets. The censor justified his decision to reject publication, because although the supply of the required gear was accelerating, the story would only serve to tell a Japanese strike-commander 'that if he bombs us now we are not fully prepared to deal with his assault'. This astonishing admission in the third year of the greatest conflagration in the history of humanity kept a restless public quiet, but did little to improve the equipment available to Sydney air raid wardens. To fill the void, the *Sun* joined other media outlets in providing yet further advice for the home-owner, advising citizens to reinforce their ceilings with hardwood to prevent roof collapse in the event of bombing.

The newspaper readers of Sydney had reason to get to work straight away. Even as they ate their porridge that morning, the Japanese were already overhead. Cruising over Australia's premier city at a sedate 160 kilometres an hour, Fujita found Sydney completely undefended, allowing him to drop down to a height of just 1000 metres, so that his observer could more comfortably count the warships and transports then at anchor. The Japanese airmen were helpfully assisted by lighthouses, still blazing away, oblivious to the arrival of the enemy. Undisturbed and undetected, Fujita completed his mission and returned successfully to the mother submarine north-east of Sydney, armed with a comprehensive picture of Australia's leading naval base. Not a shot had been fired, and the Australian military never even knew that the defences of their most important military base had been penetrated with laughable ease.

As Fujita disassembled his floatplane and re-embarked, away to the north other Japanese airmen were planning a larger and deadlier mission. For the Wirraway pilots of 12 Squadron at Darwin, 19 February began as yet another day of what they thought would be routine garrison flying, consisting mostly of long and tedious patrols along the lonely Top End coast. One of these men was a country boy from South Australia, Michael Butler. He joined up the day after war was declared. His father was an Anzac from the first war, but Butler had his eyes aloft. 'Keen on aeroplanes', Butler joined the air force, and soon found himself happy as a cadet pilot, even if that qualified him only as the 'lowest form of mankind'. Still, Butler gladly put up with the boot-polishing, the square-bashing, the inane regulations and the poor food because 'all we wanted to do was fly'.

One of Butler's mates at Darwin was another young sergeant, Bob Crawford. On the morning of 19 February, Crawford was told to find his observer and get airborne, with orders to 'protect the shipping' then at anchor in Darwin harbour—what from, he was not told. As he walked through the squadron camp to find his crewman, somebody said to Crawford, 'Look!', and there over the harbour was a gaggle of wheeling silver specks. The sound of gunfire soon broke the morning: a Japanese carrier strike on an Australian base, something the RAAF high command had discounted for nearly two years, was under way.

Crawford and his squadron mates took shelter in slit trenches and sat out the raid, which devastated allied shipping, the permanent air force base and the civil aerodrome where 12 Squadron was based. Emerging gingerly from their shelters, the Wirraway pilots watched as discipline at the RAAF base collapsed, and a torrent of men poured away to the south, fearing a Japanese landing.

Crawford and Butler stayed at their posts, only to receive ominous orders to get their Wirraways ready to attack a Japanese invasion force. Butler remembered that as a 'strike bomber', the Wirraway had little to commend it. When armed with two 112-kilogram bombs, a modest enough weapon load with which to take on a Japanese battle fleet, 'you nearly bent the wings down on them'.

Still, Crawford got orders the next day to patrol out to sea, and find what was thought to be an incoming invasion force. He was lucky, and found nothing other than further evidence of the horrible damage inflicted by the Japanese carrier pilots. On Bathurst Island, Crawford came across the smouldering hulk of the Philippine freighter *Don Isidro*, bombed the previous day and driven ashore on the beach to prevent her complete loss. As Crawford circled overhead, he took in the melancholy sight of bodies lying on the beach, and the lifeboat davits on the ship swinging free, the crew having abandoned ship in a desperate effort to escape the Japanese.

Back at base, Butler had a job that spoke volumes for the state of Darwin's defences. Instead of taking the fight up to the Japanese in modern aircraft, the young sergeant sat in his Wirraway on a baking-hot northern landing strip and acted as a wireless relay station. With radio communications obliterated in the raid, Butler and his observer parked on the airstrip at Batchelor, south of Darwin, and used their plane's radio to forward messages on to Katherine, for further transmission to the Australian high command in Melbourne.

To say the Australian defence system fell apart under the weight of the Japanese bombing raid, mounted by aircraft from four carriers in the Timor Sea and long-range bombers from land bases in the Celebes, is to imply some sort of system existed in the first place. The leader of the Japanese raid, Mitsuo Fuchida, scornfully dismissed the defences of Darwin as 'contemptible', and with good reason. As Butler and Crawford could attest, the RAAF had no fighters available when Australia was first bombed, nor were there radar sets operational that might have at least warned those on the ground to take cover, and given notice to the ships on the harbour to get under way.

Were these facts to emerge, the Australian public might rightly have demanded to know how things had come to such a sorry pass. The federal censor immediately stepped in, issuing an instruction just hours after the Japanese raid that the Australian press were only to publish stories about Darwin which were of a 'morale building character', and nothing was to be written which would 'reveal weaknesses'. The suppression of news was very successful, until the American papers published photographs of the raid more than five months later, much to the embarrassment of the Australian authorities, who wrote to their US counterparts: 'Government statements glossing over losses at Darwin will spring to everyone's mind when these pictures are seen. The fact that Australians will be the last to see them will not improve matters'. Official denial about the reality of the Darwin raid extended to the Royal Commission that investigated the failures of the defence. This made a number of findings about the lack of preparation, albeit without peering into the government decisions in 1939 that crippled the RAAF in the first years of the war, but even these were too hot to handle. Cabinet decided in April 1942 that the reports of the Royal Commission were to be given 'no publicity' and 'no further action' would be taken on the findings.

While the government began work within hours to keep a lid on the events at Darwin, RAAF chief Charles Burnett also had to give the impression he had events under control. The man most responsible for the debacle now dropped into the Darwin air force base after the Japanese raid, to give the survivors the benefit of his opinion. Writing of this tour of inspection, he attempted to convince posterity that he had been concerned for some time that the position at the Australian base was not 'as good as it might have been from the air standpoint, quite apart from the shortage of aircraft'. What an air force was meant to do without aeroplanes in which to fly and fight, Burnett did not say, nor did he mention that he was the man most responsible for the lack of such equipment. Nevertheless, he drew up on parade the personnel of the RAAF station, and gave them a pep talk. In this, he emphasised the need to maintain morale, and gave some helpful hints on 'what to do in the event of bomb raids', before concluding with a sermon on 'the importance of leadership'. With this fine contribution, Burnett got back into the safety of his own aircraft and returned to Canberra, to brief the War Cabinet on his unstinting labours to shore up the national defence effort.

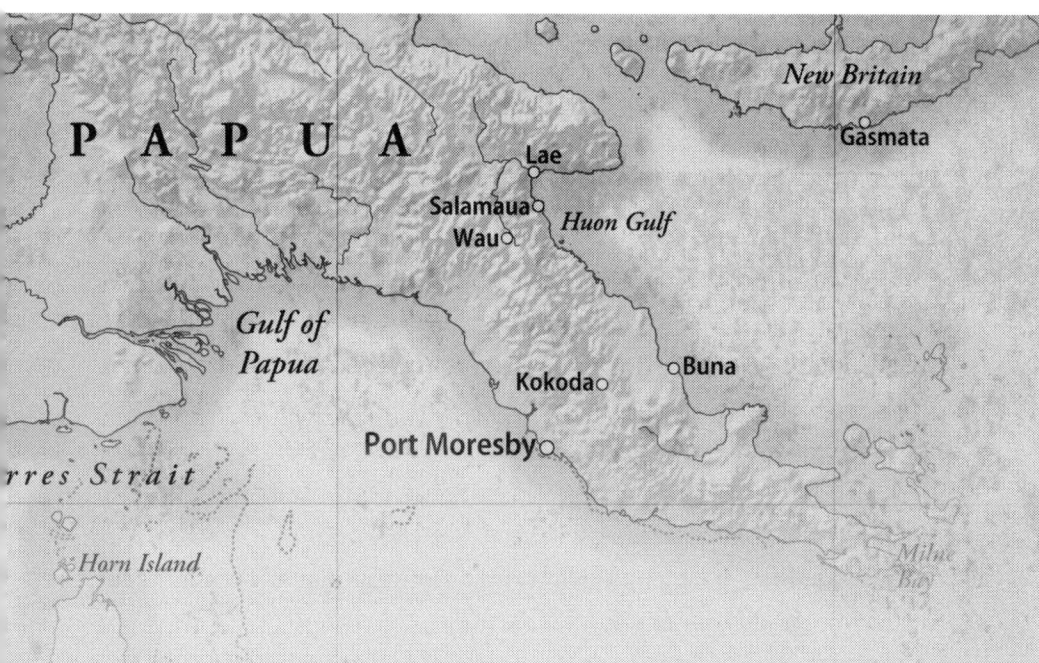

CHAPTER THREE
'... we were content to let the enemy assume the initiative ...'

In recent years, there have been attempts to downplay the seriousness of the threat to Australia, including the raid on Darwin, and the significance of the fighting in New Guinea, on the grounds that the Japanese never prepared definitive plans to invade the country. This is an idle and sterile debate, in which twenty-first-century hindsight is used to make light of the situation facing allied strategists in 1942. They did not have the luxury of examining archives in Tokyo to establish what was going on in the Japanese war machine—all they saw was a hitherto unstoppable enemy offensive, in which the invasion of the Australian mainland was a distinct possibility, among several alarming scenarios.

Whatever the comforts of current theorising, the head of the Australian Army, Lieutenant General Vernon Sturdee, concluded on 15 February 1942 that 'considerable risks are at present being taken with the security of this country', and the 'immediate problem' was how to rectify that weakness. Despite earlier, tactical decisions of allied commanders to first bolster the defences of Java by diverting there the first Kittyhawk fighters assembled in Australia, on the whole, American planners agreed with Sturdee, concluding that 'Australia and New Zealand were vital as bases for future operations, and loss of either or both would vastly multiply the difficulties of any future offensive against Japan'.

The threats were multiple, not singular: a direct attack on Australia could not be ruled out, but the Japanese might prefer to snap the trans-Pacific supply route from the United States, and drive Australia out of the war by other means, namely blockade and bombardment. To first secure Australia, Sturdee recommended the Australian army units serving in the Middle East should return to Australian shores, advice that prompted Prime Minister John Curtin to stare down the British government, which preferred that these troops go to Burma or Java.

Sturdee was right to fear for his country. While the Japanese entered the war with no definitive plans past Rabaul, their phenomenal and easy victories encouraged them to study the prospect of invading Australia.

The first months of 1942 saw a debate within the Japanese military over the merits of such an operation. Elements of the Japanese Navy favoured invasion; the Japanese Army, already over-stretched, was implacably against the idea. Sturdee could not have known as much, and correctly concluded that the decision to recall Australian troops from the Middle East doubled 'the present security of this country'.

While he convinced the Australian government that its principal response to the crisis was the immediate defence of Australia, the strategy the Japanese eventually settled on still posed a grave risk to the national interest. Rather than attempt to occupy the continent, the Japanese would isolate Australia, cutting off the vital supply line through the south Pacific to America, and blockade and bombard the east-coast ports. For this, the Japanese would embark on a new island-hopping campaign, through the Solomons to New Caledonia and Samoa. In this program, the seizure of Port Moresby was an indispensable first step, since the troublesome Australian garrison there threatened the Japanese flank as it pushed south. Accordingly, the Japanese committed themselves to an invasion of Port Moresby on 2 February 1942, and began planning for the campaign under the code-name Operation MO.

Some latter-day Australian writers belittle this threat, and thus the significance of the fighting in New Guinea. In doing so, they seem to suggest that the threat to the trans-Pacific route was of little or no account, that the risk to Australia's interests ended when the Japanese concluded invasion was not a viable operation. On the contrary, it is fair to say Australia would never have been the same place again had its big cities suffered bombing raids by Japanese carrier forces, and submarines subjected its major ports to blockade. Japanese strategists in 1942 showed a better appreciation of Australian interests than this modern revisionism, setting out the purpose of their operations in New Guinea as an effort to 'blockade the communication lines between the Australian mainland and the region ... in order to control the seas to the north of eastern Australia'. The strategic goal was part military, and part political, to lever Australia out of the western Alliance: blockade operations would 'strengthen the pressure on Australia, ultimately with the aim to force Australia to be freed from the shackles of Britain and the United States'.

Fortunately, Australian and American interests coincided. The United States needed Australian (and New Zealand) bases, if they were to roll back the Japanese advance. While the Australians held on at Port Moresby, they bought time for the Americans to fortify the trans-Pacific supply line, a route that Washington held to be of great importance. The first days of 1942 were a low point in the war for the Allies, as U-boats sank hundreds of ships in the Atlantic, many in American coastal waters, and the Soviet Union grappled with Hitler's army at the gates of Moscow. At this time of great crisis, everywhere American planners looked they were met with demands for men and guns, but amid the welter of competing priorities, the United States put the south Pacific high on their action list.

The threat the Allies faced was clear and calculable. In early 1942, American intelligence estimated that the Japanese could assault New Caledonia or Fiji—and thereby unhinge the Pacific supply route at a point close to Australia—with at least one infantry division, supported by strong naval and air forces. This was a remarkably accurate assessment. Japanese planning for Operation FS (Fiji–Samoa) began at the same time they committed themselves to taking Port Moresby. For the second-phase assault on Fiji, Samoa and New Caledonia they allocated nine infantry battalions (roughly equivalent to the divisional force expected by the Americans).

To match such a force, Washington approved plans to garrison all the islands on the ferry route to Australia, supported by strong air units that could provide local air defence against Japanese carriers. This commitment included a large garrison for New Caledonia, which arrived there in early March.

These reinforcements were desperately needed. As Darwin proved, where the Japanese could get at supply bases and routes of communication— 'soft' targets behind the main fighting line—they could do frightful damage. For this, they needed a 'war of movement', in which their carrier fleet, supported by land units, roamed through the Pacific to hit defences before the Allies had time to ready them. The Japanese were eager to do this, aiming to maintain the momentum of their advance into the south Pacific, so they could bring the communication routes between Australia and the United States under fire.

To halt this war of movement, the Allies needed to erect a barricade that would protect their rear areas, and Port Moresby served that role. If Port Moresby held on, then allied reinforcements could assemble at secure bases, like Townsville, and further south, at Brisbane, out of reach of Japanese strikes. From there, the Allies could counter-attack at will, drawing the Japanese into a war of attrition that they surely could not win. Whether to prevent an invasion of Australia, which allied planners could not rule out, or to protect the trans-Pacific supply line while it was fortified, in early 1942 Port Moresby stood out as the key to the safety and security of Australia itself.

As the Darwin defenders emerged from their shelters shocked and dazed on 19 February, far to the east events confirmed the importance of Port Moresby to the Allies, and the threat the unsubdued Australian garrison posed to Japanese plans. In northern Queensland that day, the first contingent of what would be an accelerating flow of American aircraft arrived, when the 14th Reconnaissance Squadron of the United States Army Air Corps flew twelve Boeing B-17 bombers into Townsville. However, since Townsville lacked adequate fighters and anti-aircraft guns to protect the big bombers, they were flown further inland, to Cloncurry, confirming how the vast distances of the Australian mainland offered the Allies the opportunity to build a defensive position in depth. Three days later, the Boeings were back at Townsville, to be bombed up for their first raid—target: Rabaul.

New to the theatre, the Americans needed local help, and the experienced Catalina pilots of Port Moresby stepped forward. Julius Cohen thereby added another extraordinary achievement to his wartime record, as a co-pilot and mentor to the American commander Major Richard 'Dick' Carmichael. In another American bomber went Pilot Officer Norman Robertson of 20 Squadron, playing the same role of local guide and combat tutor. At midnight on 22 February, six bombers, each crammed with fuel and four 250-kilogram bombs, took off from Townsville's Garbutt airstrip and headed north-east. One soon returned, defeated by bad weather, but the others pressed on, aiming to strike Rabaul at dawn.

Separated into two flights by the storm, the first element of two planes reached Rabaul to find it obscured by cloud and volcanic ash. Their pilots took the brave step of circling Rabaul for thirty minutes to secure a clear bomb run, which naturally allowed Japanese interceptors to scramble. When the second flight of three B-17s led by Carmichael and Cohen arrived at the target, the Zeroes were ready. Even so, as Cohen later recounted, the big Boeings made a formidable opponent, operating at an altitude where the Zeroes struggled for want of high-performance superchargers. Carmichael's machine was nevertheless peppered with holes, and a second bomber had an engine set on fire, encouraging Motosuna Yoshida of the 4th Air Group to claim a victory. However, the stricken bomber's pilot, First Lieutenant Harry Brandon, successfully extinguished the blaze and returned safely to base. One bomber from the first flight, its fuel spent in the orbit over Rabaul, crash-landed on the north coast of New Guinea, the crew emerging unscathed. The rest made it back to Port Moresby to refuel, before flying south again to the safety of Garbutt.

To follow up the American raid, two Australian Catalinas raided Rabaul that night. One failed to find the target, but the machine captained by Flying Officer Bill Bolitho reported dropping twelve 112-kilogram bombs on Vunakanau. The damage inflicted on the Japanese in this miniature edition of 'round the clock' bombing was modest, but the raid held more significance than the actual results. While Port Moresby held out defiantly, the Japanese could not, as they had at Darwin and elsewhere, get to the allied rear areas. With machines like the B-17, and the smaller, quicker twin-engined Martin Marauder B-26, the Americans could strike where they liked, secure in their Townsville base. All now depended on whether the Australian garrison at Port Moresby could keep the Japanese at bay, and prevent them from resuming a war of movement into the South Pacific.

The importance of New Guinea in these terms was also increasingly understood by the Japanese air leaders. Already on 13 February Japanese commanders in Rabaul agreed on a plan to seize Lae, on New Guinea's north coast, which would provide them with a land base from which they could bomb Port Moresby more effectively.

While they made preparations for this next move, the role Port Moresby played as a staging base in the raid of 23 February required immediate retaliation. The very next day ten enemy bombers made the first daylight raid on Port Moresby. The Australian press put on a brave face for the occasion, the *Sydney Morning Herald* invoking for its readers the image of the stereotypical laconic Aussie, calm under fire. The *Herald* would have its subscribers believe that 'in the middle of the raid, one sunburnt Digger was nonchalantly carrying groceries between a lorry and the camp, and despite the crash of bombs, he never once raised his eyes'. Osmar White also played his part in the propaganda farce, describing the

Japanese bombing as 'execrably bad'. In reality, the Japanese did rather more damage than the Australian authorities were prepared to admit to the public. Japanese bombs hit the camp of 32 Squadron hard, destroying trucks that were then irreplaceable, together with a Hudson bomber and a civil plane. A squadron mechanic, twenty-six-year-old H. C. M. Bower, from Strathfield in New South Wales, was killed.

The bombs dropped on Seven Mile also frustrated the hopes of air force men for more comfortable accommodation quarters. Plans for these had drifted on without much urgency for three years, so that by early 1942, the men still could not get a shower at the base. Along the western edge of the strip, construction workers were struggling to finish permanent and modern barrack blocks. The men making do in tents watched this work with 'pleasant anticipation', contemplating the luxury of plumbed showers and flyscreens. The raid on 2 February dashed those hopes, the concussion from the bombs shattering every piece of fibro-cement sheeting used as wall panelling on the new buildings. The base personnel sullenly went back to their tents.

The Australian response to this punishing raid was more defiant than effective. On the night of 24 February, two Catalinas bombed Rabaul, but the gesture proved costly. The machine flown by Flying Officer Ern Beaumont was shot down and the crew killed. The second Catalina nearly met a similar fate. The failure of an engine forced the flying boat, piloted by the hard-working Bill Bolitho, down to just 60 metres above the ground. Bolitho rescued his craft and crew by jettisoning the bomb load, and retired gingerly to base.

Still the Australian crews did not let up. The next night, Cohen led his men back to Rabaul, and this time pressed home the attack with a vengeance. Cohen found the Japanese defences were alert and effective, and searchlights flicked onto the Australian aircraft as soon as they appeared over the target. Approaching Simpson Harbour at 2300 metres, Cohen was determined to fight back at the Japanese, explaining later that the Catalina crews were sick of being shot at from all sides without landing a few blows themselves. To put matters right, Cohen opted for a direct, no-nonsense approach. The night of 25 February was clear, allowing Cohen to make out the wharves jutting out into the harbour. To maximise his chances of a hit, Cohen simply heeled the Catalina over, and commenced a dive-bombing run for which the big flying boat was never designed. She proved a forgiving steed, even if Cohen's crew were less impressed: co-pilot Flight Lieutenant Robert Seymour described the experience as the most terrifying moment of the war for him. At just 400 metres, Cohen ordered bombs away, and hauling back on the stick, safely exited the target area.

The results of the bombing might have been unclear, but the spirit of the Australian airmen was plain enough. Not that the work of the Catalina crews attracted any support from high command, other than Burnett's now standard invocation to hold firm in the face of the enemy. As Cohen later wrote, Burnett was still 'busily expediting' the flow of Australian aircrew to serve with the British in Europe. When Cohen read out one of Burnett's 'hold firm for the Empire' messages at the Moresby flying boat base, it was greeted by his crew with 'unrefined mirth'.

Cohen was not the only captain of a maritime aeroplane at work on the last nights of February. With his mother submarine still undetected, Nobuo Fujita continued his work down the Australian east coast, flying his little floatplane over the country's prime naval bases. In the darkness before dawn on 26 February, his flight-crew went back to work, getting ready for another remarkable reconnaissance mission.

The local press was at least ready for him. The editor of Melbourne's *Argus* summed up the first years of the war pretty well, when he told his readers: 'too often in this war we have seen what happened when we were content to let the enemy assume the initiative and then endeavour to stop him on unfavourable terrain and with inadequate equipment'.

The response of the Australian defences to Fujita's latest mission confirmed the deductions of the *Argus* in full measure. Once more, the Japanese ace negotiated the tricky catapult launch, but this time, headed north-east through the early morning darkness.

Hindered by a cloud bank, Fujita dropped down to gain his bearings, and found himself squarely over an RAAF airbase. This was Laverton, on the western fringe of Melbourne. As he had over Sydney, Fujita was reconnoitring a major Australian port, and the defences, yet again, failed miserably. The Laverton base was aware *something* was afoot, but were not quite sure what, reporting an unknown aircraft overhead at 5.45 am. The machine was not positively identified as Japanese, but described merely as a 'dark coloured twin float monoplane, with a Perspex covered cockpit'.

While the local air force scratched its collective head, Fujita circled around Port Phillip Bay to allow his observer to tally up and describe suitable naval targets for later attention. With this intelligence gathered without disturbance from gun crews or fighter interceptors, Fujita flew back to his submarine, likewise waiting for him, without harm from the defences, in windswept Bass Strait. Meanwhile, the only Australian reaction to this intrusion was suitably comical. The puzzled RAAF squadron at Laverton prepared a three-aircraft 'strike force', but sent it east to Bairnsdale, in the opposite direction whence Fujita had actually come.

Nothing underlined with greater gravity the importance of Port Moresby than Fujita's ability to cast his prying eyes along the east coast of Australia.

Without the bulwark of Moresby to hold them back, Fujita and his modest floatplane would be followed soon enough by much more damaging Japanese forces.

With that end in mind, the Japanese escalated their pressure on the Australian front in New Guinea. On 28 February, two days after Fujita's daring appearance over Melbourne, they struck once more at Moresby, with eleven bombers and five Zeroes. The bombers struck again at Seven Mile, and although they were unable to repeat their earlier success, the Zeroes followed up with a strafing attack that did a great deal more damage.

At the time, Bert Bates, an engineer at the flying boat base, was aboard one of the Catalinas at anchor in Moresby harbour, performing routine maintenance. Suddenly a motor boat pulled up alongside, sent out to retrieve the engineering crews when the air raid warning sounded. Bates clambered into the little boat, and with his comrades decided to sit out the raid in the middle of the bay. Suddenly an aircraft swung around a hill, and began a run down the harbour. 'A Lockheed', announced someone on board, and impressed with the full-throttle display of the unknown aircraft, added: 'Struth, look at 'em go!' Bates was not so sure, and when he saw the machine had a single radial engine, he was comforted by the certainty it was an Australian Wirraway. Looking again, Bates had second thoughts: 'Wirraways be buggered! They're Jap fighters!'

Indeed they were, and the Zero pilots knew their business. They dived straight at the nearest Catalina, and Bates watched as 'columns of spray shot into the air from the nearest "Cat" as the incendiary cannon bullets tore thro' and around its helpless frame'. Two more flying boats suffered the same fate within seconds, and as the Zeroes zoomed into a climbing turn for another firing pass, already the first machine 'was enveloped in flames across its entire wing'.

On shore, journalist Osmar White concluded that Japanese marksmanship had more to commend it than he had hitherto allowed. He wrote of the deadly Zero attack in a paradoxically playful way, noting

'A vast column of smoke and steam': one of the three RAAF Catalinas destroyed in the 28 February 1942 raid burns to the waterline.

how the Japanese fighters 'rolled and turned and looped with the skittish exuberance of ... pilots who see no fighters to oppose them'.

Out on the harbour, Bates was equally taken with the spectacle, but being closer at hand, found it understandably more terrifying. As his little motor boat chugged slowly back to the jetty at the flying boat base, 'on our right the first of the blazing craft was seen to be rapidly sinking, shooting up a vast column of flame and steam as it plunged to its watery grave ... shortly afterwards the second "Cat" with a brilliant burst of pyrotechnics also disappeared from sight'.

The Australian Catalina squadrons had lost heavily again, although on this occasion the Japanese paid some price for their success. One Zero crashed in the raid, and the Australians thought they had shot it down with machine gun fire. The Japanese in turn made their own intelligence error, reporting Petty Officer Katsuaki Nagatomo of the 4th Air Group killed in action. Nagatomo was in fact taken prisoner, and told a different story to the tale of Australian combat success. He fell victim not to the fire of the defences, but to a mechanical fault. As he approached Moresby at altitude, Nagatomo's machine suffered a cockpit fire over the target, well before the Japanese met any anti-aircraft barrage. With his machine ablaze, Nagatomo crash-landed, and in this inglorious way, his wartime career came to an abrupt end.

Suffering from horrible burns, Nagatomo was taken to Australia by a Catalina flown by the irrepressible Bill Bolitho. After his ordeals on the harbour, Bert Bates also flew south on this plane, and was happy to be leaving for the front line, if only for a few days. With the 'singed and bandaged' Nagatomo propped up on a bunk, Bates and his mates smoked and chatted merrily, delighted at the prospect of a return to mainland comforts.

Once there, Nagatomo was interrogated by allied intelligence officers as and when his convalescence allowed; on medical orders, these sessions were limited to an hour at a time. The resulting interrogation reports nevertheless make fascinating reading. A career pilot with

500 hours' experience, having graduated in June 1940, Nagatomo was still confident of Japanese victory. Australian intelligence officers found him 'not inclined to be helpful' during the first round of interrogations, and 'notwithstanding the pain and suffering he was suffering', he showed his captors an air of 'scornful contempt'. Indeed, such were his injuries that doctors had to intervene to bring the first interrogations to a halt. Nagatomo's bearing confirmed pre-war estimates of the quality of Japanese aircrew, including their extreme bravery—he, like his comrades, refused to wear a parachute in combat because such a device in the face of the enemy was unworthy of the samurai tradition.

The devastation inflicted on the defenders of Moresby on 28 February demanded retaliation, and Kingwell did his best to oblige. On 3 March, he sent his strongest available force—just five aircraft—against Gasmata, hoping to deny the Japanese the advantages that base offered as an intermediate landing ground. However, good aeroplane though it was, the Australians had learnt that sending the Hudson alone into airspace defended by Japanese interceptors would result in more losses than their modest force could tolerate. Kingwell therefore opted for a night raid, only to find he had traded the devil of Zero fighters for the deep blue sea of the weather.

When the five Hudsons of 32 Squadron lifted off from Seven Mile on the evening of 3 March, all seemed well—the sky was clear, the wind calm. The tropical idyll soon ended. As the Australians headed north-east, over the Owen Stanleys, they found themselves in a storm over Kokoda, literally. Soon the night was rent with startling lightning bolts, and the Hudson crews were flung about in a severe thunderstorm. One crew opted to return to base, while another flanked the storm front by flying south-east, before turning north again to successfully bomb the target. One machine got through the storm, only to miss Gasmata, and returned to Moresby, metaphorically empty handed.

At the end of this dramatic operation, two Hudsons were missing. Flown by twenty-three-year-old Flight Lieutenant Ken Erwin and twenty-one-year-old Flight Lieutenant Arthur Nicolay, these machines were thought by their comrades to have succumbed to the weather, Kingwell reporting that the Hudsons were certain to have been 'dashed against one of the many high mountains which the storm was completely enveloping'. An understandable conclusion perhaps, especially when the radio operators at Seven Mile heard an aircraft asking for bearings on the outward flight, only on this occasion Kingwell sold his men a little short. Despite his youth, Erwin in particular was a notably experienced pilot, and so able that he was among the first Australian pilots selected to convert to the Hudson, at a time when a modern high-speed bomber was a rarity in the RAAF, and thus the selection of crews to fly them was subject to especially rigorous criteria. He then fought in the early days with Lerew at Rabaul, service that included the very first Australian bombing mission conducted from that base.

In a tribute to their airmanship, both Erwin and Nicolay got through the tempest on 3 March, but it would be many years before any Australian learnt of what became of them on that black and ill-tempered night.

As the war inched its way towards Australian shores, so the list of air force casualties grew. Across the country, a succession of families received the dreaded telegram from the Air Board, advising them with deep regret that their loved one was killed in action. Where the fate of an airman was uncertain, families were told he was missing, leaving them in an awful limbo. These were the telegrams that went out to the families of the men aboard the 11 Squadron Catalinas on 21 January, until the well-meaning Reverend Hardie blundered into their private anxiety with letters asserting that the crews were in fact dead.

When the mother of John 'Jackie' Perrett, flight engineer aboard the Catalina of Thompson and Metzler, received the telegram from the Air Board advising her that Perrett was missing, she naturally kept her hopes alive, but was understandably puzzled by Hardie's certainty her son was dead. She wrote immediately to the Brisbane office of the Red Cross Bureau, then a key organisation in military affairs, since it acted as a 'go-between' among the combatant powers in matters affecting prisoners of war and missing servicemen. 'Today I received a letter from the chaplain at Port Moresby,' wrote Mrs Perrett, 'sympathising with me on the loss of my son'. No doubt like most mothers, Mrs Perrett had refused to give up hope, especially as the RAAF had only posted her son as missing. As she explained, Hardie's letter therefore came as an 'awful shock'.

The Red Cross dutifully wrote to the Air Board seeking details of Perrett's presumed death. Officials swung into action, writing back to the Perretts on 26 February, refuting Hardie and assuring the family that Jackie Perrett might still be alive. At least now they gave some context for the loss of his Catalina, explaining how the plane had come under anti-aircraft fire, but that 'nothing further was heard from the missing aircraft'. As M. C. Langslow, Secretary to the Air Board, went on to conclude, 'while indicating no special reason for believing your son may be alive', the known circumstances 'quite equally give no definite information that he has lost his life'. The Perretts were assured that every effort was being made to ascertain the final facts, and Langslow undertook to provide any further information as it came to hand.

In these circumstances, one Australian family faced their own personal turmoil, and the nation more broadly looked hesitantly towards the north. Thanks to the skill and bravery of a handful of men like Kingwell and Cohen, Pedrina and Hemsworth, Port Moresby was holding out, but for how much longer?

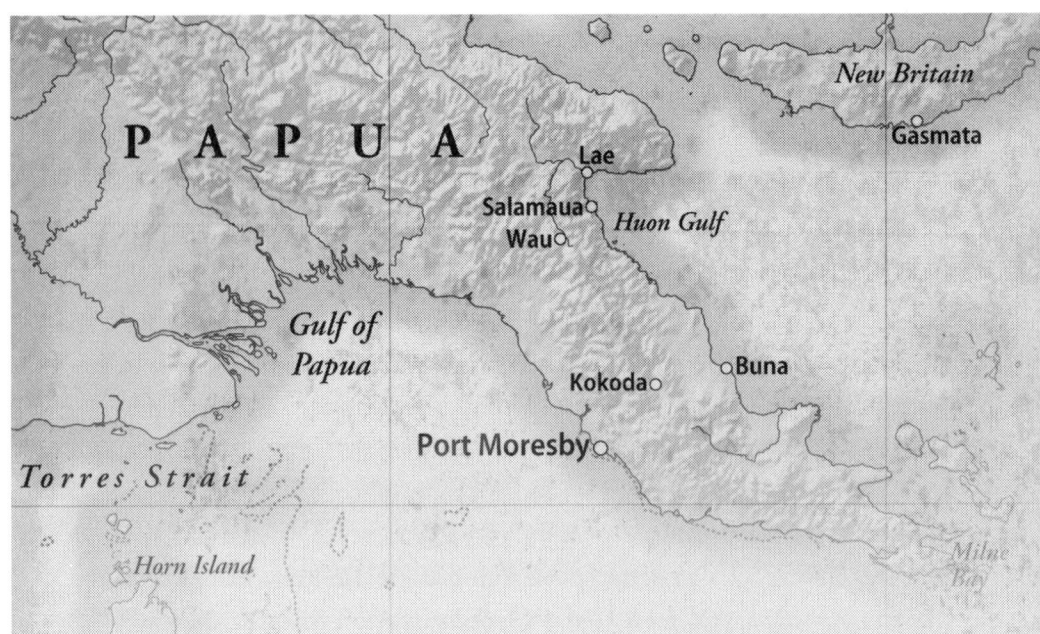

CHAPTER FOUR
'We just got our beer ...'

To establish a springboard for their final push on Port Moresby, the Japanese next set out to secure airbases on the north coast of New Guinea. In the shape of the aerodrome facilities at Lae and Salamaua, they found them ready made, but it took the Japanese six weeks to follow up their initial raids on these bases. As was their custom, when the Japanese moved to seize desired infrastructure, they did so in force.

The Japanese operation against northern New Guinea came in two related parts, with a battalion of the army's South Seas Force allocated to take Salamaua, while the navy's Kure Special Naval Landing Force seized Lae. Both received a strong naval escort, including the four heavy cruisers of the 6th Squadron, which had already performed a similar role in the operation against Rabaul. The well-established Japanese Navy air units at Rabaul would provide air support, the 4th Air Group operating a mix of Zero fighters and Mitsubishi Type 1 bombers (known to the Allies as the 'Betty'), and the 1st Air Group flying the older Mitsubishi Type 96 bombers (code-named 'Nell' by the Allies).

The over-worked Hudson crews of 32 Squadron did their best to keep track of Japanese preparations. Photo reconnaissance missions were mounted over Rabaul on both 5 and 6 March, and indeed a Hudson on patrol found the invasion convoy headed for Salamaua at sea on 7 March, but without an adequate strike force, an opportunity to hit the Japanese while the invasion flotillas were at their most vulnerable was missed.

In the early hours of 8 March, three men—Jim Birrell, Jim Keenan and Garth Raynor—occupied an NGVR look-out post at the mouth of Francisco River, just south of Salamaua airfield. Peering out into the pre-dawn gloom, Keenan was not sure of what he could see. He roused his sleeping comrades, and the three Australians returned to their post—to find Japanese barges pushing through the surf onto the beach.

The transport available to the Australian militiamen was a battered and unreliable truck, but mercifully—'for the first time ever'—it sprang into life at the first attempt. Thus propelled, the little party set about their appointed tasks, setting fire to the airfield fuel dump, destroying the town's wireless mast and cutting the wire bridge over the Francisco.

At the airfield, they found another group of NGVR men already torching the fuel dump. As the Japanese formed up at the beach and moved inland to the airfield, NGVR rifleman Tom Brannelly discharged the one and only bullet fired against the Salamaua invasion force. He shot and killed a Japanese officer at close range while the latter was giving instructions to his men. As the Japanese fanned out to seek their attacker, Brannelly and his small band jumped the back fence of the house in which they were quartered. They made off over the Francisco bridge, and after their crossing, Keenan quickly cut the wire cables and left the Japanese to find their own way over to the far bank.

Apart from Brannelly's lone shot, the more substantial opposition facing the Japanese came during their passage through the Bismarck Sea, when successive tropical storms battered their ships. Those carrying the army troops then had some difficulty entering Salamaua harbour on the night of 7 March due to bad weather. However, without a serious defence to delay them, Japanese troops were soon ashore, and the RAAF's first blow in anger did not come until the following day, when 32 Squadron's commanding officer Kingwell made a lone attack at Salamaua. He reported hitting an 8000-tonne merchant ship with anti-submarine bombs, and left it ablaze and listing. The report of damage was accurate, but that of its extent was not. Japanese archives record only slight damage to the transport ship *Yokohama Maru*, which killed three men and wounded eight more. Later in the day, Kingwell returned to the attack, accompanied by two other

Hudsons, one piloted by the unflagging Pedrina. Again, Japanese records show this raid inflicted some harm, albeit modest, with a single hit on the destroyer *Asanagi*, once again insufficient to sink the vessel.

The Australians were fighting back as hard as their scant resources would allow. But if Japanese commanders assumed the latest acquisition to their empire had been safely accomplished, they were in for a rude shock.

Unknown to them, as the Japanese were landing at Lae and Salamaua, an American carrier task force was jockeying for position to raid Rabaul. A few weeks earlier, the carrier *Lexington* had attempted such a strike, but was detected by Japanese patrol planes, and then attacked by torpedo bombers. American forces were counter-punching rather than taking the offensive, and thus it was not in the interests of American strategy to send a precious carrier into the teeth of a forewarned Japanese airbase. The *Lexington* therefore withdrew, but not before her fighters shot down fifteen of seventeen Betty bombers from 4th Air Group that attempted to sink the carrier.

When the Lae invasion force presented itself, the American fleet seized its chance, ditched the plan to raid Rabaul, and moved to attack the Japanese shipping clustered in the Huon Gulf. Safe in the waters south of Port Moresby, the US strike could launch in secret, and thus it achieved complete surprise at dawn on 10 March. One hundred and four carrier aircraft swept over the Japanese anchorages, sinking the transports *Kongo Maru* and *Yokohama Maru*, the minesweeper *Tama Maru*, and *Ten'yo Maru*, a luxury liner pressed into service as a minelayer. Japanese loss of life was equally heavy, with six army and 126 naval personnel killed.

The Lae raid confirmed two things: first, the American carriers, which had escaped the carnage at Pearl Harbor, were a long-term threat to Japanese plans, and second, Port Moresby had once again played

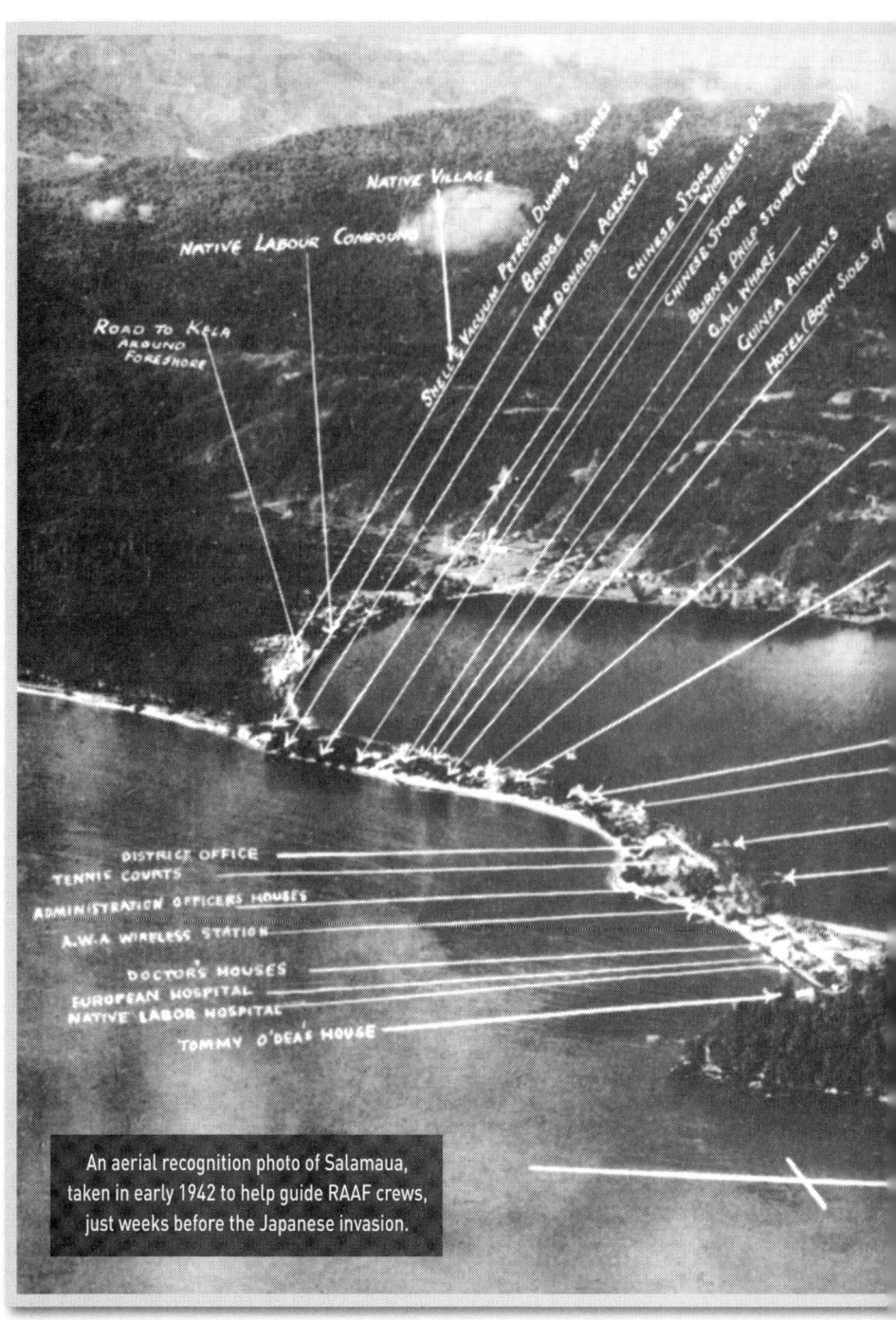

An aerial recognition photo of Salamaua, taken in early 1942 to help guide RAAF crews, just weeks before the Japanese invasion.

'WE JUST GOT OUR BEER ...'

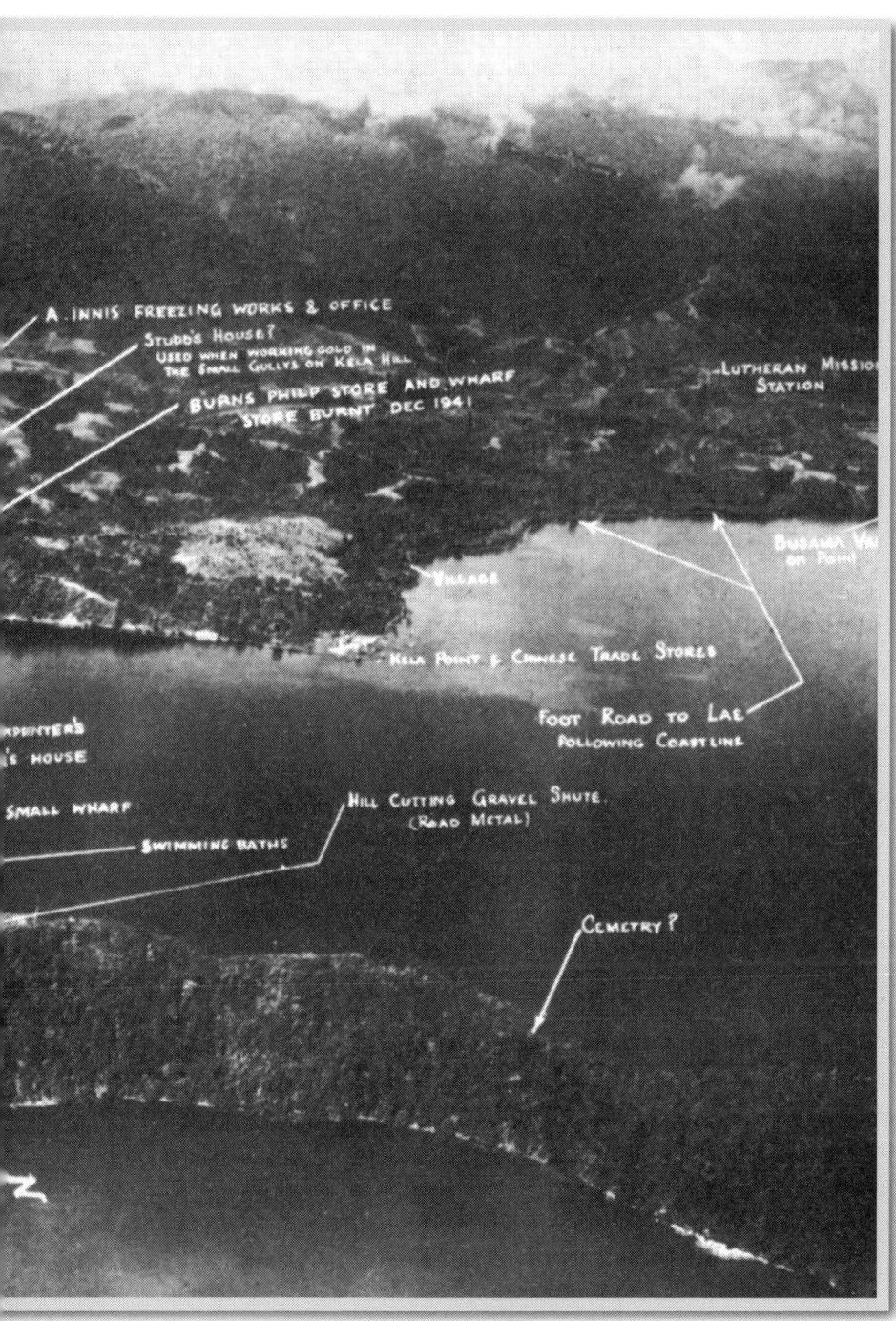

its role as a defensive buttress for allied forces in the Coral Sea area. Japanese strategists made the mistake of ignoring the first lesson, and instead of pursuing the Americans, sent the bulk of the best carriers off to harass the British in the Indian Ocean in April, but they digested the second lesson well enough. Preparations for Operation MO accelerated, only now the invasion of Port Moresby would be covered by a Japanese carrier force, to protect the troopships en route, and repeat the success at Darwin by raiding Cooktown and Townsville, the principal transit bases on the ferry route for aircraft reinforcements to New Guinea.

The Americans were already committed to the south Pacific as a key theatre of war, but the invasion of Lae prompted a reassessment of the allied position. In an appreciation dated 14 March 1942, US strategists concluded that the threat to the Pacific supply line was increasing. With the fighting in Java over in another disastrous defeat for allied arms, the competition for American resources between the south Pacific and the Netherlands East Indies also ended. Accordingly, the Americans allocated still further men and material to meet the threat to New Guinea, Fiji and New Caledonia. Yet the danger remained that the Japanese, hurt but not rebuffed at Lae, would get to Moresby before allied plans were fully realised.

While the Pentagon pondered the great decisions of strategy, elsewhere on 14 March 1942, the war ground on more prosaically. That morning, construction worker Daniel McGrath stood at the bar of the grandly named Royal Hotel on Horn Island in the Torres Strait, and took his first sip of beer. He and his mates were on the island to build defence works and expand the RAAF airstrip, to cater for the increased traffic from the mainland to Port Moresby. The size of the task had kept them busy for weeks. Dropping in to their local for a quick drink before getting back to work, the men were puzzled to find themselves interrupted. 'We just got our beer', McGrath explained afterwards, when 'all the whole bar started to shake, all the bottles on the shelves rattled ... somebody said "what's that?" and another bloke said, "it's an earth quake"'.

The tremor was in fact the reverberation from the engines of eight Betty bombers and 12 Zeroes of the 4th Air Group running in to attack the RAAF aerodrome. Although this fact is little known today, the Torres Strait islands, especially Thursday Island, which boasted a battery of coast defence guns, and neighbouring Horn Island, with its airfield, occupied a strategic place in Australian defences. In addition to their role as a staging post to Moresby, the islands formed a watch-house on the route into the Coral Sea from the west.

The Japanese had only recently come to realise the importance of these islands. They mounted the Horn Island operation on the back of intelligence gathered from a source that would have shocked the Moresby defenders. The Australians believed their losses in the raid on Gasmata on 3 March were due to the weather over the Owen Stanleys. Little did they realise at the time, but the missing bombers got as far as the target, only to be shot down in the vicinity of Gasmata. Maps recovered from one of the Australian machines showed the Horn Island aerodrome to Japanese eyes for the first time. The importance of the installation, in forming a flank guard to the Coral Sea, was then brought into sharp relief for the Japanese with the success of the American carrier raid on Lae.

However, when this crucial Australian base first came under enemy fire on 14 March 1942, yet again the RAAF had little with which to meet the threat. Equipped with near-useless Wirraways, 24 Squadron constituted the Australian air defence, and it was sheer coincidence that when the Japanese raid approached after midday, Kittyhawks of the American 49th Fighter Group were there to meet them.

Well equipped though they might have been, the Americans were nevertheless still learning the combat ropes, and their commander Captain Robert Morrisey gave his pilots the most simple orders he could craft: take off, and stick together around him. Even this basic plan soon went awry. As the Kittyhawks climbed for combat altitude, Morrisey tested his guns and found they failed, so he was forced to return to base and have them hurriedly serviced. By the time he was airborne again, the Japanese bombers were making their bomb runs. In the excitement of their first battle, Morrisey's men broke ranks and began making individual firing passes on the Japanese formation, claiming (incorrectly) to have shot down one of the Betty bombers in the process.

The Zero escort was strong and experienced. Led by Lieutenant Shiro Kawai, a career fighter pilot who commanded the air defence of the important Japanese base at Truk in December 1941, the Japanese pilots included Hiroyoshi Nishizawa, Geoff Hemsworth's adversary over Simpson Harbour the previous month.

With their own formation broken up in the pursuit of the bombers, the Americans were quickly in tactical difficulty, and could thank only the rugged design of the Kittyhawk for keeping the odds more or less even. Two Kittyhawks soon separated from the main fight, and the much more nimble Zeroes repeatedly hit them, wounding both pilots. While the Kittyhawks might have had fewer firing opportunities, when they did let fly, their heavy machine gun armament had a devastating impact on the lightweight Zeroes. The Japanese might have held tactical advantages, but when Lieutenant A. T. House drew a bead on a Zero that darted across his sights, he shot down the fighter flown by Lieutenant Nobuhiro Iwasaki, killing the Japanese pilot.

While House and Iwasaki fought their battle, Morrisey found a Zero on his tail. Unable to throw his pursuer, Morrisey was in trouble, and he was only rescued by a remarkable—and unbelievably lucky—piece of flying. Backing up after his stoush with Iwasaki, House came to his commander's aid, aiming to knock the Zero off Morrisey's tail. Closing in, House pressed the teat-trigger on his joystick, but the Browning guns now

The aircrew mess at Horn Island in 1942 matched the undeveloped state of the defences.

refused to fire. With Morrisey unable to shake the Japanese fighter, House made the brave decision to ram the Zero, and amazingly, accomplished the feat. As Morrisey swept in to collide with his opponent, his starboard wing smashed the Zero's cockpit canopy. The little fighter blew up at once, killing the pilot, Genkichi Oishi, and leaving 'pieces on fire falling everywhere', as House later described. The Kittyhawk itself spun away and House prepared to bail out, then the fighter righted itself. Barely under control, House managed to land, but only after three attempts. Of his act of derring-do, House was self-effacing: 'It wasn't much of a decision ... Morrisey had a family, he was my commanding officer, I just felt I owed it to him and the outfit'.

As the combat subsided, one of the wounded American pilots, Lieutenant Clarence Sandford, attempted to gain his bearings. Disoriented, he headed first in what he thought was a southerly direction, but when he failed to find land, assumed his compass was faulty.

In fact, Sandford flew more or less due west, and eventually flew 400 kilometres across the Gulf of Carpentaria to the Arnhem Land coast. Running out of fuel, he prepared to bail out, but thought better of it when he saw a school of large sharks below. The pause was opportune, because land now came into sight, and when he took to his parachute, Sandford was just five kilometres from the coast. Battling shrapnel wounds in his foot, Sandford struggled ashore, to be assisted by two Aboriginal men who walked the American, sunburnt and exhausted, to Yirrkala Mission. Evacuated to Darwin, Sandford went through a nine-month convalescence, and only rejoined combat operations in 1944.

Attacking an Australian target, the Japanese paid the RAAF an unwarranted compliment, mistaking the American fighters for 'Hawker Hurricanes', the implication being that until that time the RAAF flew mostly British aircraft. Thanks to an official sleight of hand, the Australian press was also encouraged to promote the idea that the RAAF was the saviour of Horn Island. The Australian government issued a press release, in which Lieutenant House was described as an 'Allied' fighter pilot. When the mainland newspapers got hold of the incredible story of a Zero falling to a selfless ramming attack, they naïvely concluded that this must be the work of one of 'our' pilots, and duly trumpeted the achievement as Australian.

The principal local contribution to the defence of the Torres Strait was in fact more mundane, and comprised a handful of coast defence guns and a small garrison on nearby Thursday Island, commanded by Lieutenant Commander Rupert Hurst. A distinguished World War I soldier, he later wrote a graphic account of the air combat as it swirled overhead. When the Japanese singled out the Horn Island aerodrome, Hurst watched from the relative safety of neighbouring Thursday Island, as the Betty bombers made their bomb run. Through a break in the heavy clouds, Hurst saw the

Japanese unload their ordnance on the airfield, and then pass over him on Thursday Island, he assumed for the purposes of completing the mission with a photographic reconnaissance of the fortress. Zeroes then followed up, strafing the aerodrome, destroying one Hudson and briefly setting fire to another before ground crews extinguished the blaze.

It was at this point that the American fighters intervened, and down below, Hurst watched as aircraft flitted in and out of the cloud cover, firing as they went. The Australian colonel was naturally delighted with the effort of his allies and the effect it had on the morale of his troops. Hurst at once sent out search parties to inspect the wreckage of the Japanese machines, one of which fell on nearby Hammond Island. When the Australians inspected the site, there was not much to find, the Zero having hit the ground with such force that debris covered an area of over a kilometre. The Japanese vastly inflated the actual results of their operation, claiming to have shot down thirteen 'Hawker Hurricanes' and destroyed three Hudsons on the ground.

The aftermath of the raid provided yet another example of Australian extemporisation. The Thursday Island garrison lacked a trained bomb disposal team. To deal with a large unexploded bomb near the Horn Island airfield, and thereby allow air operations to recommence, Hurst despatched what he optimistically called a 'volunteer suicide squad', made up of sappers from the Royal Australian Engineers. Led by Major Tom Sherman, the nine-man party went to work with admirable gusto, excavating their way down through some two metres of sandy loam to the bomb, which they found had shed two of its tail fins as it bored its way in. With the bomb uncovered, Sherman called forward a medico from the Australian Army Medical Corps to provide some technical assistance. The good doctor examined the bomb with his stethoscope, but thankfully reported 'all was quiet'.

With his quarry sleeping peacefully, Sherman showed himself to be a man of direct disposition—he simply slung a strop around the bomb, tied this improvised apparatus to a truck and set off in first gear. With the bomb hauled up to ground level by these abrupt means, a second strop was added and the ordnance then swung onto the lip of the excavation, where it was dragged away at the end of a long rope towards a large crater made by another bomb during the raid. When rough ground threatened to set off the unexploded weapon, two men were called forward to carry it to safety, although Sherman did admit in his report 'we were afraid of bumping the fuse cap', with obviously harmful results for the two load bearers.

They were presumably even more nervous than their commander, but with the bomb safely conveyed to its crater, Sherman attempted to detonate it. The application of three plugs of gelignite failed to make any impression, and the Australian engineer concluded with some disappointment that the thing was a 'complete dud'. Sherman admitted some of his methods were a 'trifle unorthodox', but curiosity was probably his principal character trait. Unable to blow up the bomb, he thought he might set fire to some of the explosive, presumably with the simple if exuberant aim of seeing what would happen. Yet again, Japanese weapons manufacture let him down. He found the greenish-yellow explosive burnt very tamely, and even then, only with 'some difficulty' could he obtain any kind of ignition. Horn Island's adventure into the realms of the Boys' Own Annual ended appropriately, with a squib. Heavy rains soon fell, filling the crater, submerging what remained of the unexploded bomb and dashing Sherman's final line of enquiry, the removal of the fuse cap for examination.

The efforts of Sherman and his men might have been amateurish, but the need to keep open the Horn Island base was real enough. The next phase of the New Guinea campaign was a race between Japanese plans for the Moresby invasion and the arrival of Australian reinforcements, and Horn Island was a crucial lane in which that contest would be run.

To secure an isolated garrison like Port Moresby requires a military infrastructure of great complexity, and not all of it is necessarily glamorous or combative. Signals units, hospitals, supply depots and the like provide the administrative shaft to what is often a very small spear-tip, and this is especially true as combat operations move into remote locations like the jungle of New Guinea and the surrounding islands.

Had Australian strategy better reflected the national interest, much of this infrastructure would already have existed by the time Japan entered the war. Now it was a question of hasty improvisation. Among Moresby's many deficiencies in March 1942 was the absence of something as mundane as a searchlight battery, needed to illuminate Japanese night bombers so that anti-aircraft gunners could see the targets they were meant to hit.

To fill this gap, on 23 February 1942 a searchlight unit was hurriedly formed out of personnel drafted from the Maribyrnong Searchlight Training Camp in Melbourne's western suburbs. Within a week, 67 Anti Aircraft Searchlight (AASL) Unit was aboard ship, bound for New Guinea. Its men enjoyed a journey that served as a metaphor for the transition of the country as a whole, from comfortable peacetime routine to a nation on the front line. Embarked on the steamer *Macdhui*, the troops luxuriated in an à la carte menu, including boiled hepuka fish with anchovy sauce, a choice of two roasts (beef or mutton, with all the trimmings), and desserts including ginger pudding with canton sauce, and raspberry jelly.

Disembarkation at Moresby no doubt came as a shock after such luxuries. The ranks of 67 AASL were lined up on parade as soon as they got ashore and dosed by medical orderlies with tablespoons of quinine, the ferociously bitter anti-malarial treatment that leaves a very different after-taste to ginger pudding. The next course in this new diet was no more palatable: salt tablets, thought to be needed to avoid cramp in the sultry tropics.

Thus medicated and nourished, the searchlight men went about their work, hauling up the big lights onto the hills around Moresby, using antique trucks where they could, and sheer brute force where the vehicles would not go. Seventeen days later, they were finished, and the Australian base had another piece in its growing arsenal.

Other progress was being made as well. While the men of 67 ASL laboured, air force technicians of 29 Radar Station went 'on air' to provide Moresby with its first radar warning set. Although technical problems meant that radar performance was poor for many months, and the mountains to the near north blocked out coverage in the sector from which virtually all Japanese raids originated, Moresby at least had another basic building block for a modern air defence system.

And even with the radar operating under some limitations, careful planning could partly compensate for what technology could not provide. As the searchlights and radar masts went up, the Port Moresby garrison also prepared a ring of 'observer' posts. These were three-man outposts circling Port Moresby at a radius of nearly 50 kilometres. Equipped with binoculars and a wireless set, the 'spotters' in these posts could give Moresby warning of incoming aircraft, including the strength of the formation, its direction, altitude and speed.

Despite being distinctly 'low tech', this system worked well in the Battle of Britain, and it would come to be an integral part of Moresby's armoury. Although simple in concept, the task of building these observer stations was not. Eight were required, in an arc from Rorona in the west to Rigo in the east, and the observers had to build their own accommodation, a grand term for structures that were cobbled together in the jungle from whatever could be found on site. The terrain was naturally difficult: in some areas, 'the country was too wild and mountainous' even for local villagers. Each team of spotters 'had to hack a site for their station out of a mountainside covered with dense jungle and wet moss often two feet thick, and then construct a rough hut' from materials found in the immediate vicinity. Rations were limited and local food scarce, but the work of these hardy men meant that the chances of a surprise attack on Moresby from the north could be reduced, if not eliminated.

The Australian position was deepening, but it lacked one vital component, without which the Japanese might yet get to Moresby before the garrison was ready.

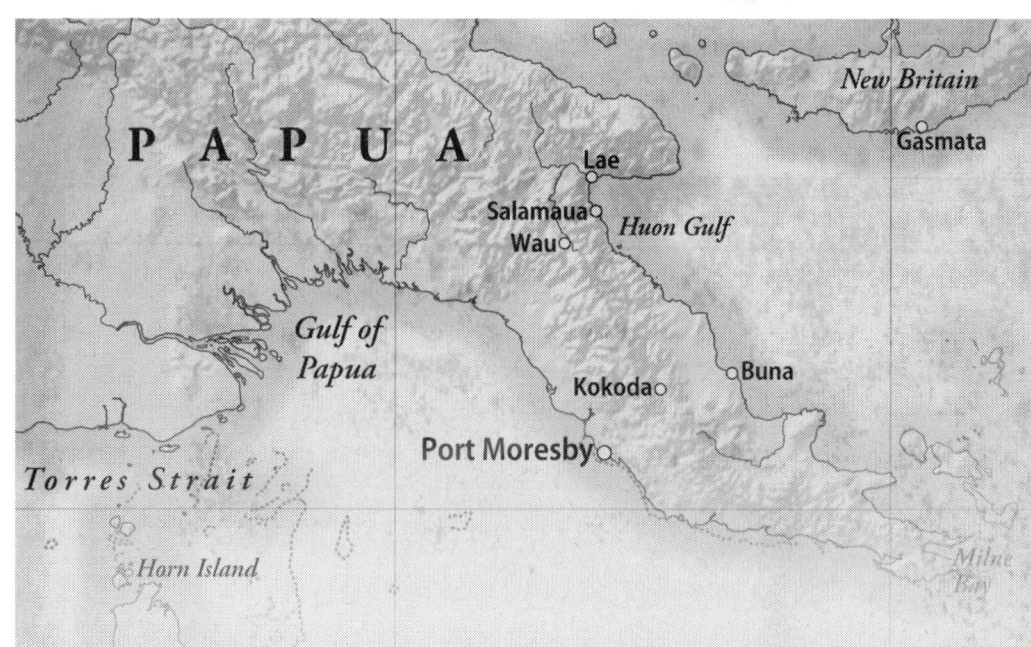

CHAPTER FIVE
'... a beautiful aeroplane to fly'

On the morning of 21 March 1942, Chief Petty Officer Heihachi Kawai lifted his big Mitsubishi Type 1 Betty bomber, the best of its type in the Japanese armed forces, off the airfield at Vunakanau, Rabaul, and set course to the south-west. With his crew of six, Kawai was out to reconnoitre Port Moresby, tracking the flow of Australian reinforcements prior to Operation MO. Running into the target, Kawai expected no trouble—he and his comrades from 4th Air Group had bombed Australian installations several times in the preceding weeks without airborne opposition.

Down below, Ray Neal, serving with the Australian army gun crew manning the coastal defence battery at Paga Point at the entrance to Moresby harbour, looked up as he had many times before, tracking the Japanese intruder through binoculars, frustrated, again, that the garrison had no air cover to call its own. The day was dry and sunny, in Neal's estimation, a 'typical tropical afternoon with 60–70 per cent cloud cover'.

However, both Neal and the Japanese bomber crew would find something very atypical about the day. Now over the harbour, Kawai's gunners suddenly saw two fighters diving down to attack in a classic firing pass from astern. They were P40 Kittyhawks, each armed with six .50 calibre machine guns, more than sufficient to deal with the Mitsubishi. Like all Japanese combat planes, the Betty saved weight by omitting armour plating and self-sealing fuel tanks (such tanks are fitted with a lining of rubber, so that when they are punctured, the rubber vulcanises to provide a temporary seal).

From below, the long-suffering Australian garrison watched the fight unfold. Osmar White was one of them, and he happened to be standing next to a senior air force officer. As they watched, tracer fire arced across the blue sky. In pressing home the attack, one of the fighters passed so close to its prey that collision seemed inevitable, to which the RAAF commander muttered darkly, 'Jesus, there's no future in that, you bloody young fool'.

At the coastal guns by the harbour, Neal was entranced, and watched as a 'bright burst of fire' broke out inside the Japanese bomber, developing rapidly into an aerial bonfire. The Betty staggered, and fell away trailing black smoke. In a long death ride, it dropped to earth, crashing into the sea to 'make a large splash' near the Basilisk Beacon to the south of Moresby harbour. There were no survivors.

At Seven Mile airfield, the base from which the Kittyhawks had scrambled, and all around the harbour, men gathered on ridges and hilltops, celebrating wildly. To the troops, these planes were the 'Neverhawks', or the 'Tomorrow-hawks', merely the promise of things to come rather than actual machines. Now myth had become reality, and the air war in New Guinea was a different fight, but where had these fighters come from, and who was flying them?

The 'back of beyond' is a quintessential and evocative piece of Australian idiom. Even today Yalleroi, way past Emerald in central Queensland, more than earns the title. In 1939, it consisted of barely six buildings, including a general store-cum-hotel, relics of its past glory as a former staging post of Cobb & Co.

As well as quenching the thirst of hard-bitten jackeroos, the pub provided lodgings to Arthur Tucker, a nineteen-year-old who served the local primary school as a student teacher. Listening to the radio one September evening, along with the store owner, Tucker heard Australian Prime Minister Robert Menzies perform his melancholy duty, announcing to the country that as Great Britain was once again at war with Germany, so too was Australia.

For young men like Tucker, stuck in routine jobs, in some cases at the end of the world, war provides—perhaps regrettably—an avenue of escape, to adventure, travel and excitement. In young Arthur's case, the lure was also technological. He had always been interested in aeroplanes, so the dawn of the new conflict provided a once-in-a-lifetime opportunity to fly. And the RAAF was interested soon enough in Tucker, because he was the sort of specimen to put a gleam in the eye of any recruiting sergeant. During his various postings around the Queensland outback, young Tucker, a rugby footballer, held his own against teams of granite-like cane-cutters and flint-hard jackeroos. Better still, to go with his physical toughness, Tucker also happened to be a crack shot with a rifle, winning prizes for his shooting club in district junior championships.

Country boys were not the only ones in search of adventure. In Melbourne, twenty-one-year-old John Piper also looked at enlistment as an opportunity to learn to fly. A carpet salesman studying commerce part-time at the University of Melbourne, Piper had wanted to fly but never found enough money to learn. He at least had some military experience, having served in the militia for a few years. To begin with, life in the air force was not much different from this part-time soldiering: 'I'd be one of the few people that has marched every inch of the Essendon Aerodrome, doing left turns and right turns, and disappearing into the distance'.

John Pettett, a Randwick boy from Sydney's eastern suburbs, found like Piper that the privilege of earning his wings first required a long period of mind-numbing regimentation. Pettett made a good case for admission to the RAAF thanks to his technical skills. He left school early in the Depression to work in the engineering department of Radio 2UE, but went back part-time to get his matriculation certificate so he could pursue engineering studies. Pettett was another inspired by romantic notions of the air—his favourite film of the 1930s was *Dawn Patrol*, the Hollywood tribute to the 'chivalrous' air war over the Western Front in 1918.

He too applied to join the air force the day after war was declared, but like many others, was frustrated by the slow pace with which the

STORM OVER KOKODA

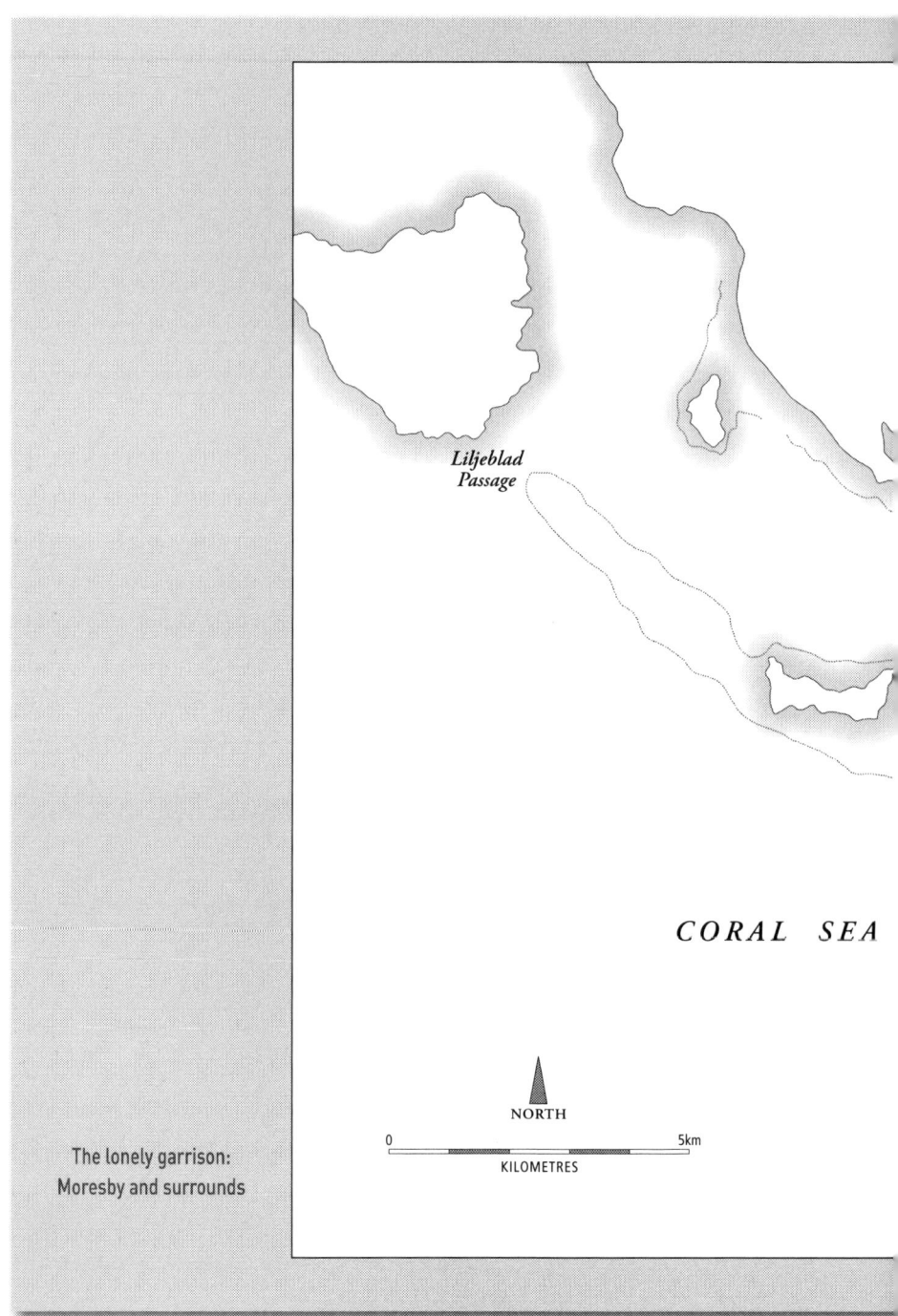

Liljeblad Passage

CORAL SEA

The lonely garrison: Moresby and surrounds

'... A BEAUTIFUL AEROPLANE TO FLY'

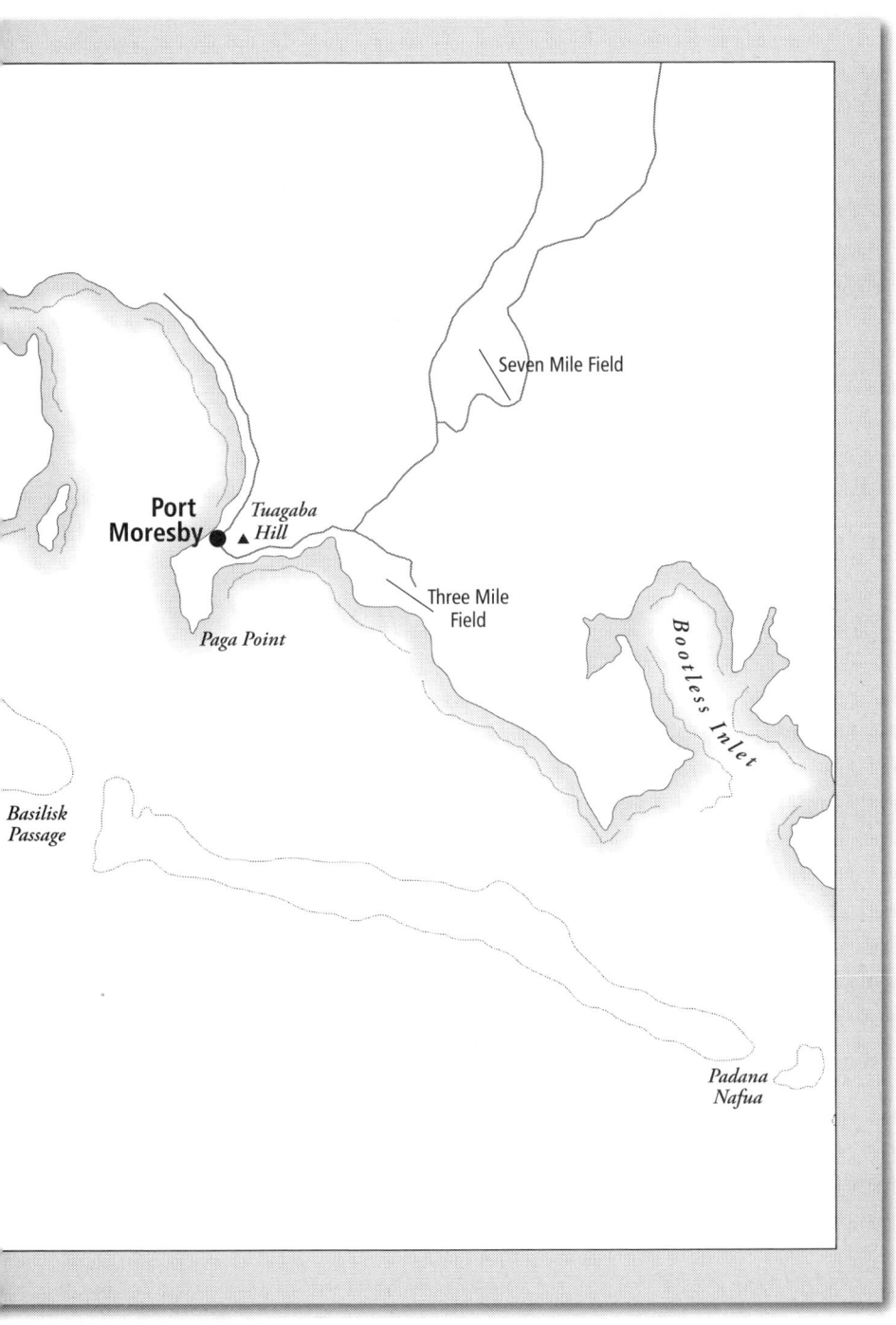

101

war effort built up. He only went into training in January 1941, but his flying school was at least close to home, conveniently located at Sydney's Mascot aerodrome.

Pettett soon found that flying was dangerous, even before he got to a combat zone. With his instructor Pilot Officer Bob Cherry, Pettett was engaged in instrument training in his Tiger Moth biplane on the morning of 6 June 1941. As he dropped out of cloud down to 300 metres, he was shocked by a 'great crash and a bump'. Gathering his senses, he saw a piece of the lower wing missing, and when Cherry called out 'tighten your straps', Pettett realised they were in peril. Cherry 'sideslipped' the stricken Tiger to the ground. During the wild descent, Pettett noticed they were over the Lakes golf course near the airfield. Himself a golfer, Pettett had an odd thought—noticing a fire burning in the middle of the fairway, he sympathised with the inconvenience this must be for handicappers teeing off on a Saturday morning. The thought did not linger, as the little Tiger Moth, with its undercarriage dangling like so many sticks from the fuselage, just 'dug straight in' when they hit the ground. Up on its nose went the biplane, causing Pettett to bang his own nose on the crash pad that lined the front of the cockpit. The plane flipped over, leaving Pettett dangling in his straps, dazed and convinced, 'I was finished'.

Pettett was not done for, but two of his comrades were. The fire he had seen on the way down came not from garden clippings in a golf course clean-up, but the funeral pyre of a second Tiger Moth, which lost its upper wing on the machine of Pettett and Cherry in what was virtually a head-on collision. On the ground, the proprietor of the golf course kiosk, J. Davenport, saw the machines touch briefly, and then one spin away with part of a wing missing. Hopelessly out of control, it burst into flames on impact, such that when Davenport arrived panting on the scene, nothing could be done to save trainee Tom Hodge and instructor Sergeant Jack Holt. Davenport had done his best, but he was soon followed by 1500 gawping onlookers, whose macabre interest in

'... A BEAUTIFUL AEROPLANE TO FLY'

Left to right: Arthur Tucker, John Pettett and John Piper.

the sight was such that they required an armed guard to keep them back. Pettett, despite his battered nose, was flying again that afternoon.

Most young men training in the RAAF in 1940 were destined for service with the British air force via the Empire Air Training Scheme. A small minority were posted to home-based squadrons, and one of these was John Piper, who went to 22 Squadron at Richmond. There, he flew shipping patrols, chaperoning the great ocean liners leaving Sydney Harbour, carrying with them the Australian Army to the Middle East. However, somebody in command saw something in Piper to think he had a talent for single-engined fighters, because he was one of four RAAF officers sent to Singapore in 1941 to do a specialist fighter tactics course. The Australians got some theoretical insight into high-performance combat, but still lacked the crucial ingredient of operational experience: 'all we did was whiz around the place doing beam attacks and quarter attacks, just standard textbook things really'. Returning home, the theory was wasted, because there were no fighters to fly. Piper went back to

103

flying Wirraways, this time at Brisbane's Archerfield base, and waited for something to happen that might take him closer to the fighting.

Eager young pilots like Piper could not gain combat experience in the RAAF because so few regular RAAF squadrons were serving overseas. Only two such units were flying combat missions in 1940—10 Squadron, which we have already met, flying Sunderland flying boats from British bases, and 3 Squadron, flying a succession of fighter types in North Africa.

This was a distinguished unit, and its record showed what the RAAF might have done had pre-war plans to send an expeditionary force of Australian career pilots to Europe come to fruition. Fighting first the Italians, and later the Germans, as well as the Vichy French in Syria, 3 Squadron developed an enviable reputation, and produced many of the very best fighter pilots in the RAAF, including a young officer by the name of Pete Jeffery.

In its hour of need, the RAAF did not have many like Jeffery to turn to, but he was just the sort of pilot for the crisis of 1942. Just weeks before Pearl Harbor in November 1941, in the desert fighting to relieve the siege of Tobruk, Jeffery proved his mettle in spectacular fashion, landing in the open desert to pick up a fellow pilot downed by the enemy. With two men crammed into the cockpit of a single-seat fighter, Jeffery returned safely to base, a feat that earned him a Distinguished Service Order (DSO).

In the days after the raid on Darwin on 19 February 1942, every kind of rumour swept around the Top End's military camps: the Japanese were on the horizon, the American Army was on its way, the Australians would pull back to the south, and so on. The only thing Bob Crawford and Mick Butler did not hear by way of rumour was the order they eventually received.

A week after having seen what the Japanese could do, they were told to report to Archerfield, selected as two of the handful of pilots to join the most important combat unit the RAAF has ever formed, a squadron of single-engined fighter planes, needed urgently to defend Australia and its northern territories. This was a development made possible by luck rather than good management. For two years, RAAF high command had denied the need for fighter aircraft. The Americans had already spurned one Australian attempt to ask for their charity, but now with enough Curtiss P40 Kittyhawk fighters to go around, they relented, and diverted seventy-five of these machines to the RAAF, sufficient to form three squadrons.

The job of establishing these from scratch went to Pete Jeffery. Having completed his tour of duty in Libya, Jeffery returned to Australia, and took on the most important work the RAAF then had to offer. The first of the new units was numbered 75 Squadron, but with so few experienced combat pilots to draw on, the RAAF could find only a handful of key leaders like Jeffery to send to it. Others like Butler and Crawford had an impressive total of flying hours in their log-books, and some like Piper had even completed specialist fighter courses, but only Jeffery and some key lieutenants had the combat experience needed to convert flying skill into operational effectiveness.

Frighteningly, some of 75 Squadron's first intake of pilots came straight from flying schools. Arthur Tucker had recently completed an operational training course at Nhill in Victoria, but was expecting a posting to Canada for further training before going on to Great Britain for service under the Empire Air Training Scheme. The national emergency interrupted that particular career path, and Tucker found himself sent to Bankstown airfield in Sydney's south-western suburbs.

When he got there, Tucker was in for a shock. Bankstown was home to an inexperienced US unit, the 7th Pursuit Squadron, and Tucker and a handful of other Australians joined the Americans for familiarisation training on the Kittyhawk. This was a training program in name only. An officer handed Tucker the aeroplane's instruction manual, told him to read it, and when he could start the engine, take off. Fortunately Tucker found guidance in an older pilot also slated to join the new fighter unit, Alan Whetters, who had been flying since 1936, for part of the time as a flight instructor. With many hours of flying time in his log-book, Whetters went first on the Kittyhawk conversion course, and returned with the reassuring news that the American fighter was 'just like a Wirraway, only with a longer nose—you can't go wrong'. With these encouraging words, Tucker taxied down to the end of the strip. After the initial surprise generated by the surge of power when he opened up the Kittyhawk's throttle, something with which he was quite unfamiliar, he found Whetters was indeed correct; the Kittyhawk was a 'beautiful aeroplane to fly'.

There were good reasons for Whetters and Tucker finding the Kittyhawk a first-rate aeroplane. Its bloodlines went deep into the history of American aviation. Perhaps even more than the mighty Boeing company, the Curtiss-Wright Corporation, the firm that made the P40, was the premier US aircraft manufacturer of the inter-war years.

This was an enterprise rich in aeronautical achievement. Its founder, Glenn Curtiss, stood alongside Orville and Wilbur Wright as one of the original giants of American aviation. Curtiss may have left school in his early teens, but his inveterate mechanical tinkering was an expression of the practical energy of the American pioneer. This was a culture of meritocracy, and with the technologies of the internal combustion engine still new and developing, even young inventors with little money had a chance at success provided their ideas and engineering skills were good enough. While a teenager, Curtiss was improving equipment for his first employer, the Eastman company (later the giant Kodak corporation). But it was the petrol engine that really set Curtiss on the path to fame and fortune. Before turning to aviation, he set world land speed records on board motorcycles of his own design and construction. Invited to participate in an experimental association to build aircraft by the inventor of the telephone, Alexander Graham Bell, Curtiss at once transferred his design genius to the new technology. His first aeroplane, the delightfully named 'June Bug', flew to the astonishing altitude of 3100 metres on 4 July 1908, winning Curtiss the first of several prizes for aeronautical achievement, and $2500 (equivalent to about US$60,000 today) for his pains. This flight and others also gained Curtiss the distinction of holding the first pilot's licence in the United States.

Now besotted with flying, Curtiss struck up a relationship with the US armed forces, training both army and navy pilots. In 1910, a pilot employed by his firm flew from a US warship for the first time. With this massive new customer in prospect, Curtiss looked to take the aeroplane in new directions. Before the outbreak of World War I, he invented the flying boat, which made such an impression across the Atlantic that Winston Churchill, then head of the British admiralty, promptly bought the type for the Royal Navy. A development of this machine had the distinction of being the only US-designed and built aircraft to see combat in the Great War.

With the United States drifting into the war, Curtiss could see that a huge expansion of American military aviation required a new trainer, and quickly. Thus was born the JN4 Jenny, which was built in prodigious numbers, and was so tough and easy to fly that it served after the armistice as the archetypal mount for the barnstormers that brought flying to the backblocks of America in the inter-war years.

Unlike British manufacturers, Curtiss made a relatively smooth transition to peacetime markets, but not at the expense of technical progress. His D12 in-line engine revolutionised high-powered aero-engine design in the 1920s, powering a line of record-breaking Curtiss seaplane racing aircraft. Curtiss also took to building high-performance combat aircraft, beginning with the P1 Hawk fighter of 1923. Curtiss himself died of complications while undergoing surgery in 1930, aged just 52, but he lived on through the success of the firm that bore his name.

The immediate ancestor of the Kittyhawk was the Curtiss P36, an all-metal fighter that first flew in May 1935, before either the Hurricane or the Spitfire in Britain. The American aircraft industry between the wars was a cut-throat marketplace. At the time, aviation relied very largely on either government orders for warplanes, or government subsidies for fledgling airliners. Either way, the new technology was heavily shaped by the political and cultural values of governments, who looked at the aeroplane as a way of expressing what they stood for. This meant the aeroplane needed to represent the 'American way', and competition and merit were keenly held virtues for many in Washington, who were sceptical of big monopolies. Thus, anti-trust legislation was used to break up emerging combines of aircraft manufacturers and airlines in the early 1930s, and military orders were awarded strictly on the merits of the machine in question and its builders.

The result was a government procurement system that encouraged and rewarded innovation, and the Curtiss P36 exemplified the fact. Built by the Curtiss corporation with its own money, the P36 actually came second in the army flight trials for a new fighter, and initially a rival machine got most production orders. But re-engined with an in-line, water-cooled Allison motor, the P36 morphed into the P40, and a legend was born. For the new, water-cooled engine, Curtiss designers installed the necessary radiator under the fighter's nose, giving the plane the dashing and aggressive lines that later served as the canvas on which both American and British squadrons would paint the famous 'shark's mouth'. Curtiss had produced a fast, rugged fighter, whose principal virtues were firepower and toughness. The Kittyhawk was too heavy to be a traditional 'dogfighter', but the weight also provided one tactical advantage—diving speed. As Australian ace Clive Caldwell would later remark, the Kittyhawk could go 'downhill faster than almost any other aeroplane with a propeller', and in the combats to come over the south Pacific, this was a characteristic that would keep many allied pilots alive.

The Kittyhawk thus had pedigree, but getting a machine propelled by 1000 horsepower into the air, and back on the ground, in one piece was still a challenge for novice pilots. As young Australians got to grips with their new steed, problems were inevitable. In one of his few flights before flying north into combat, Tucker struck problems with his propeller's automatic pitch controller, which meant he could not change his propeller blades to the 'course' setting and thus slow the fighter down for landing. Approaching the runway too fast, Tucker 'bounced' no less than sixteen times, with his unsympathetic flight commander calling out each bounce on the radio. Tucker noted sanguinely, 'we never got on after that'.

Further north, Michael Butler, Bob Crawford and John Pettett were going through the same process at Brisbane's Archerfield base. Butler flatly concluded of the training program, 'I don't think you could have made it any shorter'. Like Tucker at Bankstown, Butler had an instruction sheet thrust in his hand, sat a brief verbal 'exam', and was then told, 'off you go'. His total hours on Kittyhawks before flying to New Guinea came to just eight, including some formation flying, but absolutely no gunnery training. He fired the guns on a P40 for the first time on the ferry flight en route to Moresby.

Pettett at least had the benefit of knowing some of his squadron mates. He was one of a number of pilots from the resident RAAF unit at Archerfield, 23 Squadron, who were posted to the new Kittyhawk unit. Apart from Pettett, along to 75 Squadron went Jeff 'Pop' Woods, a twenty-six-year-old school teacher from Perth, and Ally 'Bink' Davies, just twenty-one, also from Western Australia.

With pilots under training at bases around the country, Jeffery's first priority was to assemble the squadron. He himself arrived at Bankstown on 7 March, and immediately announced plans to fly north, to consolidate 75 Squadron at Townsville.

This was a tall order, but in war, needs must. Tucker by this time had just three flights in a Kittyhawk in his log-book, none of them involving instrument flying in a P40. Sending inexperienced fighter pilots on the long flight from Bankstown to Brisbane, and then on to Townsville, without this training was a risk, and Jeffery assumed he would not meet bad weather on the way. If he did, and his pilots were forced to fly through cloud, the results might be disastrous. Unable to fly on instruments without reference to a horizon, novice pilots can quickly become disoriented, lose control completely and enter an uncontrollable spin that too often ended in a fatal crash.

On the morning of 7 March, Jeffery took his pilots into the air from Bankstown, leading three other pilots in one flight, while Pilot Officer Jim Norton and John Piper each led a 'V' of three. It did not take long for the weather forecast to go badly wrong. Barely had the Kittyhawks got beyond the Hawkesbury River, just north of Sydney, when they faced an ominously dark cloud bank.

Each flight stayed together as best they could, but formation flying in cloud is a difficult art. Tucker, on the port wing of Norton, put his trust in his leader, ignoring his own instruments to keep tight on the other man's wingtip. Perhaps had Jeffery known more about his pilots, the leadership of this section might have been reversed, because while Norton had only come out of flight school in January, Tucker had at least come from a training unit where his instructor insisted on extending the curriculum to give students more than the basics, by teaching them some 'blind flying'. Tucker drew on this extra training now. Sensing that things were going awry, Tucker dared to peek at his instruments, and found to his alarm that 'our speed was up and we were obviously in a tight descending spiral to the right'. He opted to break formation, straightened up on instruments alone, and climbed back up through the cloud. Breaking through, he climbed too high, and for the very first time, stalled a Kittyhawk. As the fighter spun earthwards, Tucker drew on aeronautical first principles, turned his controls against the spin and regained control.

With his breath back, Tucker climbed up again, and when he regained clear air, found a Kittyhawk in the distance. Reasonably enough after the travails of the morning, he concluded 'company would be nice', and set off in pursuit. Catching up, he found the other pilot suddenly diving quickly, eager to exploit a break in the storm front down below. Tucker followed suit, and levelled out close to the ground despite the pelting rain. Following the example of his newfound leader, who proved to be John Piper, Tucker lowered his flaps and undercarriage without having yet sighted an aerodrome, but happily found himself on descent into the advanced landing ground at Evans Head, on the New South Wales north coast. 'Suddenly hangars shot past on the left hand side', and Tucker touched down, chastened but unharmed.

While Tucker ducked and wove his way to safety, down below, the sleepy mid-north coast timber town of Wauchope went on with its war. The locals had done their best to prepare for any eventuality, albeit with mixed results. A local unit of the Volunteer Defence Corps (VDC)—Australia's answer to 'Dad's Army'—quickly formed after Pearl Harbor. When a Japanese submarine was reported to be sending troops ashore on the nearby coast at Lake Cathie, the VDC swung into action, piling into cars and trucks and making for the battlefront. On arrival, the Wauchope reservists swept the area and found it clear of the enemy, and only then realised that in their haste they had left their ammunition at home.

Saturday afternoon, 7 March 1942 was drinking time. Wauchope's timber mills, its lifeblood, had closed after another long week of hard work and calloused hands, and the mill workers were thronging into the local pubs to greet the weekend. On the outskirts of the town, a young farming couple, Albert and Essie Freeman, tended to their chores. The weather was cool; rain had threatened all day, but little had yet fallen. As Albert and Essie went about their work, a plane suddenly came up from the south, headed in the direction of Kempsey, a larger township to the north. The young farmers were unfamiliar with the sound of high-performance aircraft, but even to them it seemed that the aircraft's engine was running rough. As it disappeared below the tree line, they thought the machine was sure to crash, at which moment, another plane appeared equally suddenly from the direction of Wauchope.

This time, there would be no doubt as to the outcome. The second plane passed them side on, and just cleared the trees on the eastern ridge of their property. Heading west at frighteningly low altitude, it clipped a tall dead tree in a cleared paddock. The plane flipped onto its back, hit the ground and slid upside down until it passed between a large stump and a nearby log. The resulting impact tore off the wings.

Stunned by the rapidity of events, Albert gathered his wits, and called out to his wife, 'If he's alright, I'll bring him in'. In preparation for the rescue, he asked for the tonic of the age to be made ready—'Put the kettle on!' Making his way to the crash site, Albert paused when the plane burst into flames and the ammunition on board began to detonate. Essie called out, 'Come back, you'll get shot!', but Albert gamely persisted, desperately seeking some way to get close to the cockpit and liberate the young pilot trapped inside. The sound of the exploding ammunition was such that a team of bullock drivers nearby thought that Wauchope was being bombed.

When all hope was lost, Albert Freeman at last relented and moved away to safety, to watch the flames slowly consume the wreckage. Jim Norton, the leader of Tucker 'V' on that fateful ferry flight, died in these horrible circumstances. A twenty-six-year-old butcher, Norton had only joined the air force in April 1941. He left behind a widow and two young sons.

The first machine seen by the Freemans met an equally unhappy end. Lloyd Holliday had no more experience than Norton—he too had only completed his Wirraway course the previous January. Holliday got as far as Kempsey, before he too was killed in a crash. A third Kittyhawk was lost, flown by Pilot Officer Ron O'Connor, the third pilot in Norton's 'V'. Having only flown a Kittyhawk for the first time on 17 February, it was small wonder he found the flying conditions that day such a challenge. O'Connor came down at Kyogle, but managed to walk away from the wreckage. Despite these losses, Jeffery got the bulk of his aircraft to Brisbane.

While at Archerfield, Jeffery set about completing the establishment of the squadron, something that requires much more than a list of pilots. An air force squadron is a self-contained administrative unit, meaning it must feed, clothe and care for its men, and maintain its machines. Its roll-call therefore extends from cooks to doctors, and engine fitters to armourers.

En route to Townsville, Jeffery had none of these specialists, but at Archerfield he did by chance begin to assemble the squadron's medical team. Apart from playing host to a Kittyhawk training course, the airfield was also home to an Elementary Flight Training School (EFTS), the basic entry point for new pilots. On the staff of the Archerfield EFTS was a young doctor, Bill Deane-Butcher, who happened to know Jeffery's brother Rod, also a doctor, from their training days together in Sydney in 1939.

Revered: Bill Deane-Butcher's medical prowess—and common humanity—made him one of the most admired figures in the campaign.

Deane-Butcher was an outstanding young doctor, and faced a painful choice in 1940 between continuing his medical career at Sydney's Prince Henry Hospital, or joining up. The fate of one of his colleagues settled the matter. When the Nazis overran France, this young doctor—a Jewish refugee from Germany—took cyanide, believing that Hitler was certain to win the war. Deane-Butcher agonised no more, and enlisted, receiving from the hospital's chief medical officer a glowing testimonial along the way: 'I hold a very high personal regard for [Deane-Butcher] and consider him to be one of the finest young medical officers ever associated with this institution ... he is a man of fine bearing, gentlemanly conduct and a high professional outlook'.

Enlistment was one thing, and active service another. Eager to move on to more glamorous war service than that offered by the chance to tend to the ailments of cadet pilots at the controls of Tiger Moth biplanes, with 75 Squadron passing through, Deane-Butcher took the opportunity to press his case with Jeffery for selection as the unit's medical officer.

Military appointments are often impersonal postings from on high, but when new formations are being put together under the pressure of operational demands, unit commanders often take what they can find, and personal contacts, however slender, are usually the only references available. Calculating that a friend of his brother was likely to be sufficient recommendation, Jeffery looked Deane-Butcher up and down, and gave him the job.

With his new unit moving north to Townsville, Deane-Butcher followed, but was initially disappointed. Arriving in north Queensland, he expected, following images of Battle of Britain pilots lounging in deck chairs waiting to scramble, 'to find a well-appointed base with "75 Squadron" emblazoned over the guard gate'. The motley collection of tents he found in a paddock was naturally something of a let-down.

In small numbers, pilots arrived, and the squadron ground crew assembled, many drawn from 24 Squadron, already based at Townsville.

Some of those reporting for duty came from colourful, if not odd, backgrounds. From the RAAF headquarters at Townsville came Ted 'Cathedral' Church as the squadron's equipment officer; he first came to the tropics as a butterfly collector for an English museum, and was ribbed by his air force colleagues as a collector of 'pheasant plumes' evermore. The pre-war careers of other squadron staff were more prosaic. Don Swann, the unit adjutant, left his trade as a signwriter to join the RAAF, and with the down-to-earth outlook of a practical man, proved a level-headed administrator in the trying times ahead.

A number of key personnel were already at Townsville waiting for Jeffery. They included two of the most prominent personalities in the early life of 75 Squadron. Like Jeffery, each was a veteran of the fighting in North Africa with 3 Squadron, and each now took up an important leadership position. John Jackson was slated to succeed Jeffery as squadron commander once the new unit got to Moresby, while Peter Turnbull was appointed a flight commander. The other flight command went to John Jackson's younger brother Les, until then with 23 Squadron at Archerfield, and a graduate, along with John Piper, of the fighter training course at Singapore.

Aged thirty-four, John Jackson was something of an 'old man' for a fighter pilot in 1942, but his more advanced years relative to those around him, along with a 'deep friendly voice', brought a much-needed sense of authority to the new fighter squadron. Jackson was already an experienced private pilot before the war. The son of a prosperous Queensland seed merchant, Jackson went to school at Scots College, Warwick, south-west of Brisbane. Impressed by the 1934 London–Melbourne Air Race, Jackson saw how a light aeroplane could accelerate his business as a stock agent, and promptly headed south to Sydney, to learn to fly and to buy his first machine, a Klemm Swallow. By 1937, he had graduated to a fast, streamlined Beechcraft Staggerwing, and was mortified to realise when he enlisted that this was faster than most of the aircraft then equipping the RAAF.

'... A BEAUTIFUL AEROPLANE TO FLY'

John F. Jackson, DFC (right), during his service in Libya.

There was something of the patrician about John Jackson, but his well-to-do background had a distinctly Australian tinge to it. He liked a game of cards, with a bet on the outcome. Although happily married with two young children, Jackson nevertheless enjoyed the night-life of Alexandria, touring 'all around the cabarets ... a regular den of evil'. Still a country boy at heart, Jackson found some of the bathroom fittings of his first-class hotel puzzling, wondering at the mysteries of a bidet—'a weird-looking arrangement with a plug in it'. Jackson narrowed the purpose of this foreign porcelain down to 'some feminine arrangement', and concluded uncertainly, 'I think I know what it's for, but will record it later when I find out from one of the hotel blokes'.

Jackson soon had the respect of those he would lead in combat. He took his pilots into his confidence, sharing his plans over drinks at Townsville's beachfront Strand Hotel. His own experience of preparing

117

With all too little formation flying practice like this to prepare them, 75 Squadron pilots went to war.

for action no doubt helped. Most of his young pilots were about to face the Japanese without adequate training, a route Jackson had already travelled against the Italians in Libya. On the eve of his first combat sortie, Jackson had to admit that although he had graduated as a 'full-blown operational pilot', the fact remained that 'all the air gunnery I've done is practically nil'. Jackson survived to learn his craft the hard way—on the job, flying combat missions in a variety of fighters, some of them elderly to the point of ancient, against the Italians, Germans and even, during the invasion of Vichy Syria, the French. The experience that Jackson gained along the way would be crucial in the testing days ahead.

On 9 March, the Japanese landed at Lae. Clearly, Moresby was next. If 75 Squadron was to fulfil its destiny, Jeffery and Jackson had only days to get the unit into something like combat shape. Flight training at Townsville began on 11 March, concentrating on formation flying, as the few senior pilots worked hard to get a disparate collection of pilots into a cohesive whole.

Ready or not, the squadron had to get to Moresby. On 17 March, an advance ground party of thirty-three men left for New Guinea under Ted Church; with somebody at the 'other end' to service the aircraft, Jeffery flew to Moresby on 19 March via Horn Island, accompanied by wingman Flying Officer Barry Cox. (An experienced Wirraway pilot, twenty-six-year-old Cox would prove one of the most dependable and loyal pilots in the weeks to come.) Having checked on the state of Seven Mile airfield at Moresby, Jeffery flew back to Cooktown in north Queensland on 20 March, where John Jackson was in transit to Horn Island.

With the whole squadron assembled there, the stage was set for the most important wartime development in the history of the RAAF. On 21 March, in two flights, the first led by Jeffery, and the second following four hours later with John Jackson in charge, the Kittyhawks took off from Horn Island, bound for Port Moresby—and near disaster. Approaching Seven Mile airstrip, with flaps and undercarriage down, Jeffery's flight of four fighters suddenly found themselves under fire. Skittish army machine-gunners, accustomed to seeing only Japanese fighters, peppered the Kittyhawks with bullets. One of these ripped through the headrest of Jeffery's machine, missing his head by little more than a centimetre.

All of the machines were damaged, but the two most airworthy Kittyhawks were scrambled that afternoon when the Betty bomber of Heinachi Kawai approached Moresby to conduct its reconnaissance of the base. These were flown by Flying Officer Wilbur Wackett, son of the famous Australian aircraft designer Lawrence Wackett—then at the helm of the country's only stand-alone aircraft factory, the Commonwealth Aircraft Corporation—and Barry Cox, again flying as a wingman.

Thinking the base still undefended in the air, Kawai commenced his photo run at the low altitude of 3300 metres. Still more than a kilometre below, Wackett and Cox climbed hard, and soon gained sufficient height to dive in for classic stern and quarter attacks. Set ablaze, the Mitsubishi went down, and as it did so, radio operators at Moresby jammed Japanese signals so that the presence of defending fighters went undetected at Rabaul.

75 Squadron had its first combat success, and the RAAF was finally ready for its greatest trial.

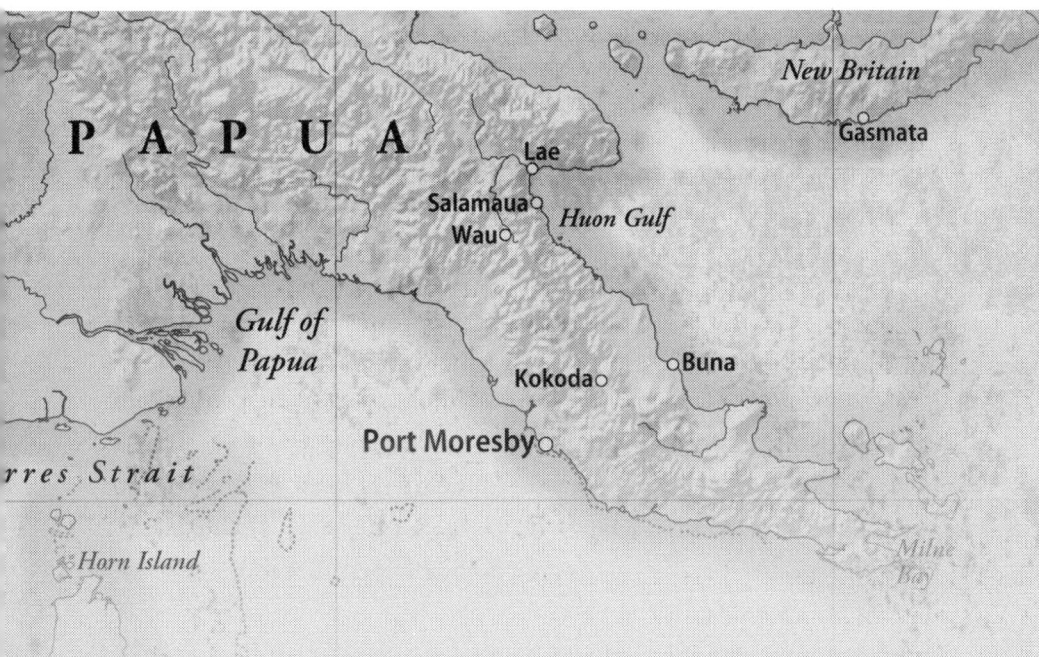

CHAPTER SIX
'Step on it! Can't you drive any faster?'

Having dealt the first blow, Jackson was determined to strike hard while surprise remained with his squadron. Before dawn the next day, he ordered his pilots into the air, not to intercept an incoming enemy, but to take the battle to the Japanese.

On the eve of this decisive event, 75 Squadron spent a fitful night. Some personnel were still arriving; Deane-Butcher and a young Tasmanian pilot, Geoff Atherton, disembarked at Moresby harbour from a Catalina flying boat at dusk on 21 March. In the darkness, carrying their kitbags, these latest arrivals stumbled over rocks and climbed up through shoulder-high grass to the squadron encampment. There they found a large tent furnished only with benches and bare wooden tables, but the scene had some domestic atmosphere. 'Flickering lamps provided our first glimpse of home', wrote the doctor afterwards, and waiting for them, 'there was a cup of tea and an enormous smile from a sweating bare-chested cook'.

Having taken his tea, Deane-Butcher repaired to his tent, and found war in the tropics a strain even before the guns began firing. He lay awake, fearing an enemy ambush at any moment, and felt the sweltering black night close in around him: 'the mosquito net was stifling ... the dark in the bush is really dark'. Deane-Butcher's tent at least held up to the weather. John Pettett, one of the pilots rostered for Jackson's surprise attack the next morning, spent most of the night trying to keep dry, digging a trench around the perimeter of his tent to drain the water away as the rain came bucketing down.

With this minimal rest, Jackson assembled his squadron in the darkness before dawn, and briefed them on his plans. For the attack on Lae, he divided his Kittyhawks into two flights. One led by Peter Turnbull would fly 'top cover', while the second, with Jackson himself in the lead, would strafe Lae aerodrome, targeting Japanese aircraft where they were parked and vulnerable to attack.

These well-laid plans barely survived take-off. Whether through inexperience, the dim pre-dawn light, nerves or all three, one pilot misjudged the take-off. With the squadron on take-off roll, Guy 'Cocky' Brereton found himself drifting off the runway. In his rear-view mirror, Johnny Piper saw the accident unfold, as Brereton's Kittyhawk swung wildly out of line. Brereton was lucky, to the extent that his fighter ploughed into a mound of gravel by the runway, deposited there for the construction works still under way.

While the rest of the squadron took to the air, the Seven Mile rescue team rushed in trucks and cars to Brereton's badly bent aeroplane, which began to smoulder as they approached. The butterfly collector turned equipment officer, Ted Church, happened to be in his utility with Deane-Butcher as a passenger. Speeding to the crash site, the two men found Brereton unconscious, with a 'very nasty gash' on his forehead, caused when his head smashed into the reflector gun-sight mounted on the lip of the cockpit. With flames beginning to crackle, Church and Deane-Butcher worked frantically to free their comrade, and the desperation that they applied to the task is best judged by the damage Church received in the process. With Brereton's safety harness jammed, Church yanked and pulled with such vigour that when the harness finally gave way, he smashed his wrist-watch, a prized possession given to him by friends when he enlisted.

Assisted by Deane-Butcher, Church eventually dragged Brereton's limp form from the wreckage before it was finally engulfed in flames. 75 Squadron thereby kept a valuable pilot, and the University of New England a future Professor of Agriculture, but one of the precious Kittyhawks was lost. Stitched up by Deane-Butcher, Brereton was flying again within a week.

John Jackson showed the importance of operational experience to combat leaders on that first mission to Lae. Keeping his squadron together up and over the Owen Stanleys, Jackson headed not straight to the target, but out over the Huon Gulf to the east. Thereby he not only approached the Japanese base from an unexpected direction, but with the rising sun behind him, he could hope that the glare would blind the Japanese anti-aircraft gunners for a few vital seconds while the attack went in.

Not that the Japanese were such sloppy soldiers that they left their base unprotected. As they swept in, the Australians met a standing patrol of several Zeroes. This engaged the Australians' low flight, with some success, shooting down the Kittyhawk of Bruce Anderson. He was the only 75 Squadron pilot with combat experience against the Japanese, having flown in the doomed attempt by 24 Squadron to use Wirraway training planes as 'interceptors' in the defence of Rabaul two short months before. Tragically, this experience counted for nothing now, and Anderson was killed.

Nevertheless, Jackson's tactics were sound. The Japanese attack on the 'low' flight placed the 'top cover' led by Turnbull in an enviable tactical position. Wilbur Wackett, leading the second pair of Kittyhawks in the escort flight, saw Turnbull waggle his wings, drop his belly tank—the detachable fuel tank carried as an external load beneath the fighter's fuselage—and dive down to engage the Zeroes.

Wackett and the others followed Turnbull down, and with the advantage of height, pressed home their counter-attack. Unfortunately for Wackett, only one of his guns fired when he opened up on a Zero, but he thought he saw his rounds striking the port wing of his target, 'about five feet from the wing tip'.

John Pettett, flying wingman to Turnbull, had more success with his guns. He watched as a Zero pulled away from its firing pass on the Kittyhawks below into a climbing turn, the sort of manoeuvre in which the nimble Mitsubishi excelled. Pettett marvelled at this 'quite amazing manoeuvre', which the Japanese pilot probably thought was putting him into a position to make another pass at Jackson's flight streaming in to attack Lae. However, without seeing Turnbull diving down to assist, the Zero pilot succeeded only putting himself into Pettett's gun-sight: 'suddenly this thing popped up, more or less in front of me, and all I instinctively did was pull back on the stick, and pull the trigger ... allowing what I thought was enough deflection, and that machine went down'. Pettett, then and later, was unremorseful: 'I certainly had no feelings at all for the Japanese pilot ... he was there to try and kill me ... I had no compunction'.

Turnbull himself claimed a second Zero, but Wilbur Wackett, victorious the previous day and now disadvantaged by his failed guns, was in trouble. Apparently from nowhere, a burst of Japanese fire smacked into his engine. Recalling the moment two years later for an air force publicity piece, Wackett wrote, 'the next thing I knew ... bullets were smashing up the cockpit and holing the wings of my plane. One bullet struck my wrist watch. Then I found myself covered in horse hair from the padding of my head rest. I could hear bullets pinging the back of my armour-plate'. Diving steeply into cloud cover, Wackett thought he had the situation under control, switching on his emergency fuel pump and changing the petrol supply to another tank. Coming out of the cloud at 300 metres, he saw two Zeroes, both in flames, crash into the water, but then his engine failed completely.

Wackett was in a desperate predicament, more than 12 kilometres from land and too low to bail out safely. Ditching an aeroplane like the Kittyhawk, with its big 'chin' radiator at the front of the fuselage ready to scoop in water and throw the plane onto its back, was a risky business, especially at the airspeed at which Wackett hit the sea. Banging the fighter down onto the waves at 160 kilometres an hour, Wackett got lucky. He was 'slightly stunned', with cuts on his forehead and shin and numerous nicks and scratches, but otherwise unharmed. The Kittyhawk sank so quickly that by the time he had unfastened his safety belt and oxygen and wireless mask, he was well under water. With the aid of his parachute pack, which provided some temporary buoyancy, Wackett bobbed to the surface. After he 'looked longingly at the land' away in the distance, Wackett concluded 'there was nothing for it but to swim', and so he struck out for safety.

Thanks to Wackett's intervention and the efforts of the rest of the escort flight in holding off the Japanese fighters, Jackson was free to set about what the squadron had come for. With the rest of the strafing flight behind him, the Australian squadron leader lined up on a row of Japanese fighters beside the Lae runway. Drawing up aircraft on the ground in this way greatly simplified refuelling and maintenance, and confirms that the Japanese were quite unaware of the recent additions to Australian airpower at Moresby. Had they suspected the likes of Jackson might be coming, the Japanese commanders would surely have dispersed their machines around the Lae base. Now they were lined up in a way that amounted to target practice for 75 Squadron, and Jackson and his men did not let the opportunity pass. Indeed, such was the surprise achieved by the Kittyhawks that Jackson elected to make a second pass, in defiance of usual strafing tactics not to re-engage a target already attacked for fear of retaliatory anti-aircraft fire. Having swept down along the line of the runway from the sea, Jackson made his own climbing turn and came back the same way, firing as he went, and then exited the target area, out across the relative safety of the Huon Gulf.

This was a raid pressed with great determination. So committed were the Australians to their task, they skimmed the Japanese base to within millimetres of disaster. On his first combat sortie, John Piper went so low that he scraped his wing on the propeller of a grounded Japanese bomber, striking the tip of the blade with such force that it ripped one of his heavy Browning machine guns clean from its mounting. He flew back to base, gingerly. Once there, his exciting day ended when, having landed safely, he tipped his Kittyhawk onto its nose by braking too quickly while taxiing back to the Australian flight line.

Piper might have dented his Kittyhawk in a variety of ways, but the raid in which he played such a dashing part was devastatingly effective. The Australians claimed twelve aircraft destroyed on the ground, in addition to the Zeroes shot down by Turnbull and Pettett. Nor did the attack finish with the departure of the Kittyhawks. With the teeth of the Japanese fighters temporarily pulled, two Hudsons of 32 Squadron took the opportunity to join in and bomb the airfield. The chance was squandered, one machine unloading short of the target and depositing its bombs harmlessly in the harbour, while the other was unable to bomb at all due to a mechanical fault. Four American B-17s did better from medium altitude by blowing up an ammunition dump and inflicting further damage to Japanese aircraft still smouldering from the work of Jackson and his men.

Such is its confusing speed, air warfare is beset by 'over-claiming', as pilots think their fire has done more damage than it achieves in reality. At Lae on 22 March, there was little imbalance between the claims made by 75 Squadron and the actual results. Japanese records confirm eight Zeroes and one bomber were destroyed on the ground, and two Zeroes shot out of the sky, in one of which Petty Officer Keiji Kikuchi of the 4th Air Group, a fighter pilot of two years' standing, lost his life. The Japanese also surmised correctly that their opponents were Australian. As they had over Horn Island on 14 March, they misreported the Kittyhawks as British Hawker Hurricane fighters.

As Jackson led his men south back to base, down below Wilbur Wackett was struggling to stay alive. Just turned twenty-one, Wilbur—the only son of leading industrialist Lawrence Wackett—had been raised as one of Australia's elite young men. Through the 1930s, he attended both Sydney and Melbourne Grammar schools, a change in schools being required by his family's move south, when Lawrence set up the Commonwealth Aircraft Corporation factory at Fisherman's Bend, at the mouth of the Yarra River. With these educational advantages, young Wilbur did not let his family down, gaining a welter of athletic titles, mainly in sprinting, and sufficient to be crowned his school's junior athletic champion.

Wackett would need all his athleticism now. Supported by his 'Mae West'—the universal term for life vests in the British and Dominion air forces, in honour of the buxom Hollywood starlet—Wackett struck out for the coast near Salamaua. The swim proved a hair-raising marathon. First, his 'heart skipped a beat' when a large shark breached the water close by. When others began to circle him, he sought psychological if feeble protection, by rolling down his shirt-sleeves and pulling up his socks! He was more effective in lying quite still in the water until the shark moved on.

Resuming his swim, Wackett briefly considered throwing away his revolver and water bottle, but reasoning he might need them if he managed to gain the enemy-held shoreline, he decided against it. By midday the sun was very hot, and his lips and eyes burnt from the glare and salt. Tiring, he lay on his back to rest, but found the current carrying him away from land, so that whatever he gained in recuperation, he lost in distance. After what he calculated to be eight or nine hours, by which time his strokes were very weak, Wackett was approaching exhaustion, but fortunately also the shoreline. A hundred metres from land, he saw two villagers near a canoe dragged up on the beach, but they declined to come to his aid. He eventually struck bottom three metres from a rocky shore, and clambered up to sit on the sand beyond the tide-line. Not surprisingly after his maritime ordeal, Wackett lacked composure—to see whether his revolver still worked, he fired off a round, which served only to terrify the villagers just up the beach. Had a Japanese patrol been nearby, no doubt this act would have had much more severe consequences.

Having announced his arrival in this way, Wackett was disappointed to find the villagers were not disposed to help him. 'Several women screamed when they saw me and rushed into their houses', but at length 'two friendly boys' agreed to help him.

With their assistance, Wackett trudged for days into the interior. Festooned with leeches every time they crossed a water course, and tortured by 'millions of mosquitoes', he owed his life to the bushcraft of his guides and their common humanity: one of the boys stayed up all night to massage Wackett's cramped and bruised feet while the Australian took what restless sleep he could. Succoured by the wild roots dug up in the jungle by his helpers, Wackett reached the village of Bulwa, to find an outpost of the NGVR. Now with army help, Wackett trekked overland for weeks, finally striking the south coast, to be carried to Moresby by canoe, by then feverish with malaria.

As Wackett set out on his marathon journey, Jackson led the rest of 75 Squadron back to base. There, the young Australians gave excited reports of the combat to intelligence officer Stu Collie, a Melbourne lawyer before the war and later the squadron's most ardent publicist, while ground crews serviced the machines. Their work was difficult and dangerous. Keeping the Kittyhawks in the air was the job of Bill 'Spanner' Matson, a career air force engineer. His skill was legendary; the 'miracle man' of Seven Mile, he made 'engines go with a total disregard' for the nominal requirements of technical manuals.

Apart from the threat of Japanese air raids, conditions at Port Moresby were challenging from an engineering perspective. Ground crews performed all of their work on the aircraft outdoors, and the New Guinea sun made the planes' metal skins so hot they could hardly be touched. Dust was another constant problem. Merely unpleasant

Bill 'Spanner' Matson, pictured later in the war at Milne Bay.

to eyes and mouth, the grit was anathema to the inner workings of the Kittyhawks.

With the labours of Matson and his men complete, 75 Squadron was soon ready for more action on 22 March, but further flying that day only confirmed the difficulty the Australians would have in maintaining a reasonable number of serviceable aircraft for operations. In the afternoon, reports of an incoming enemy plane required John Piper to scramble in pursuit, but he managed to hit a drum on take-off. Piper nevertheless continued on and, when the feared raider failed to materialise, he maintained a standing patrol over Seven Mile for two hours before attempting a landing with his damaged fighter. Piper did remarkably well—yet again—by holding up the wing on one wheel, while the airspeed fell away, before easing the wingtip down on the side where he had no undercarriage. This skilful bit of flying kept damage to a minimum, but still Matson and his men had one more problem to work on.

Their list of engineering patients soon increased to two. Replacing Piper on patrol, Jackson sent Sergeant Bill Cowe aloft, with Sergeant Stan Havard flying as his wingman. Havard was barely out of flight school, and it showed. Straying too close to his leader on take-off, his plane was caught in the attendant slipstream and Havard lost control. The rookie fighter pilot survived with a bruised ego but the damage to his fighter was more substantial, and 75 Squadron lost another precious Kittyhawk to long and difficult repairs.

The defenders of Port Moresby could ill afford these losses to inexperience, because the Japanese, now aware Port Moresby was home to fighter interceptors, were out for revenge. To crush the air defences of the Australian base without further ado, on 23 March nineteen bombers escorted by four Zeroes mounted a raid directed at Seven Mile airfield.

The bombing achieved little, but the subsequent strafing runs by the Zero escorts proved punishing. Ted Church was on the dispersal line when the bombers unloaded, helping to move aircraft into the protective

131

dispersal pens in which the fighters were parked. Having done what he could for the grounded fighters, Church set off down the runway to find cover for his utility truck, itself too valuable to lose. Accompanied by Jock Russell, an officer on the staff of RAAF Moresby, Church suddenly became a target himself for the Zeroes screaming low over Seven Mile. 'We suddenly heard the spit-spit-spit of machine guns and the louder report of cannon immediately behind us', Church later wrote, at which point Russell offered the helpful advice, 'Step on it! Can't you drive any faster?'

Church replied with an understandable profanity, and at the same time nearly pushed the 'accelerator pedal through the floor boards'. Veering off the runway, the two men bailed out of the truck and scrambled up a hill to watch proceedings.

The Zeroes might have missed Church's fleeing truck, but grounded aircraft were much easier to hit. Two Kittyhawks were soon set ablaze, and another damaged. The losses could have been worse but for an extraordinary act of bravery on the part of one of the ground crew, Alan Ramsay. With the airfield reliant on a single refuelling tanker under his command, Ramsay was at work topping up the tanks of Kittyhawks when the strafing attack began. The fighter he was refuelling was hit and set ablaze, and despite the obvious risks, Ramsay stuck to his job, disconnecting the tanker amid the flames and driving it to safety. Ramsay was Mentioned in Despatches for the feat.

For Deane-Butcher, the raid marked a baptism of fire, and understandably he found the experience terrifying. 'We lay face down in the fine low grass', he recalled, as the Zeroes swept overhead with all guns blazing, and Deane-Butcher was taxed by the problem of how best to protect the two parts of his body he most valued, namely his head and his genitals: 'I speculated madly on how to cover all my vital parts under one tin hat'.

Not all the Australians were under cover. Peter Turnbull, unable to get into the air thanks to an unserviceable motor on his Kittyhawk, even joined in the defensive barrage with a .38 revolver, jumping up out of a slit trench as the Zeroes went by, unloading in their general direction and then taking cover again when the Japanese came in for a fresh firing pass.

One Japanese fighter was hit, but probably not by Turnbull's defiant gestures. The machine-gunners who so nearly killed Pete Jeffery two days before, now vented their anger more accurately, in the direction of the Japanese. They put up a hail of fire, with success.

However, their success all but spelt the end for the long-suffering Ted Church. Thinking himself safe with Jock Russell on their hilltop, Church watched as one Zero pulled up in a steep climb, and then inextricably dived directly at them. With no worthwhile target to hit, it was obvious that the fighter was screaming down out of control. As Church ruefully noted, a machine travelling at nearly 500 kilometres an hour 'covers a lot of ground in a few moments'; unable to get away in time, the two Australians also had nowhere to take cover on their barren outcrop. All they could do was lie flat, and as Deane-Butcher had already found, a tin hat did not cover much: both Church and Russell were acutely conscious that 'a lot of body [was] showing outside the protective dome' of their helmets.

Once in its death dive, the Zero never deviated, and crashed into the hill immediately above where Russell and Church lay in fright. The fighter exploded on impact, and 'burning oil and petrol spattered our shirts and shorts, pieces of aircraft flew in all directions'. Breathless, the two men slapped out the hot oil on each other. Struggling for words, Church eventually managed the obvious observation, 'that was a bit too close for general comfort, Jock'.

Inspecting the wreckage, the Australians were initially puzzled to find no sign of the pilot. The body of Petty Officer Kyoichi Yoshii, a graduate of the Japanese fighter program as far back as December 1936, was eventually found 400 metres away. Despite having been thrown clear such a distance, Yoshii was largely unmarked, although what killed him was perfectly obvious: a bullet wound to the right temple. No doubt Yoshii's colleagues back at Lae mourned his loss, but the Australians took the opportunity for some souvenir hunting. Jock Russell purloined one of the Zero's 20-millimetre cannons, not much damaged apart from the dents and bent fittings caused when the impact blasted the gun from its mounting, while Church settled for the fighter's joystick.

Although the modest ground defences did well in this action, they could not prevent the destruction of parked aircraft. 75 Squadron could not afford to lose fighter aircraft at this rate, and something had to be done to better protect the precious Kittyhawks on the ground between sorties. Japanese raids also posed a productivity problem for Matson, since between ten in the morning and two in the afternoon (the prime time for Japanese raids, taking into account the distance from Rabaul where the heavy bombers were based), his ground crews had 'one eye on the air and the other on the job'. As a result, even without raids, jobs that might have taken a few hours to complete dragged on, and then when bombers did make an appearance, naturally men took cover and repairs were delayed until the all-clear sounded.

Ever resourceful, Matson set out to solve the problem. As the Japanese were after targets around the airfield, he took the simple step of removing the Kittyhawks from its environs so that the engineering work could go on undisturbed. 'Well,' he remembered in a later interview, 'we had a look around, and found a place, almost on the side of a steep hill, where we could get some chance of hiding [the Kittyhawks]'. This proved very successful. Early each morning, or just before dark, those aircraft requiring a 'long job' were towed up the hill and camouflaged with branches and palm leaves. This meant the ground crews only had to stand down for the 'red warning' (when enemy aircraft were actually in sight), and could return to the job 'after the Nip had dropped his bombs'. The passage of the fighters to and fro seemed perilous—at times it seemed they might do more damage to the aircraft by moving them—'but we managed it without mishap'.

Matson was not the only one working hard at keeping 75 Squadron in the battle. The conditions facing Deane-Butcher were equally challenging, but his principal enemy was not the Japanese, but disease. Within hours of arriving in New Guinea, the men of 75 Squadron began falling ill.

The reasons were not hard to find. A monotonous diet of tinned food was one. Tinned bacon, baked beans and 'goldfish'—herrings in tomato sauce—were the standard fare, lubricated by tinned butter that took on the consistency of sump oil in the heat, and offered about the same appeal. What was not tinned came dried, including egg powder, deservedly labelled 'yellow death', and worst of all, dehydrated mutton, which was soaked overnight and the vile-smelling result converted into what passed for meatloaf. In the eyes of Arthur Tucker, all of this was 'dreadful stuff'. The squadron cook did not pretend otherwise, inviting the pilots to breakfast every morning with a blunt invocation:

Come and get it, fuck ya's,
or I'll shove it fuckin' up ya's.

For pilots like Tucker, the available diet proved an agony at high altitude. At ground level, the wind generated by such cuisine might be socially embarrassing, but at 6000 metres, the loss of external air pressure meant the internal gas distended the bowel in distinctly unpleasant ways.

The incidence of stomach disorders climbed alarmingly. Gastroenteritis was the chief problem, and again the pilots suffered especially badly. In Tucker's log-book, his first combat mission was annotated simply 'shits'—not because he was afraid, but because he lost control of his bodily functions, and his motions were 'trickling down

[his] legs'. Still, the men had to fly and fight. Tucker's regime involved taking a spare pair of shorts to the operations tent every morning, so that when he landed, 'you'd clean your aeroplane up, wash your shorts' and start the whole process again. For some, the fear of imminent death had other effects on their bodily functions. There was no braver man than Les Jackson at Port Moresby, but when he was on the roster list to fly, he invariably threw up his breakfast, often in the cockpit while on standby in his fighter.

Apart from the unpalatable diet of preserved food, the main culprit for the ill health that plagued Seven Mile was the poor hygiene around the Australian base. On his arrival, the overflowing grease traps of the airfield's kitchens horrified Deane-Butcher. Together with the nauseating condition of the latrines, these were an obvious breeding ground for disease of all kinds.

With the aid of a team of medical orderlies led by Jack McIntosh, a former St John's Ambulance officer from Brisbane, Deane-Butcher worked to tighten up housekeeping around the base. They soon perfected a preferred design for the latrines. The delightfully named 'six holers' described the capacity of the facility, and they were partly thus sized for the relative ease with which they could be dug to the requisite depth. Deane-Butcher then took direct action to keep them clean—in went a liberal dose of kerosene, followed by a lit match. This method had the desired effect, at least until one of McIntosh's young orderlies used petrol instead, and blew up one toilet complex.

The sun set and the dust duly settled on Moresby after the Japanese attack on 23 March. As light faded, far away to the south, the Australian Air Board in Melbourne received some startling intelligence. A radio broadcast from the infamous Radio Tokyo gave Australian authorities the first intimation that some of the aircrew reported missing in the loss of the Catalinas two months before might be alive.

This news came in the form of personal messages from some of the men involved, read for them by a Japanese announcer, but with enough family detail to suggest that against all the odds, they might still be alive. One of the messages purported to come from Paul Metzler. In contrast to the horrendous treatment that most allied prisoners of war received from the Japanese, the broadcast messages permitted to a handful of men like Metzler were apparently an attempt by the authorities in Tokyo to convince the Australian public that Japanese military administrators were honourable and compassionate.

Metzler addressed his message to his wife, and the Japanese announcer began in stilted tones, unfamiliar with Australian idiom: 'Good day, Kit'. Metzler's note went on to explain that 'Japanese fighter aircraft shot us down over the ocean, but I am alive and well'. The message requested that Kit and Metzler's family send food, clothes and tobacco through the Red Cross, and of course, 'please try to write'. And finally, across the years, we can hear a husband attempt to buoy the spirits of his beloved wife, so far away: 'Keep your chin up, Kit, and I will pay you a surprise visit one of these days'.

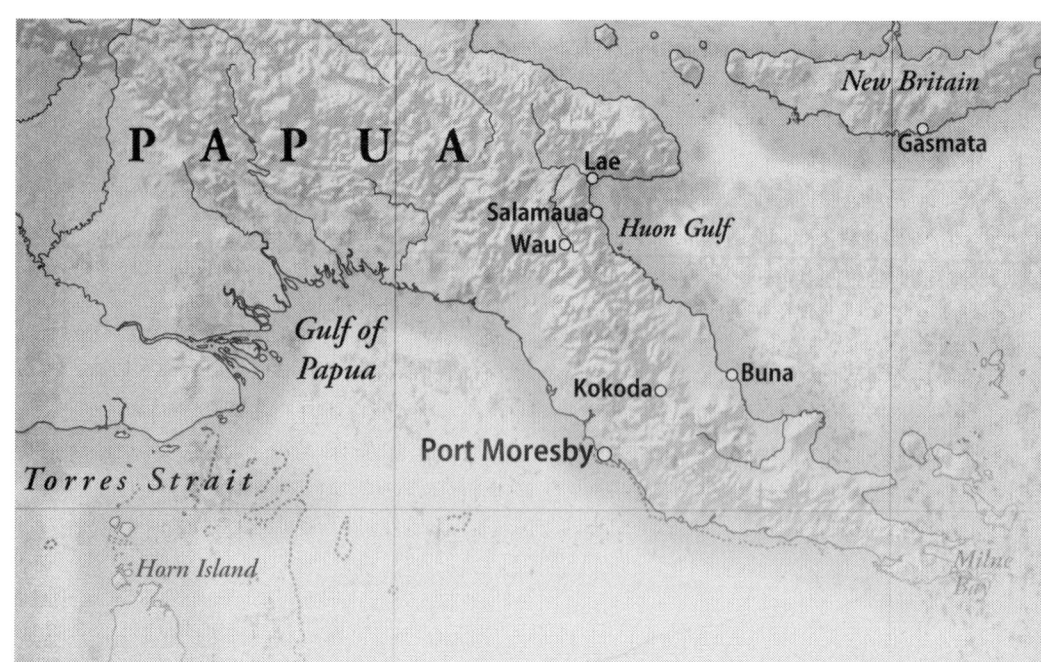

CHAPTER SEVEN
'Hey, Daddy, I want a diamond ring ...'

When the Japanese failed to eliminate 75 Squadron in one blow, operations settled into a pattern, as each side struck at the other's airfields with whatever strength they could muster, hoping to dictate subsequent events by claiming air superiority. To that extent, 75 Squadron had already achieved an important operational goal by forcing the Japanese into a campaign of aerial attrition that they could ill afford.

For their airfield raids to be successful, each side also needed effective reconnaissance. On the Australian side, John Jackson often undertook these missions on his own, in brazen and dangerous solo flights over Lae. The Japanese alternative was more conventional, using Betty bombers as photo reconnaissance aircraft. With Kittyhawks now in residence, these missions were extremely dangerous for the Japanese bomber crews, a point already made with the success of Wackett and Cox on 21 March, and reinforced at first light three days later, when Piper shot down a lone enemy bomber into Hood Bay, 100 kilometres east of Moresby.

This was the first action on what would prove to be a busy day for 75 Squadron. Mid-morning, the squadron operations tent received a report of an inbound Japanese raid, and to meet it, Les Jackson and Ron Bailey scrambled. They faced daunting odds, as a large formation of bombers escorted by three Zeroes bombed Seven Mile, without much impact. Jackson managed a fleeting head-on pass at the Zeroes, and received for his trouble a bullet through the mainplane of his Kittyhawk, but otherwise the action ended inconclusively.

The ability of 75 Squadron to scramble aircraft to meet incoming raids would prove a decisive tactical advantage, just as it had for the Royal Air Force in the Battle of Britain. Whereas Fighter Command had obtained this tactical intelligence from an expertly designed and operated radar system, at Port Moresby radar was proving of more limited utility. With high mountains to the north, 29 Radar Station could not guard the key approach route, and while the ring of observer posts close to Moresby helped fill the gap, the warning these spotters provided was usually measured in minutes. This was sufficient to get gun crews to the ready and to allow men to take cover, but at this short distance, 75 Squadron had too little time to get into the air before the Japanese arrived. Although the fighter controllers at Seven Mile could not obtain reliable early warning near the Australian base, what if an observer, hundreds of kilometres away, were to provide intelligence reports of aircraft actually taking off from the Japanese airfields?

This was exactly how the pilots of 75 Squadron minimised the number of surprise attacks on Seven Mile, and for these warnings they owed most to an unassuming hero by the name of Leigh Vial. A district officer in the civilian administration on New Britain, Vial enlisted as a coastwatcher after being evacuated to the mainland. The Royal Australian Navy commissioned most of the coastwatchers, but the Director of Naval Intelligence, Eric Feldt, found his own bureaucracy so time consuming that to speed things up, Vial was commissioned in the RAAF. With these formalities out of the way, Vial returned to New Guinea on his first assignment.

Vial's job was to spy on the Japanese bases at Salamaua and Lae, but getting into position was a prodigious labour in its own right. He walked from Moresby to the outskirts of Salamaua, a trek that took twelve days and an investment of stamina and endurance that would daunt even the hardiest commando.

Once in place in a tree-top observation post immediately overlooking Salamaua and with views across the Huon Gulf to Lae, Vial's principal weapon was a set of binoculars. From this fragile vantage spot, he spied on the Japanese aircraft taking off to raid Port Moresby, and radioed this intelligence through to RAAF commanders. He was sustained by local produce, principally yams and taro root, and by deliveries of supplies by the NGVR, operating forward towards the coast from its base at Wau. Secrecy cloaked these supply runs. Vial radioed through his requirements and specified a drop site. When an NGVR patrol found the appointed

'HEY, DADDY, I WANT A DIAMOND RING ...'

Leigh 'Golden Voice' Vial spent months in a tree-top observation post like this one, in the hills above Salamaua.

location, usually by a river, the militiamen then walked upstream in the water for several hundred metres to the drop-off point, to avoid leaving a trail that the Japanese might be able to follow. So accurate were his warnings that Vial soon acquired the nickname 'Golden Voice', and as well as to the Kittyhawk pilots, Australian successes in the skies of New Guinea owed much to his brave and lonely vigil.

Vial's work gave the Port Moresby defenders invaluable early warning, but that would count for little if 75 Squadron ran out of aeroplanes. In the first four days of fighting, the unit lost five aircraft to enemy action, wrecked two more and sustained enough damage to several others to have them in Bill Matson's tender care for prolonged periods.

On 25 March, Barry Cox, already one of the squadron's more seasoned pilots, attempted to lead a flight of reinforcement aircraft from Townsville, but the results only confirmed the losses the Australians could expect when inexperienced pilots were given command of high-performance aircraft. Sergeant Stan Havard, who had already 'pranged' a Kittyhawk at Port Moresby, did not fare much better as a ferry pilot. He only got as far as Cooktown before coming down in a forced landing on an isolated beach, thereby marooning one of the precious Kittyhawks. To recover it, Cox took matters into his own hands, requisitioning a motor launch and chugging up the coast to find his forlorn squadron mate. Putting the young sergeant back on the launch, Cox completed the rescue mission by taking off in the Kittyhawk, braving the imminent and disastrous prospect of nosing over in the soft sand of the beach. He got away with the feat, but another 75 Squadron pilot would not be so lucky in similar circumstances a month later.

By these hair-raising means, Cox reassembled his reinforcement flight, only to have another young pilot crack a tail-wheel on landing at Cooktown on 29 March. With spare parts flown in by a 32 Squadron Hudson in use as an escort plane for the single-engined fighters, Cox finally managed to get off for Horn Island the next day, but it had taken the best part of a week to accomplish what should have been possible in a few days. 75 Squadron eventually got its first replacement aircraft, and it was sorely in need of them.

In Cox's absence, losses continued to accumulate. On 27 March, Jeff 'Pop' Woods led Ron O'Connor, the only survivor of the crash-landings around Kempsey and Wauchope just three short weeks earlier, on a standing patrol north of Port Moresby.

Circling at 4000 metres above Mount Frank Lawes, 45 kilometres north of their base, the Australians found a number of Zero pilots engaged on their own patrol. The action began when Woods became aware of a Japanese fighter astern and 300 metres above. In a standard defensive manoeuvre, Woods turned back into the looming attack, but having gone 90 degrees to starboard, he then found two more Zeroes above and on his port beam. By this stage, Woods had lost his wingman, and firing briefly in front quarter attack at the two Zeroes closest to him, he took cover in cloud at 3000 metres. Emerging from this sanctuary, Woods saw a parachute drifting down at between 1000 and 1500 metres, and below it, a fire blazed up from the jungle, which he presumed to be a crashed P40.

Indeed it was. John Jackson was also in the air by this stage, and reported seeing the same parachute. Back on the ground, Jackson organised a search flight, which Woods volunteered to make once his machine was refuelled. Taking off again at midday, he could find no sign of either wreckage or a parachute in the rough country. A fortnight later, an RAAF corporal reported having seen a Zero circling a parachute in the vicinity and hearing the sound of gunfire as the chute came down.

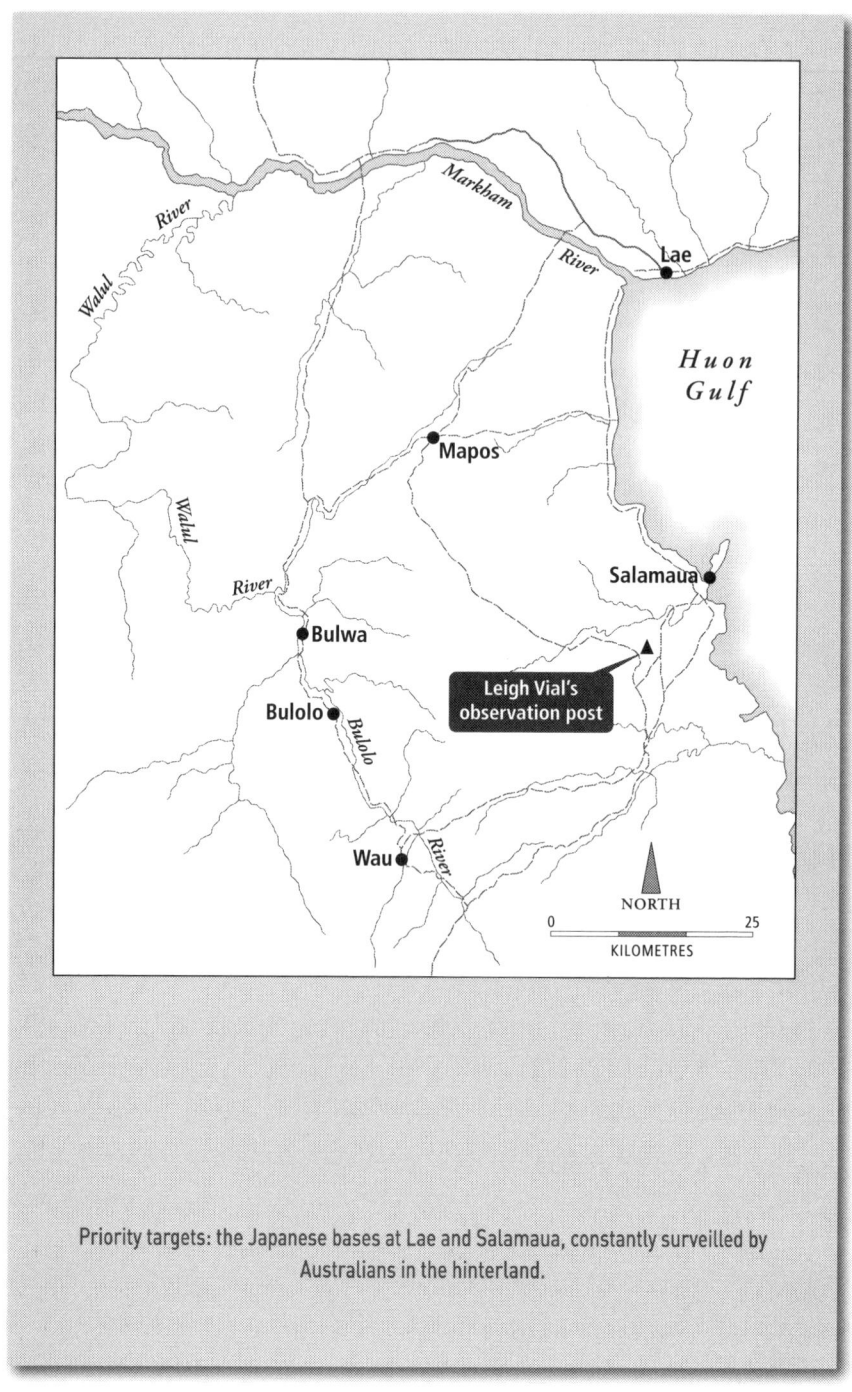

Priority targets: the Japanese bases at Lae and Salamaua, constantly surveilled by Australians in the hinterland.

Nothing further was ever seen or heard of O'Connor, but his grief-stricken mother never gave up hope. When she died in 1968, her son Ron remained the sole beneficiary of her will, and it remained for the Public Trustee to obtain confirmation of his death from the Air Board before officials could wind up her affairs.

The Australians soon found that the sort of close-quarter manoeuvring against the Zero which cost O'Connor his life was a tactical situation to avoid at all costs. The Japanese fighter had been designed for just this type of combat, but there was more to the Zero than dogfighting. Indeed, the Japanese fighter must rank as one of the greatest pieces of aviation engineering ever conceived.

The Zero was the brainchild of Jiro Horikoshi, who was given the task of designing the Japanese Navy's next carrier fighter in 1937, at the age of just thirty-three. Horikoshi's youth personified the Japanese industry as a whole—it was only in 1931 that the Japanese authorities committed themselves to achieving national self-sufficiency in the air, through what they called 'Project Aviation Technology Independence'. Prior to that decision, the Japanese Navy relied heavily on imported technology, most of it from Britain, from whom they bought their first carrier planes and flying boats in the 1920s.

Horikoshi was one of the talented designers who changed all that, first with the Type 96 fighter, then with the Zero. His achievement was to meet what he dramatically called a 'challenge of impossibilities'. When the Japanese Navy issued its new fighter requirements in 1937, nothing like it had been seen anywhere in the world. After heavy losses to its unescorted bombers in the fighting over China in 1937, the Japanese decided their raids needed fighter escort, which meant long range. This pointed towards a heavy fuel load, which would leave the machine lacking in the manoeuvrability needed to take on opposing fighters. To that conundrum Japanese naval planners added a requirement for heavy cannon armament, so that the new fighter could also serve as an interceptor against incoming enemy bombers. Their specification also demanded a top speed of more than 500 kilometres an hour, and to finally spice the design recipe, the new machine needed to operate from aircraft carriers. This in turn demanded a relatively large wing for low-speed control, but that promised to confound the requirement for a generally fast machine, which normally meant the smallest possible wing area.

When Horikoshi first examined the navy's new design specification in May 1937, he 'dropped into his chair [and] tossed the document' onto his desk in despair. Attempts to talk the navy out of some of their demands were unavailing. If the Mitsubishi firm for whom Horikoshi worked were to get the contract, he eventually concluded his design team had to simply 'get on with it'.

This they did with a vengeance. It is conventional wisdom that the Zero used a relatively low-powered engine because Japan's industrial limitations meant that was all that Horikoshi had available to him. In fact, Horikoshi looked at a higher-powered, 1070-horsepower motor and rejected it, because it compromised his overriding design philosophy: weight reduction. A big motor would be heavier in itself, and, requiring more fuel, it would also need to cart around a greater weight of petrol. Horikoshi opted instead for a lower-powered motor, and aimed to get the three fundamental operational requirements—range, speed and manoeuvrability—by a relentless and ingenious program of weight reduction.

He achieved his ambitions by combining design breakthroughs with what we would now call material science. Looking at the structure of his new fighter, Horikoshi realised that up until then some aircraft parts had been unnecessarily strong for the loads placed upon them. These loads are measured as units of gravity—for example, 3G represents three times the normal gravity load. Long, slender metal parts stretch or bend under the loads imposed on them when an aeroplane manoeuvres, and then return to their original shape. Components of this type might return to their shape at up to (say) 9G, and only finally fail at 10G, the so-called destructive load point. However, stubby, thick metal parts do not flex in the same way. They might permanently deform at 6G, but not finally break until they reach the destructive load of 10G.

From this comparative analysis of component design, Horikoshi found a new method of saving weight, without compromising the strength of his airframe. If he designed his new fighter to operate at loads of (say) 6G, it was obvious that the thin, slender parts of the airframe would be stronger than they needed to be. They could be thinned out still more, so that both types of component shape carried equivalent loads.

To this insight Horikoshi added a new duralumin alloy that was even lighter than the traditional material but just as strong. By these means, he lowered the weight of the prototype Zero to just 1800 kilograms, but still managed to employ a relatively large wing for carrier landings and overall manoeuvrability.

To further enhance the agility of the design, Horikoshi introduced several innovations. First, the wingtips on the Zero were bent down on the lead edge. The tapered wings used on the Zero usually 'stall' first at the wingtip, and by turning them down, Horikoshi delayed the onset of the stall and thereby gave future Japanese fighter pilots the ability to turn in seemingly impossibly small circles at low speed.

Finally, Horikoshi improved the control response of the Zero. As the speed of an aeroplane increases, the quicker flow of air makes the effect of control surfaces like the elevator more dramatic. When a pilot applies a force on his stick, the amount of travel in the elevator is the same whether it is at low or high speed, the problem being that when travelling fast, this same amount of movement on the elevator may be too great, making the controls 'over-responsive'. Horikoshi solved this problem by installing thinner cables in the Zero, thereby deliberately engineering an amount of flex in the control runs that converted the pilot's movement on the stick, down through the fuselage to the elevator. At low speed, these operated conventionally, but at high speed, the thin cables flexing under stress absorbed some of the pressure of the faster air over the elevator, thereby limiting the movement of the elevator and thus eliminating the problem of over-responsiveness.

In all, the Zero was an engineering marvel. It combined features achieved nowhere else in the world, and made a lie of racist assumptions in the West that the Japanese were merely technical imitators. Later in the war, one pilot from 75 Squadron had the opportunity to inspect a captured Zero, and was in awe of the strength achieved by such a lightweight design. The little fighter had its weaknesses, which the Australians would uncover in the harsh classroom of air combat, but the Zero was a machine to fear.

In tackling Horikoshi's work of genius, 75 Squadron took the obvious first step of avoiding the traditional turning dogfight that the Zero specialised in. Under Jackson's seasoned leadership, the Australian Kittyhawk pilots relied instead on the Kittyhawk's own virtues of high dive speed and firepower. The preferred tactic soon evolved—wherever possible, gain a height advantage, dive to make a firing pass, and with the high airspeed gained in the dive, zoom back up to safety. And if they got into trouble, the Australians resorted to diving away as their standard evasive manoeuvre. With this defensive tactic, they had a technical advantage over the Zero, in the shape of the Stromberg carburettors that controlled the fuel supply to their motors. These were so-called 'direct injection' carburettors, which pumped fuel into the Allison motor regardless of whether the fighter was upright or inverted. In comparison, the Zero was equipped with a simple float carburettor, which relied on gravity to feed the fuel into its engine. Thus, when the Japanese first pushed or turned over into a dive, it lost power as the negative gravity momentarily cut off the supply of fuel. Kittyhawk pilots soon learnt that diving away from a Zero gave them a speed advantage, and a much-needed escape route.

Admittedly these good intentions were hard to observe in practice, because the Kittyhawks needed a height advantage that was difficult to achieve. While 'Golden Voice' Vial did his best to alert 75 Squadron to incoming raids, such an 'eyes and ears' system of ground control was obviously scarcely foolproof. Whenever the Australian fighter pilots received only a local warning from the immediate vicinity of Seven Mile that Japanese aircraft were nearby, they took to the air at a severe disadvantage. In these situations, the Zeroes could catch the Australians still climbing for height at low airspeeds, and fall on them from above in fast firing passes that were hard to counter.

This was just the situation facing John Piper and his wingman Ron Bailey when they scrambled to intercept five enemy aircraft reportedly inbound for Port Moresby on 28 March. At 3000 metres, they saw three bombers in a 'V' formation still high above them. The Japanese were between three and six kilometres away, so Piper continued to climb. Closing on the bombers from below, Piper saw at the last second two Zeroes sweeping down from out of the sun, in a classic fighter pilot's 'bounce'. He rolled away, but in a remarkable piece of 'full deflection' shooting, one of the Japanese pilots managed to hit his fighter several times, even though the Zero was directly above him. Piper survived, but as he regained control, he saw a Kittyhawk diving away with a Zero on its tail.

Once more, the defenders never saw the Australian fighter and its pilot again, although local villagers did report seeing an aircraft crash. This vague report was the only intelligence on which to mount a search, but 75 Squadron nevertheless set out to find one of its missing pilots. The effort proved in vain. The remains of Ron Bailey, aged twenty-one, a champion footballer and athlete in his school years and only recently married, were never found.

For the men of 75 Squadron, in between the terrifying excitement of aerial combat and bombing raids were long periods of boredom in uncomfortable surroundings. Recreation facilities were virtually non-existent, and Deane-Butcher did his best to fill the gap, realising that a psychological outlet to the stress of battle was important to the health of the young men in his charge. He encouraged singing at night as one means of relaxation, and penned a number of songs himself to give the squadron its own repertoire. Deane-Butcher also liberated whatever comfortable furniture he could from the abandoned homes around Port Moresby, to give the pilots the physical means to lounge around and unwind.

Otherwise, there was little to keep the men entertained. The squadron did have a wind-up gramophone, but it was limited by the available playlist—this consisted of just one record. On the B-side was an instrumental version of Frenesi, and on the A-side the hit tune 'Daddy, I want a diamond ring'. This topped the charts for eight weeks in 1941, and featured in the movie *Two Latins from Manhattan*. Nowhere was a song on higher rotation than in the operations tent at Seven Mile. Time and again, men cranked up the gramophone, amid the bomb bursts and the strafing Zeroes, to let the waiting pilots sing along to its incongruous lyrics:

> *Hey, listen to my story 'bout a gal named Daisy Mae*
> *Lazy Daisy Mae*
> *Her disposition is rather sweet and charming*
> *At times alarming, so they say*

She has a man who's tall, dark, handsome, large and strong
To whom she used to sing this song

Hey, Daddy, I want a diamond ring, bracelets, everything
Daddy, you oughta get the best for me

Hey, Daddy, gee, don't I look swell in sables?
Clothes with Paris labels?
Daddy, you oughta get the best for me

Here's 'n amazing revelation
With a bit of stimulation
I'd be a great sensation
I'd be your inspiration

Daddy, I want a brand new car, champagne, caviar
Daddy, you oughta get the best for me

Hey, Daddy, I want a diamond ring, bracelets, everything
Daddy, you oughta get the best for me

Apart from singing, the available diversions were very limited. Those determined to take a drink could find alcohol, but the attractiveness of a tipple depended on a man's palate for warm beer. John Pettett was one who could not touch a drink in these conditions. He and his tent-mate, 'Bink' Davies, set out to down a bottle, but with stomachs clogged with baked beans and tinned bacon, this would be one mission they were unable to complete.

Les Jackson, the squadron's 'wild child', had no such inhibitions. With Deane-Butcher and squadron intelligence officer Stu Collie, he got on the grog, with damaging consequences for Collie. While Jackson ploughed on into the night, warm beer in hand, Collie fell asleep in the hammock slung between the posts of their hut. To enliven proceedings, Jackson swung the hammock back and forth, until he up-ended the stupefied and hapless Collie, who fell a metre and a half to the floor in a crash of bruises and curses.

Diversions off the base were also limited. Looters had long since despoiled the Port Moresby Hotel. John Jackson, an avid home film-maker, found an outlet for his hobby by collecting footage of what the Australians considered the strange customs of the local villagers. His film of the scenes around Moresby and the Seven Mile strip are today in the archives of the Australian War Memorial.

As is often the case with young men, some of the impromptu attempts at entertainment were hazards in their own right. Some of those with an interest in fishing found unorthodox means to pursue the pastime. John Pettett was one, and on the rare days when he was not scheduled for operations, he set out on Port Moresby harbour aboard one of the Halvorsen motor launches used by the air–sea rescue service. Safely anchored, Pettett and his mates began to haul a harvest from the tropical waters—with hand grenades the preferred method of capture. Stunned by the explosions, scores of fish floated to the surface—on one occasion they caught 560 tailor. As well as the somewhat hazardous entertainment value, the fresh fish gave the squadron cooks something to work with other than tinned herrings.

While Pettett and his pals bombarded the marine life, the Japanese were rolling out their plans and bringing in reinforcements to support them. On 29 March, the Japanese 25th Air Flotilla began arriving at Rabaul. The next day, Japanese troops went ashore at Buka in the Solomons, and immediately began the construction of a fighter airfield. At the same time, other Japanese units seized Kieta on the east coast of Bougainville,

Every bit a fighter pilot: Les Jackson (pictured *right*, later in the war).

followed by Faisi in the Shortland Islands to the south. With this tentacle-like advance stretching south-east of Rabaul, the Japanese were coming closer to dominating the Coral Sea, and thereby advancing their planned envelopment of the Port Moresby bastion.

It fell once more to the hard-working Hudson crews of 32 Squadron and those aboard the Catalina flying boats of 11 and 20 Squadrons to keep track of these developments, with the now-customary heavy losses that went with confronting the Zeroes. They did so with few resources. As Japanese naval fleets criss-crossed the waters around New Guinea on 30 March, 32 Squadron could prepare just a single Hudson for operations. Like John Lerew before him, Deryck Kingwell insisted on leading from the front, and when orders came through for an immediate reconnaissance of Salamaua, he pulled rank on the duty pilot, Bob Green, and took command of the flight himself. Not to be outdone, Green insisted on joining the mission as co-pilot, and with the flight crew finally settled in this battle of wills, the Australians set out.

With their photographic run over Salamaua completed, they may have thought the sortie would be uneventful, until three Zeroes intervened. The Australians optimistically claimed to have shot down all three Japanese fighters, Kingwell even managing to put in bursts of fire from the bomber's front guns. Nevertheless, the Hudson crew did not escape lightly. The Japanese scored hits of their own, and as a result, the scenes in the bomber were mayhem. Glass splinters injured Kingwell's eye and bullets shot off rear gunner Sergeant J. V. Townshend's little toe, while the roof of his turret disappeared in a welter of Japanese shells.

However, it was the gallant Green who suffered most. A bullet shattered his right leg, fragments badly cut his left forearm and right hand, and splinters opened wounds in his left groin. The Hudson itself was equally battered, with both tyres shot out. With Green incapacitated, Kingwell did well to defy his own wounds to bring the bomber back to base safely.

When the Hudson pulled up on the flight-line, the ever-present Deane-Butcher and Church were on hand to help. They climbed up into the bomber, to find it a charnel house. 'Blood was everywhere,' wrote Church, 'the inside of the aircraft was a shambles and the fuselage looked like a colander'. Green, unconscious from his dreadful wounds, was ferried rapidly to hospital, while Kingwell, his face a mass of congealed blood, was led away, still muttering imprecations against the Japanese.

Two things characterised John Jackson's command of 75 Squadron: first, his personal bravery, and second, his determination to carry the fight to the Japanese whenever he could. Operations on 4 April demonstrated both elements of his leadership. At dawn, alone but determined, Jackson completed a reconnaissance of Lae, something of an aerial Daniel into the lion's den. With up-to-date intelligence of Japanese aircraft movements, he followed up with another strafing attack. The mission originally comprised five Kittyhawks, but Barry Cox became lost in cloud and returned to base. Pressing on, Jackson and his men swept in again over the Lae airfield, claiming to leave four bombers and three Zeroes ablaze as they withdrew from the target area. Japanese records confirm they had indeed inflicted significant damage, if not exactly to the extent they believed. Australian fire burnt out two Zeroes; eight others and nine bombers were damaged to a greater or lesser extent. Without any loss to his own squadron, this was a fine return for Jackson in the simple arithmetic of military calculation.

The next day, the newly arrived 25th Air Flotilla attempted to repay the Australians in kind, but with less success. Seven Kittyhawks scrambled to intercept seven bombers, with nine escorting Zeroes. Les Jackson claimed one Zero shot down in flames, a loss confirmed by Japanese records; the Japanese in turn thought (erroneously) that two

Not much entertainment: 75 Squadron pilots keep themselves amused on the flight-line.

Australian aircraft were also destroyed. In fact, 5 April was something of a red-letter day for the Australians. Not only was the Japanese raid safely dealt with, but seven replacement Kittyhawks arrived to replenish his earlier losses.

75 Squadron sorely needed the new machines, because the Japanese were steadily intensifying their operations against Port Moresby. They sent in another raid on 6 April, comprising seven Betty bombers and five Zeroes. The Australian Kittyhawks scrambled, this time accompanied by two American P39 Airacobras of 36th Pursuit Squadron, flown by Lieutenants Charles Faletta and Lewis Meng. The Americans were posted temporarily to Port Moresby to familiarise themselves with the base and its operations. Faletta was less than enthusiastic about the posting. When the commanding US General in Queensland called for volunteers for the short tour to Moresby, Faletta quietly avoided stepping forward, but 'he sent me anyway'.

John Jackson himself led the Australian welcoming party, and this 'heavy set fella' made an impression on Faletta. The Americans were flying the most exotic operational fighter to fly in World War II. It was designed as a 'one-shot bomber buster' with a massive 37-millimetre cannon firing through the airscrew hub, and to make way for this huge gun the Airacobra's engine was fitted amidships, driving the propeller through a massive shaft that ran below the pilot's cockpit.

Faletta and Meng found the big cannon more trouble than it was worth on 6 April, and both were plagued by gun stoppages. Together with the Australians, they managed hits on five of the bombers, but failed to bring any down, and in turn, 75 Squadron lost two aircraft, fortunately without loss of life. Les Jackson crash-landed on a coral reef, the Kittyhawk settling in two metres of water with its tail and wings sticking out above the sea. To assure searching aircraft that he was all right, Les Jackson jumped up and down on the wing, much to the amusement of his brother, who was one of the search pilots. Not realising that it was his brother, John Jackson noted the downed pilot was a 'happy sort of chap', who seemingly enjoyed the watery dance. Les eventually swam ashore unharmed, after his brother dropped him a life-jacket to sustain his progress. 75 Squadron lost a second Kittyhawk, which went down in a swamp north of Moresby, but the pilot managed to walk out.

The Americans' initial stay lasted only a matter of days, but this was long enough for Les Jackson to exploit their naïvety for the purposes of a good time. With an eye on the stock of beer kept by the Airacobra pilots, Jackson arrived at a simple method to obtain his share. The standard air raid warning at Seven Mile airfield consisted of three rifle shots. With the American contingent resting in their quarters, Jackson let off the volley of warning shots, and when his unsuspecting allies made for the nearest slit trench, he swooped for the beer and liberated sufficient bottles for his next party.

In between such escapades, the war continued. On 7 April, 75 Squadron sent six Kittyhawks to escort American Dauntless dive-bombers to Lae. These aircraft were from the 8th Bombardment Squadron of the US Army Air Force. Newly arrived in the theatre, and based at Kila or Three Mile strip near the harbour, the Americans struggled to make the Dauntless aircraft a success in the trying conditions in New Guinea, but this was not for the want of a close partnership with the Australian fighter pilots. Running into attack at dawn, the joint allied operation was successful, forcing the Japanese to cancel a planned fighter sweep of their own against Port Moresby, and damaging nine aircraft on the ground. The Australians made no claims for aircraft shot down, but Japanese records show one of their pilots was killed in action on this day. He had fallen victim to the rear gunner of one of the American dive-bombers.

Unfortunately, even successful operations like this one were not inflicting enough decisive damage to prevent further Japanese forward moves. While Moresby's aircrews were hammering Lae, along the allied 'right flank' in the Solomon Islands the Japanese were busy again. On 7 April, they seized Buin, a strategically placed village on the southern tip of Bougainville. To complete their hold on the Bismarck Sea to the north of New Guinea, the next day another Japanese force took Lorengau on Manus Island.

As Japanese commanders made these moves, the quality of the personnel they now deployed reflected their determination to force the issue. While troops went ashore at Lorengau, elsewhere on 8 April 1942 a new contestant entered the New Guinea air war, when Japanese fighter pilot Saburo Sakai, an ace with the elite Tainan Air Group, arrived at Lae. As he circled the airstrip with eight other pilots, he groaned at what he saw. 'Where were the

Samurai! Saburo Sakai pictured during the fighting in the Philippines, January 1942; he found even less to smile about in New Guinea.

hangars, the maintenance shops, the control tower? Where was anything but a dirty small runway?' Bordered on three sides by mountains, the Lae base seemed to Sakai nothing but a 'forsaken mudhole'.

The Japanese themselves were partly responsible for this depressing atmosphere. When Sakai landed and taxied into the dispersal area, he found the one small aircraft hangar riddled with bullets, and the wreckage of burnt-out Australian aircraft littered about. The harbour presented the same melancholy air, with a smashed merchant ship sitting in the mud, its mast jutting from the water with funereal effect. Lae, concluded Sakai, was the worst base he had ever seen.

At the end of a long and over-stretched Japanese supply line, Sakai never enjoyed even a modicum of creature comforts at Lae. However, his presence in New Guinea reflected the determination of Japanese commanders to bring the fighting over Port Moresby to a successful and rapid conclusion. Sakai and his comrades in the Tainan Air Group were the best the Japanese Naval Air Force had to offer. Already a combat veteran from two tours in the war against China, the first as early as 1938, Sakai then fought over the Philippines and the Dutch East Indies after Pearl Harbor. This first phase of the Pacific war ended for the Tainan Air Group on Bali, a tropical paradise compared to what would follow in New Guinea, but a combat backwater by March 1942.

Notwithstanding the value of the Tainan Air Group, the Japanese were already finding their conquests difficult to administer and sustain. To distinguish their empire from the rapacious European competition, they called it the 'Greater Co-prosperity Sphere', a euphemism designed to appeal to pan-Asian solidarity. Whatever the propaganda, shipping shortages meant that Japanese operations at the extremity of their advance were conducted on a shoestring, as Sakai and his comrades found to their cost when they were redeployed from Bali to Rabaul, in preparation for the final move to Lae. Crammed into the hold of a tramp steamer, the pilots of the Tainan Air Group endured a two-week ordeal. 'The ship creaked and groaned' as it ploughed through the swells of the equatorial sea. Aboard ship, conditions were 'torturous', the heat 'unbearable' and the smell indescribable. Sakai himself fell violently ill, and cursed his high command for risking the cream of Japanese fighter pilots in a 'seagoing monstrosity'.

Disembarkation at Rabaul did not greatly cheer things up for the new arrivals. The volcano above Simpson Harbour was still active, and 'every few minutes the ground trembled and the volcano groaned deeply', hurling out stones and thick choking fumes. Sakai spared himself further misery and admitted himself to the newly established Japanese field hospital, where he convalesced while aircraft needed to equip the group were shipped in by sea. When the new fighters were ready, Sakai discharged himself from hospital and defied a lingering weakness to move forward to the front at the new Lae base.

Arriving at Lae on 8 April, it did not take long for Sakai and his comrades to make an impression on the fighting over New Guinea. Two days after the arrival of the Japanese aces, John Jackson was called to perform another of his lone and perilous reconnaissance missions over the Lae base. At first all seemed well. The operations tent at Seven Mile recorded him safely away at 6 am on 10 April, and an army outpost north-west of Moresby reported him heading towards Lae not long after. But by 9 am, Jackson had not returned, and fears began to mount among the men of 75 Squadron.

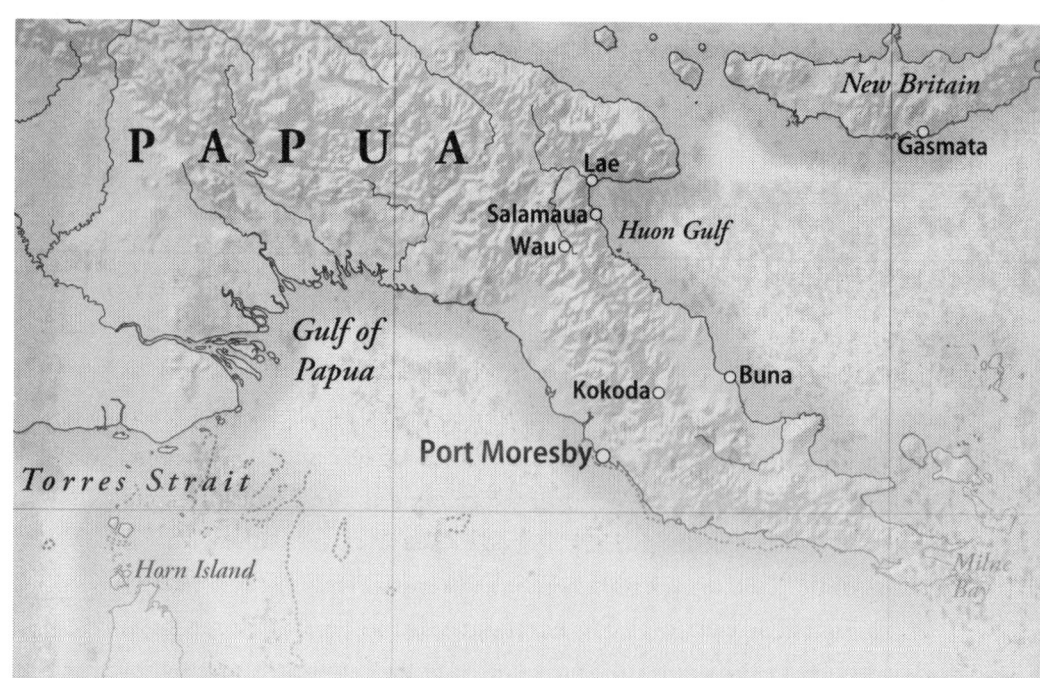

CHAPTER EIGHT
'... shot my plane to bits'

By mid-morning, the controllers at Seven Mile had to admit the inevitable, and the duty officer posted John Jackson missing at 9.30 am. 75 Squadron did not even have time to commence a search for their missing leader, because within minutes the squadron scrambled to meet an incoming raid. Nine Kittyhawks took off, and with only local warning, the Australians found themselves yet again below the Japanese formation, which consisted of seven bombers and six Zeroes. Despite this disadvantage, 75 Squadron fought well. Geoff Atherton claimed to shoot down a bomber, his first success in combat. This was the start of a glittering career for the young Tasmanian, in the course of which he acquired a reputation among his peers as one of the very rare fighter pilots who was truly fearless.

The more experienced John Piper also inflicted some injury on the raiders, damaging two bombers in a stern chase in the direction of Kokoda. He reported getting 'plenty of smoke' out of one, before scoring hits on another, but both Japanese bombers survived. Piper was convinced his ammunition was to blame—the Australians, with equipment borrowed from the Americans, did not have the full suite of ammunition types to make the Kittyhawks fully effective. Thus, Piper sent round after round of armour-piercing and tracer bullets at the Japanese, when a mix of explosive and incendiary shells would have spelt a quick end to the unarmoured Betty bombers.

Piper was unable to force the issue before being knocked out of the fight himself. With his cooling system holed by Japanese bullets, Piper had to glide down to base from 8000 metres, but managed to put bursts of fire in the direction of two Zeroes that crossed his path. Faced with the tenacious defence of the Australians, the Japanese bombing was ragged, and Seven Mile escaped unharmed.

Having fought off this latest Japanese incursion, 75 Squadron set about organising search flights to find Jackson. By this time, the Australians at least had something to go on. At 11 am, flight controllers heard a slow Morse code message, repeatedly tapping out the word 'Lori'. Since this was the name of a village 80 kilometres north-west of Moresby, on the direct route to Lae, Jackson's men drew the logical conclusion that this should be the starting point for the search. Determined to provide Jackson with supplies to face a stay in the jungle, they enlisted the help of the American dive-bomber squadron, with whom they shared the base at Seven Mile. The two-seat Dauntless dive-bombers used by the Americans could drop Jackson a medical kit and food in a way that a Kittyhawk could not, if only he could be found. The Americans, having enjoyed the benefit of Jackson's cover over Lae, were naturally happy to help, and accordingly a Dauntless set out at 11.45 am, its rear cockpit crammed with supplies and medicine. This well-intentioned mission came to naught. Bad weather ended the search early. Determined to do their best to help Jackson, the Australians opted to defy the weather in the later afternoon, when Barry Cox went out alone in a Kittyhawk. He fared no better than the Americans, and the search was abandoned for the day. As night fell, if Jackson were alive, or lying wounded in the jungle, his men were powerless to help.

As John Piper glided down out of the battle over Kokoda, on the waters of the Huon Gulf, John Jackson was fighting for his life. After inspecting the airfield at Lae, three Zeroes pursued him out to sea. He initially hoped to outrun the Japanese, but unusually found his Kittyhawk unable to manage the feat, perhaps because the tuning of his motor was slightly awry. Worse was to follow for the Australian squadron leader. Turning to fight, Jackson found his guns quickly jammed. The Japanese had him at their mercy, and true to their standards of marksmanship, as Jackson later wrote to his family, they soon 'shot my plane to bits'. With his Kittyhawk a 'mass of holes, windscreen all shot away and on fire', Jackson was too low to bail out. The only way out now was to ditch into the sea. He did this, only to find his fighter quickly sinking beneath him, the next problem being that his oxygen mask kept him firmly attached to the aeroplane. When this at last gave way, the sight of land a kilometre away heartened Jackson, but with the Zeroes circling menacingly, he expected to be strafed in the water at any moment. When, 'after what seemed an eternity', the Japanese departed, Jackson found his next opponent—a large crocodile, which poked its snout at him as he swam to shore. The animal fortunately chose not to pursue the enquiry further, and Jackson, a powerful man, struck out for the beach, which he reached without further drama, albeit shoeless and exhausted. Small wonder Jackson concluded 'Providence alone ... saved me'.

Nearby, at the Lae airbase, the Japanese fighter pilots celebrated their latest victory. They were in good spirits, despite the primitive conditions. The operations room of the Tainan Air Group was no more luxurious than that of their opponents at Port Moresby. It consisted of a shack, with coconut mats hung from beams to provide walls, curtains and doors. The available equipment matched the décor. Lighting came from candles and kerosene lamps, while the only source of electrical power—from batteries—was reserved for the telephone system. And there would be no trucks to race scrambling pilots to the flight-line. The car park at Lae comprised 'an ancient, rusty, creaky Ford sedan', presumably pilfered from the departed Australians, 'one decrepit truck, and one fuelling vehicle'.

The Japanese needed their martial code, because the daily routine at Lae was tough indeed. Every day at 2.30 am, guards roused the Japanese ground crews from their beds to begin work, followed an hour later by the aircrews. This punishing regime applied day in, day out, and for all the hard work, the available diet, 'monotonous and unvarying', provided no compensation at all. At the end of the tenuous supply line, the Japanese even lacked enough rice, and mixed in barley to eke out the available stock. Protein was a rarity: 'a dish of rice, soybean-paste soup with dried vegetables and pickles' constituted meal after meal.

Like the Australians, the Japanese also struggled with hygiene. They went to great lengths to keep clean, fashioning bathtubs out of fuel drums and bathing religiously each night. The same attention was devoted to laundry, since 'every man took special pains to wash out all his underclothes in the basins every day.' The only entertainments were games the men could arrange themselves, principally chess and checkers. Despite the multitude of privations, as Saburo Sakai recalled, 'our morale was high'. For soldiers, the reason was simple enough: 'we were here not to have our personal requirements met, but to fight'.

John Jackson was in New Guinea to fight as well, only on the afternoon of 10 April 1942, he was fighting not the Japanese, but the jungle near Salamaua. Staggering ashore after his long and perilous swim, he found the local villagers understandably terrified of the Japanese, and only two young men would help him. They were not locals, but Christian converts who hailed originally from the Rabaul area. The available records identify them only by their given names, but to Edmund, an Anglican, and Arthur, a Methodist who could speak no English, Jackson would owe his life.

With Japanese motor boats now prowling off shore, Jackson set out in the footsteps of Wilbur Wackett and John Lerew, on an epic struggle for survival in the harshest conditions imaginable. Moving inland to avoid the enemy patrols, the three men slogged their way through wetlands, waist deep in 'slime and mud'. Without shoes, and no doubt already exhausted by the swim to shore and the traumas that preceded it, the Australian soon found the going hard. By the end of the first day, Edmund and Arthur were carrying Jackson across the worst of the stony jungle creeks. As they settled down for the night in the jungle, rain began to fall, and although instructed in the use of a banana leaf as an umbrella, Jackson failed to master the knack of holding it. Forced on in search of shelter, the trio found a hut and, nourished by a meal of roots and coconut, fell into an uncomfortable sleep.

On 11 April, Jackson awoke to the sound of bombing in the distance. Encouraged, he offered the hope that his boys were 'giving them "tally ho"'. They, and their American partners, were doing just that, attacking the Lae airbase in a dive-bombing raid that set a fuel dump ablaze for 24 hours, and so disheartened Japanese commanders that they ordered their bomber force to desert Lae and return to Rabaul, from where they faced much longer flight times to reach Port Moresby.

For 75 Squadron, this success came at a cost. The seven Kittyhawks were arranged in two formations, with John Woods leading a top cover of five fighters, while John Piper and his wingman Sergeant David Brown formed a 'close cover' for the American dive-bombers, to ward off any Zeroes that managed to make it past Woods and his men.

As the allied formations approached Lae from the sea, the Japanese rose to protect their base. Piper saw three Zeroes dive on the Americans below, and he led Brown down to intercept. As he did so, three more Zeroes tangled with the flight led by Woods, and the action became general.

Still loyally covering the Americans, Piper closed in on the first gaggle of Zeroes and claimed two shot down, one breaking up mid-air and falling into the sea. In turn, Peter Masters came down from above to engage other Zeroes pursuing Piper.

Masters was a rising star in 75 Squadron. Only recently turned twenty-two, he was the son of Baptist missionaries and was born in what is now Bangladesh. With Piper hard-pressed, his intervention was welcome, and effective. He took a Zero off Piper's tail by attacking in a left-hand dive that took the combatants over the hills to the south of Lae. This was a true fighter pilots' combat, in which Masters and his opponent turned into each other, seeking the dominant tactical position of a firing pass from astern. Masters could not afford to indulge in these tactics for long against the more nimble Zero, so he resorted to deflection shooting, in which a bead is drawn ahead of the target. Only experts were capable of this kind of shooting. 'With a lot of rudder and all my strength on the stick, I got about one aeroplane's length lead on the Zero and kept pulling the trigger'. Pieces flew off the Japanese fighter from the area of the engine cowling and the cockpit canopy, together with what Masters thought to be a piece of wing. The Zero spiralled down out of control. The Australian later saw the machine scattered on the ground at the end of the Lae runway. After this breathless action, Masters beat a retreat, triumphant: 'I felt no remorse, with adrenalin running free and heart pumping'.

For another of the Australians, the adrenalin was also flowing, but in a different context. After the combat began, Piper lost sight of his wingman, young David Brown. A short, brown-haired twenty-four-year-old from Castlemaine, Victoria, Brown attempted to exit the combat area, but only got as far as Salamaua before coming down close to the shore. The Zeroes did not hit Brown's Kittyhawk, which fell victim instead to the scattered anti-aircraft fire coming up from the ground. The last moments of his flight suggest the shell fragments punctured the fighter's cooling system, allowing him to travel some way before the engine finally overheated. The ever-present NGVR patrols kept a close eye on events, reporting to

Port Moresby that the Japanese salvaged the Kittyhawk, presumably for an intelligence inspection at Lae or Rabaul.

Unfortunately, the Australian militiamen were unable to help Brown. Like other Australians in his position, the young sergeant resolved to do his best to escape. With revolver in one hand and knife in the other, he began climbing a hill behind Salamaua. Regrettably, a Japanese infantry patrol was in the area, and its commander, Nachei Okabe, ordered a section of eleven men to run Brown down. Still armed but cornered, Brown surrendered when the Japanese turned a machine gun on him. Okabe at once inspected the Australian for papers and equipment that might offer intelligence information. When the Japanese dispossessed Brown of the photo he carried of his fiancée, Okabe wrote that the young Australian was 'visibly affected'. Japanese propagandists later made much of the incident. Newspaper articles in Japan claimed that Brown 'cried like a baby' when the photo was taken from him, behaviour that the propagandists claimed only confirmed the weakness of Australians.

On the evening of 11 April, Okabe handed Brown over to Lieutenant Commander Mitaya, commander of the Japanese air units at Lae. For Brown, this marked the beginning of a journey into darkness that proved among the most horrific travelled by any of the Australian aircrew in the battle for Moresby.

Before the allied strike force set out for Lae, the signallers at Seven Mile heard the same mysterious Morse code message that had raised hopes of finding Jackson the previous day. Having shut down at dusk on 10 April, whoever was transmitting 'Lori' resumed broadcasting at dawn the next day. With the previous day's search flights hampered by the weather, it was logical for the Australians to resume their efforts to find Jackson on the back of this seemingly sound intelligence. Thus, and despite the loss of Brown, when the strike force returned from Lae that morning, it fanned out to maximise the ground covered. Still the searchers found nothing. Exasperated, that afternoon the Australians resorted to sending up a signals officer in the rear cockpit of a Dauntless, in a final attempt to find the source of the puzzling Morse signal. Even with this additional technical support, the flight proved futile.

While his friends in Moresby did what they could, the subject of their efforts was doing it tough in the hinterland behind Lae. To ease the pain on Jackson's bruised and lacerated feet, Arthur and Edmund made a pair of crutches for him and cut up a bag to serve as modest sandals. With these to aid him, Jackson staggered on all day, but such was his increasingly feeble condition, the men from New Britain were literally pushing him along by day's end. What passed for nourishment was little help in easing his distress. Arthur and Edmund resorted to roasting some green bananas as a semblance of an evening meal, but not surprisingly, Jackson found these 'pretty tasteless' and they did little to restore his spirits. Another night in the jungle loomed, and still he was no closer to rescue.

When Jackson awoke on the morning of 12 April, the condition of his feet alarmed him. After two days tramping through the unforgiving landscape of northern New Guinea, 'they were like two pulps and I could hardly touch them let alone stand'.

Had he been aware of the latest search flight mounted from Moresby, Jackson might have taken some encouragement from it. After the search effort had spent two fruitless days pursuing the curious, if not bogus, Morse code signal from 'Lori', Jackson's brother Les decided to take matters into his own hands, and came close to success. Working back from John's target destination, Les took off at mid-morning on 12 April.

He searched the valleys south of Lae and Salamaua at low level, until the perennial bad weather forced him back to Seven Mile. He was at least on the right track, but the chances now of finding John, on the move beneath the jungle canopy, were slight indeed. If Jackson were to emerge from the wilderness, it would be thanks to his stamina and the dedication of his helpers. The origin of the mysterious 'Lori' signal was never found.

Still the war went on. On 13 April, 75 Squadron was back in action over Lae, taking the fight to the Japanese in concert with the American Dauntless crews. This time the Allies were searching for an oil tanker, reported to be running fuel supplies into the Japanese base. Again, the Australians formed their escort into two flights, with three Kittyhawks led by Piper sticking close to the bombers, while four others flew top cover.

When the oil tanker could not be found, the strike shifted to the airfield, at which point another vicious combat ensued with the ever-present Zeroes. The Australian trio flying close cover—Piper, Bink Davies, and Oswald 'Ozzie' Channon, a twenty-four-year-old from the New South Wales country town of West Wyalong—bore the brunt of the fighting. Coming into the airfield at 4000 metres, Piper saw three Zeroes below. After alerting the squadron, Piper led his section down to engage, and he and Channon both claimed the destruction of a Zero, although Japanese records suggest only that two of their machines were damaged. Channon saw Davies at 1500 metres turning steeply to avoid the fire of a Zero, not a good tactical option for a Kittyhawk.

Both Channon and Piper then reported last seeing Davies in a spin below 1000 metres, after which they lost track of their comrade.

With no definite news of his fate, Davies was reported missing. His mate John Pettett took the news especially hard, and the uncertainty no doubt compounded the gloom in the mess tent that night at Seven Mile.

It was not until 1946 that the RAAF officially declared the young Western Australian killed in action, by which time Bink's father Rowland had tracked down Piper for a long-sought-after chat about his son's last flight. All Piper could add was his belief that the spin of Davies' Kittyhawk would have resulted in a crash near the Japanese airfield, rather than out to sea, where post-war RAAF search parties had until then concentrated their efforts.

John Jackson had a glimpse of the combat that cost Davies his life, 'perched on a mountain overlooking the sea' behind Lae. Again, the distant bombing brought news of the latest allied raid, but on this occasion, Jackson had the motivating sight of four of his Kittyhawk pilots sweeping overhead. With this fillip to his morale, Jackson could also take heart from the modest improvement to his equipment, thanks to the tireless and tender efforts of Edmund and Arthur. When a pair of sandshoes one of them donated to Jackson proved too large, they cut them down into sandals, and the results were immediate and beneficial. Newly shod, Jackson wrote of his feet, 'the swelling has gone down and they feel a ton better but I have some decent stone bruises'. As the tramp went on through the jungle to the south and the prospective safety of Wau, Jackson did his best to keep himself going, bathing his feet every hour or so in the jungle streams.

Physically healthier and in a better frame of mind, Jackson and his guides set out early on 14 April, hoping to make a good day's progress. The intent was admirable, but due to the rugged terrain, progress was initially slow. After a breakfast of roasted taro, the three men struggled for the rest of the day through a succession of seemingly endless climbs into the mountains. As they crossed the creeks and streams pouring down from the hills, they found themselves festooned with leeches, 'by the billion' as Jackson succinctly described it. Not that he cared, because they 'could have been snakes sucking at me and I wouldn't have felt them, my feet were so sore'. Jackson's initial enthusiasm and stamina soon waned, and he was reduced to a stumble, eking out just ten or fifteen centimetres a step. As he concluded, the mountainous country ensured that, 'you can walk all day in New Guinea and in the afternoon, see, no distance away, the place you left in the morning'.

At least on this occasion, perseverance had its rewards. By noon on the fourth day, the trio came across the villagers of Mapos, and for even the happily married Jackson, the sights were almost too much for sore eyes: 'all the girls wear nothing from the waist up and look most alluring'. The cultural life of the locals also intrigued Jackson, since he had chanced upon what he took to be the festival season: 'All day I could hear the Kundu drums beating'. As Jackson approached the village, the local songs preceded him: 'the people yodel or call out in a musical sort of chant the story of my arrival'. Now among the relative comfort and safety of the villagers, Jackson briefly left the war behind and immersed himself in the richness of their world. When a dance ceremony unfolded before him, Jackson was fascinated: 'the male dancers, with not much on, painted with ochre and wearing fearsome looking headdresses mostly with birds of paradise feathers and other bright-plumaged birds, dance around in a circle beating their hollowed drums with lizard or snake skins stretched across one end'.

Grateful though he was, Jackson was delighted the next day to have the 'tuttul', or second man of the village, arrive with supplies of tea, sugar and condensed milk. With news of the NGVR in the area, Jackson scrawled out a note that the villagers obligingly agreed to carry to the Australian soldiers. And not least, Jackson now had a basin in which to bathe his bruised and bloodied feet.

For the Australian pilot, salvation was now close. After a day's luxurious rest, at 9 pm on 15 April, two NGVR men appeared to bring Jackson in: Sergeant Stuart Fraser-Fraser and Rifleman George Kerr.

With Jackson unfit to walk out, the NGVR men organised a carrier party from among the villagers to bear him on a stretcher to the main Australian outpost at Wau. When Jackson arrived there, his bearing and stoicism made a deep impression on the ranks of the NGVR, hard men themselves; one of them, Sergeant Ted Blakey, wrote later, 'what a man he was'.

While the NGVR and the Moresby base liaised over how to get Jackson back to Seven Mile, his men were under increasing pressure. The RAAF had plans to reinforce 75 Squadron, for which reason the commander of its second Kittyhawk unit, 76 Squadron, had arrived in Moresby to familiarise himself with operations. Squadron Leader 'Barney' Creswell was an experienced pre-war air force officer, but the shadow of Australia's attachment to the Empire Air Training Scheme remained. Creswell arrived at Moresby with thousands of hours' flight time in his log-book, but not one operational sortie to his name. Attempting his first among the battered defenders of Seven Mile was not ideal, and the mission Creswell chose was ambitious in the extreme. Flying wingman to Jeff Woods, Creswell set out at dawn on the most dangerous operation possible, a reconnaissance of Lae. The pair managed to over-fly the Japanese base then turned south, but Zeroes were hunting them. Over the Wau area around 8 am, a Zero made a sudden firing pass at Woods, who attempted to warn Creswell before diving away. New to combat, Creswell was seemingly oblivious to the mortal danger he faced.

On the ground, NGVR patrols looked on, reporting that the Zero fired only one short burst, upon which smoke immediately issued from Creswell's Kittyhawk, 'which tried to pancake but crashed' into a hill. The fireball that ensued incinerated Creswell. The NGVR recovered his remains and buried him at the Bulwa cemetery.

The fateful sortie to Lae was only the first Australian loss on what the Moresby defenders would find among the most gruelling days of the campaign. Later in the morning, 75 Squadron scrambled to meet a raid. Les Jackson led the nine-strong Australian formation, and the combat that followed would generate one of the great mysteries of the battle.

Approaching Moresby that morning along with twelve other Zero pilots was Saburo Sakai, on his first escort mission to Moresby. As the Japanese bombers commenced their bomb run, the accuracy of what he took to be American anti-aircraft fire impressed Sakai. In fact, the barrage was the work of the Australian 23rd Heavy Anti Aircraft Battery, and their shooting forced the Japanese bombers to unload from high altitude, thereby blunting their accuracy. Sakai looked on as an Australian salvo bracketed the Japanese bombers, which were 'hidden completely by a series of bursting shells'. It seemed like the flak had struck dead centre, but miraculously, the seven Japanese bombers emerged in formation from the 'boiling smoke.'

The Australian gunners had done their best, but still the Japanese bombs did frightful harm. Among them were more than 100 anti-personnel bombs, known as 'daisy cutters'. By exploding 30 centimetres or so above ground level, the thin-walled daisy cutters sent out a lethal burst of shrapnel, with devastating results. That morning, many of these fell on the transport pool at Seven Mile airfield. Sergeant Harry Brumby was a horrified witness to what followed. As he came on the scene, his first sight was a 'boot with an ankle and foot in it'. A daisy cutter had exploded barely three metres from two army men, who 'had each leg chopped off and hundreds of pieces out of their bodies, arms and legs and heads'. Hurrying on to the scene, Bill Deane-Butcher collected up two other wounded men who stood some chance of life, and loaded them into an ambulance. Bereft and no doubt in shock, Brumby 'sat down and cried', distressed by the thought of 'two more mothers who had to suffer as a result of this ghastly ungodly war'.

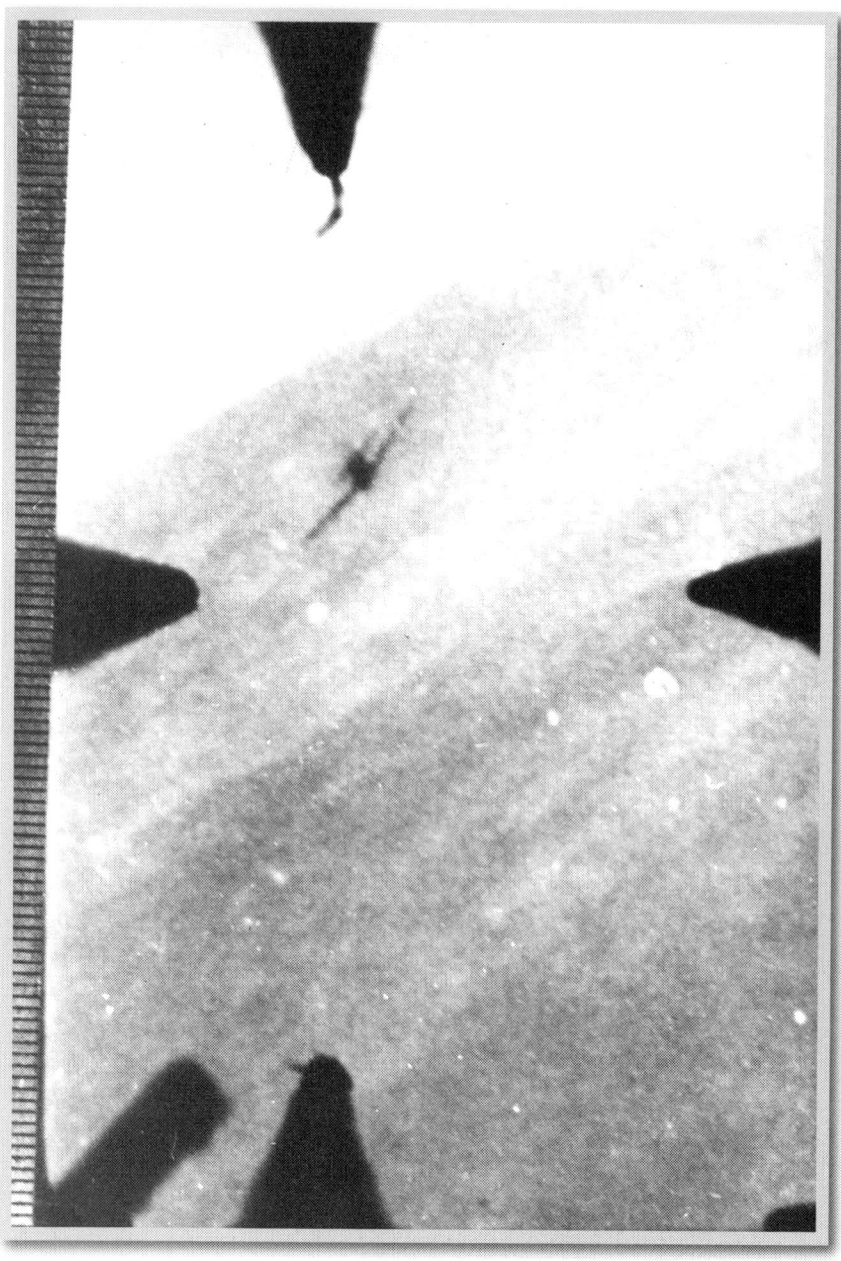

Admittedly a still from Arthur Tucker's camera gun later in the war, this amazing photo nevertheless gives some sense of the swirling, instantaneous combats over Moresby.

While Deane-Butcher set off in his ambulance, high above the pilots of 75 Squadron sought to extract some kind of revenge on their Japanese adversaries. What followed was a combat between the Kittyhawks and the Zeroes, in which the accounts of the Australian and Japanese pilots cannot be reconciled. In his post-war memoirs, Sakai wrote that six Kittyhawks dived on his Zero formation from above; the Australians reported they were still below the Japanese raid when the action began. In the confused fighting, Sakai saw a Zero flown by his friend Gitaro Miyazaki descend well below the Betty bombers. Miyazaki should not have been flying. A champion judo exponent, Miyazaki was a career pilot, graduating from flight school in 1937 and joining action over China in September 1938. As was the case with their Australian opponents, the difficult climate and poor diet resulted in endless stomach disorders. Miyazaki insisted on flying the mission on 17 April, despite the gastroenteritis that gripped him and Sakai's concerns for his 'emaciated' appearance.

Now below the bombers he should have been escorting, Miyazaki was in an extremely vulnerable tactical position. As Sakai looked on helplessly, a lone Kittyhawk dived with 'incredible speed' through the bomber formation, missing a collision on either wingtip by millimetres. Hurtling down, the Kittyhawk managed a single burst into Miyazaki's Zero, which drifted 'slowly down, trailing flame', until with a mighty explosion, the fighter was blown into 'tiny pieces of wreckage ... we failed to see even a piece of metal falling'.

Fifty years later, Peter Masters gave an account of this action that virtually replicates that of Sakai in his memoirs. This would seemingly confirm Masters as the pilot responsible for Miyazaki's demise, the problem being that Japanese records show that the Japanese pilot actually died in combat on 1 June 1942, not in late April as Sakai later wrote. Sakai's recollection of these events in his memoirs appears to be faulty. Could Peter Masters have read Sakai's autobiography and confused this action with another, similar combat?

We will now certainly never know. The other Kittyhawk pilots also made claims against the Zeroes. When a Japanese fighter pulled up in front of Arthur Tucker, the young Queenslander accepted the invitation to open fire and scored hits on the Zero before it fell away. Machine gun bullets hit Tucker's own machine nine times. The Kittyhawks of Cocky Brereton and Bill Cowe also returned home laced by Japanese rounds, while Alan Whetters was lucky not to fall victim to a Zero that chased him down towards Moresby. The intervention of Les Jackson saved him. The younger Jackson manoeuvred expertly onto the tail of the Japanese fighter and chased it for nearly 40 kilometres, before opening fire at 60 metres. The Japanese pilot turned into the attack, but Jackson saw his bullets striking the fuselage of the Zero, which reared up. As Jackson swept by, he clearly saw the engine cowling of the Zero shot away, with black smoke billowing out. He last saw the Japanese fighter spinning down at a height of just 300 metres. The Tainan Air Group reported the loss of Petty Officer Yoshimi Sakai in action on this date, and he may well have met his fate at the hands of Jackson.

While the dogfight dissolved as quickly as it had formed above him, Bill Deane-Butcher was setting out in the ambulance with his cargo of wounded men, bound for the army hospital at Rouna Falls on the outskirts of Moresby. The going was heavy on the rough track. Deane-Butcher administered morphine to alleviate the suffering of his two patients, one of whom quickly lapsed into semi-consciousness. While the grievously wounded soldier babbled out a nightmare conversation with his wife and children, the doctor fought his own demons. The day was hot and oppressive, and Deane-Butcher—sick himself with gastroenteritis—did his duty only with a supreme effort of will. When at last the ambulance pulled up at the hospital, the wounded were carried into theatre. Deane-Butcher's efforts proved in vain, and both men died. Distraught and ill, the doctor collapsed from his exertions.

75 Squadron needed its medical officer more than ever as the battle reached its climax. Deane-Butcher later complained that the unit had a 'cult of toughness' in the face of ill health and danger, and this resulted in pilots flying when unfit. Complaints only attracted a label of weakness. John Jackson was a hard man himself, and his brother Les equally so. The squadron's code of stoicism would produce growing tensions in the ranks at Seven Mile.

Japanese bombers were not the only raiders doing damage. As the American strike force based at Townsville gained experience, so their combat performance improved. In their light Zero fighters, the Japanese pilots found the powerful US bombers formidable adversaries, and their own tactics did not help. Superlative dogfight pilots, the Japanese nevertheless lacked the close teamwork needed to tackle heavily armed formations of bombers, and their propensity to remove the radios from their fighters (to save weight) did nothing to help tactical co-ordination. The result was often chaos, as the Japanese fought as individuals, making repeated lone passes against the Americans, when mass firepower was the only way to bring down the rugged B-17 and B-26 bombers. Of one battle against a B-26 formation over Lae, Sakai wrote bitterly 'it was the clumsiest air fight I had ever seen ... instead of making concerted attacks against one or two planes ... our pilots were overzealous and threw themselves all over the sky. Repeatedly several planes jerked frantically out of their firing pass to avoid a collision with another Zero or to evade the fire of a friendly fighter'. The armament fitted to the Zero did not help. Although packing a punch, the 20-millimetre cannons fitted to the Japanese aircraft were slow-firing weapons. Indeed the Australian Kittyhawk pilots could see the individual shells as they swept by, and found an analogy in the national sport: 'flaming red cricket balls'. The result was fearsome to behold, but the rate of fire was such that as Sakai lamented, Zero pilots faced the equivalent of trying to 'hit a dragonfly with a rifle'.

On 18 April, the Japanese at Rabaul would feel the growing improvement in American capability with a vengeance. Three B-26 Marauder bombers of 33rd Bombardment Squadron ran in at low level, targeting the supply ship *Komaki Maru*, the rust-bucket that had carried Sakai and his comrades to Rabaul. Now tied up to a wharf in Simpson Harbour, the ship was loaded with munitions and aviation fuel. When the first two American bombers sped in they caught the defenders by surprise, and hit the *Komaki Maru* with two 250-kilogram bombs. The third American bomber came in to the target late, and on its own. With the defences forewarned, this machine was met by a Zero flown by Lieutenant Jun-ichi Sasai of the Tainan Air Group, who shot down the American bomber. Two of the crew, Theron Lutz and Sanger Reed, bailed out and survived. They would give the Japanese valuable intelligence information during interrogation, and later meet up with David Brown under melancholy circumstances.

This victory over one of the bombers was small consolation to the Japanese for the carnage wreaked by the American planes. Hineo Inetsugu—an enlisted man from Hiroshima serving with the Kure Special Landing Party, one of the elite marine formations allocated by the Japanese to their island-hopping campaign in the Solomons—recorded in his diary the results of the bombing. The Allies later captured this, and a transcript of it now resides in the Australian War Memorial. Inetsugu recorded the devastation that followed, as the American bombs transformed the *Komaki Maru* into an inferno:

> *Today, as the whole sky over the city was clouded with ashes, it was not until the planes were nearly above the city that we were able to see. They went by in a straight line towards the west. On account of this, we thought the enemy planes had gone, but in 15 minutes they returned again from the west, dropped*

bombs and strafed us with machine gun fire. Our AA guns and machine guns fired fiercely but were unable to score. 3 planes pursued them, and disappeared in the volcanic smoke. After that, looking toward the west pier, a cloud of dark black smoke was rising. The blaze looked dreadful. Looking carefully at the blaze, the mast of a ship could be seen directly in front. So I knew for the first time that the ship was hit by a bomb.

In a little while, the truck with the casualties came to my post and inquired the way to the hospital. Seems as though there were many casualties. After returning to the tent, listened to stories from each sentry who had returned. The ship arrived yesterday loaded with many bombs and ammunition and was to be unloaded this morning. About 11, the entire ship was wrapped in flames. The ammunition exploded violently, and it was dangerous to even approach the vicinity ... the ships that were near, all changed their anchorage. Since it would not do to leave it a target for enemy aircraft, the patrol ship and cruisers which were staying in the harbour fired upon the burning ship to sink it, but the projectiles could not hit below the water line ...

The noise in the darkness caused by the explosion of the projectiles hitting and the rise of flames sky high made a gruesome scene ...

The stern of the ship exploded and sunk [sic]. Just the top part of the ship remained above the water. A little after 7 o'clock there was a great reverberation. Probably the big bombs which were loaded on the stern exploded all at once ... we fell in immediately and climbed into the cars in groups. It appeared that the fire from the ship's conflagration spread to the warehouse which was on the right bank. Upon going there, we saw that the burning fragments from the explosion flew to the warehouse. All at once, it was gravely serious, because there were many provisions and ammunition within ... the ammunition exploded repeatedly and the oil flared up and it was a sea of flames. The disastrous scene was gruesome and indescribable. Many times, I have seen pictures in the news of bombed and exploding oil tanks but to actually see it, is a horror utterly beyond imagination.

The Japanese attempted to reply to this mayhem with another raid on Port Moresby. Eight Kittyhawks rose to the challenge, and found a Zero formation approaching Moresby from the north-east. At 5000 metres, the Japanese again held the height advantage, and used it successfully to dictate terms. In the fighting that followed, Richard Granville was shot down and killed. Alan Boyd, a newly arrived but experienced replacement pilot, having served a tour with 3 Squadron in the Middle East, saw Granville's machine dive away steeply, trailing smoke. An army search party found the wreckage of his Kittyhawk, crashed at Iawewera, south of Kokoda, with Granville's body still aboard. The twenty-three-year-old from Parramatta, in Sydney, was buried at the Bomana cemetery, draped in an Australian flag crafted by women from a local plantation.

After losing a string of pilots, 75 Squadron needed a morale booster, and got two on successive days. On 22 April, Wilbur Wackett finally returned to Seven Mile, after his month-long trek back from Lae. The next day, John Jackson also returned to base, and in typically dramatic style.

As they had in the search for the Australian squadron leader, the Americans stepped forward to bring Jackson home when he was reported recovering in Wau. Escorted by Johnny Piper, a Dauntless bomber flew into the Wau landing ground and Jackson clambered into the rear cockpit. Returning to Seven Mile, the American pilot, Lieutenant V. A. Schwab, lowered his landing gear and flaps, only to find a lurking Zero hot on his tail while on final approach. With Jackson manning the rear guns and returning fire, Schwab got down, but not before the Dauntless collected a 20-millimetre cannon shell, which lopped the top off one of Jackson's fingers. After a fortnight of ordeals, the wound left Jackson unperturbed, describing it as 'just a mere scratch'. Jackson was probably luckier than he knew. Sakai in his memoirs describes a strafing attack on Moresby on 23 April, in which his wingmen were fellow aces Nishizawa and Ota, and if they were responsible for the firing passes on Jackson's Dauntless, they usually scored more hits than the one cannon shell that winged the Australian's finger.

Those on the ground were less phlegmatic than Jackson. Mechanic John Koy leapt into a trench, followed by medic Bill Topping, and when a line of Japanese bullets ripped across the top of the shelter, one round spun up in the air, landed on Topping and burnt his bare stomach. Deane-Butcher also hurried to the strip, understandably excited at the return of his commander, only to find himself caught in the line of fire. He took cover in the nearest bomb crater, but his entrance proved easier than his later exit. The crater was much deeper than he thought, and while men gathered around the unflappable Jackson to hear his story, Deane-Butcher 'with some difficulty and great loss of dignity', clambered out of his makeshift shelter to join in.

While the men of 75 Squadron celebrated Jackson's return, away on the outskirts of Lae, a three-man NGVR patrol was about to mount an astounding close-range reconnaissance of the Japanese base. Lieutenant Bob Phillips, Corporal Alex Moore and Rifleman Nev Bensley were typical NGVR men—older than most army men (Bensley was forty-one), tough and familiar with the terrain in which they moved.

On the morning of 23 April, they put these skills to use, moving up to the very boundary of the airfield to spy on the aircraft based there and the work practices of the Japanese. They got so close that they gave Moresby details of the registration numbers painted on the Zero fighters, including 'V101 to V104, V106 to V108, V110 to V112', and so on. The NGVR were not to know, but these were the markings of Sakai's Tainan Air Group. Phillips counted the number of aircraft—twenty-seven fighters and five unidentified bombers. Staying long enough to comment on the arrival times and work habits of maintenance crews and runway labourers, the Australians even gave a precise technical specification as to the length of a Zero's take-off run when loaded with a drop tank. For allied aircrews attacking the base, they gave a detailed layout of Japanese anti-aircraft guns, and finished up by inspecting a bomb dump, from which Moore recovered the labelling used to mark each weapon type (an act of close-range bravery for which he was deservedly Mentioned in Despatches). Theirs was a job of watching, not raiding, and mission completed, Phillips, Moore and Bensley crept back into the jungle from which they had come, to radio back to Moresby the most intimate details of Japanese capability and defensive preparedness.

After a night's sleep, Jackson sat down to write a poignant letter to his sister and mother. He described how his love of family had helped sustain him in all that he had just endured: 'During my recent experience I could often feel your loving thoughts about me and I'm certain they and your prayers have protected me'.

Jackson was not the only Australian writing home at this time. In a prisoner of war camp, Paul Metzler was also putting pen to paper, following up his radio broadcast the previous month. In his letter, Metzler confirmed for the Australian authorities those who had survived the loss of the Catalina, and those who had perished. The dead included John 'Jackie' Perrett, whose family had first been tormented by Reverend Hardie's false confirmation of his loss, and then by the RAAF's correction that he might be alive. Metzler's letter now extinguished all hope.

In war, the needs of the living sometimes accompany the awful news of bereavement. Thinking out loud in his letter, Metzler considered asking his wife Kit for more than spiritual comforts, hoping that she might mail him a pipe, tobacco, nuts and chocolate. On reflection, though, he decided his privations at the hands of the Japanese were of less account, concluding that his shopping list 'was before Australia was menaced, [so] please don't worry about it, I don't want anything. I am far more concerned about you by this time'. As had been the case with Jackson, all Metzler's thoughts were with his family: 'Well in case no word has reached you I am still alive and kicking. I know you will get in touch with my people, so give them my kind regards'. The psychological toll of captivity was clearly pressing on Metzler, and feelings of inadequacy unnecessarily haunted him: 'You can imagine how we feel here. At the moment Australia needs every man, civilians included. It is our business, and instead we are here'.

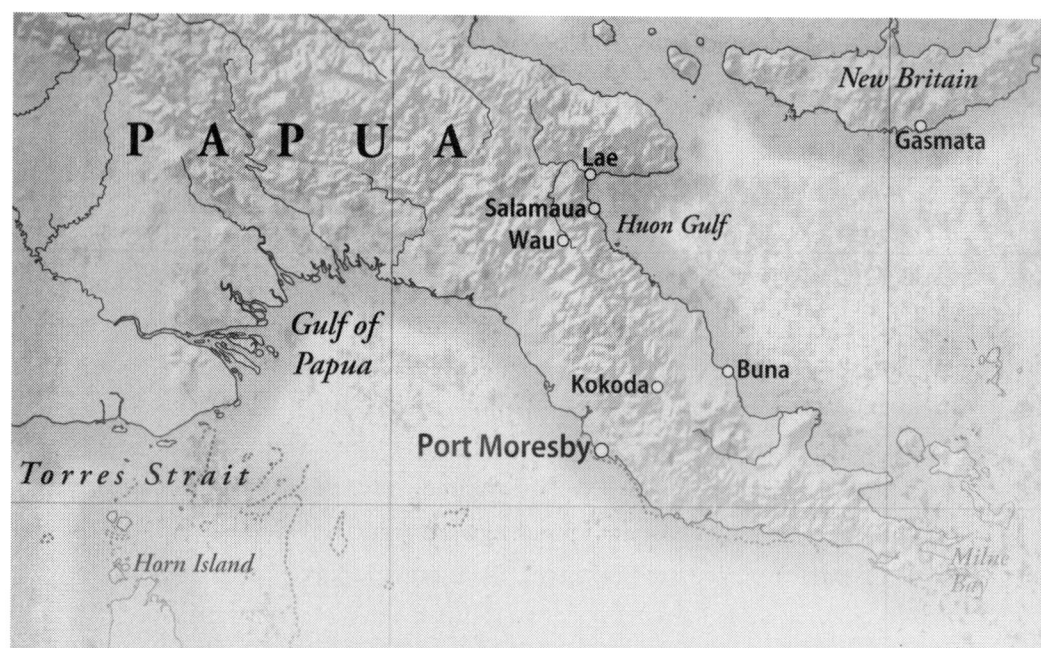

CHAPTER NINE
'... I've never been so scared in my life'

John Jackson might have returned, but all was not well among the defenders of Port Moresby. On the same day he returned to Seven Mile, the squadron had the pleasure of a visit from RAAF chief Charles Burnett. Burnett was due to return to the UK to resume the retirement interrupted by his disastrous tenure at the helm of the RAAF, and his inspection of the squadrons at Moresby was among the last of his official duties.

Burnett had already given his views about the state of RAAF morale after the bombing of Darwin, but unfortunately, no record exists of what he had to say about the state of affairs at Moresby. However, by coincidence or otherwise, within days of his visit, RAAF commanders in New Guinea forced a calamitous change of tactics on 75 Squadron, something that they justified by the extraordinary conclusion that the Kittyhawk pilots were not fighting hard enough. Both the senior air force men in New Guinea were combat-experienced airmen, but neither was a fighter pilot: Charles Pearce, overall air force commander in New Guinea, and Bill Gibson, commander of the Moresby base, had completed tours on flying boats with 10 Squadron in England in 1940–41, searching for German U-boats in the grey wastes of the Atlantic. Gallant though such service was, it did not necessarily prepare an officer to deal tactically with the special challenge of constantly meeting Zero fighters at a height disadvantage. Perhaps encouraged by Burnett, they apparently believed that Jackson and his men needed to take the fight up to the Japanese, specifically by dogfighting with the Zeroes.

This growing sense of command frustration with 75 Squadron was the environment into which John Jackson returned. The fact that he remained in command after his recent ordeal, when any commonsense view of his condition might have led to a period of convalescence and leave, suggests that both he and his commanders thought that he personally, and the squadron he led, had 'something to prove'.

Tensions were also increasing on the other side of the battle line. At Lae, the rigid caste system of the Japanese military, which ensured officers a comfortable life in isolation from their men, was beginning to gall the combat pilots who were daily risking their lives against the Australians over Moresby. With supplies of all types hard to come by, the daily tobacco issue at Lae proved a lightning rod of discontent. While the Japanese high command denied non-commissioned combat pilots a regular ration, officers happily maintained their own consumption, to the fury of Saburo Sakai. The Japanese ace took matters into his own hands and sent his mechanics into the nearby village to buy some local tobacco, which was off limits to the airmen for fear it might contain narcotics. When Sakai and his squadron mates were caught smoking the local product, their commander, Lieutenant Jun-ichi Sasai, initially attempted to quell the insubordination. When Sakai and fellow ace Nishizawa refused orders, Sasai went with the flow—and raided the officers' store to supply his men with the Japanese product.

While petty disputes of this sort strained relations between the front-line pilots and their high command, the morale of Sakai's squadron stood out, and it was Sasai's sympathetic leadership that kept it high. Having survived ill health as a child, Sasai took an intimate interest in the welfare of his men, tending the sick as they struggled in hospital with all manner of diseases, but especially the loathsome tropical ulcers that ate at a man's flesh. When the daily dose of the dreaded quinine tablets turned the stomachs of his squadron, Sasai led the way by chewing on several at a time while keeping a smile on his face. The young lieutenant 'disdained the demands of the naval caste system', which staggered his grateful men, because as Sakai wrote, 'this was a mountainous matter in the Japanese officer code'.

Despite their privations at the primitive Lae base, the Japanese were winning the race to assemble sufficient resources to establish air superiority over Port Moresby, as the fighting on 24 April would suggest. Still reliant on the intermittent sighting reports from Leigh Vial and the other coastwatchers, 75 Squadron resorted to standing patrols to prevent being caught on the ground. Necessary perhaps in the circumstances, this tactic nevertheless came with powerful drawbacks, since it required a lot of fruitless flying, and left isolated patrols of Kittyhawks at the mercy of Japanese fighter sweeps.

So it proved on 24 April. At noon, Les Jackson and Bob Crawford were circling Moresby on patrol at 2500 metres, when they saw an American B-26 Marauder under attack from Zeroes. Sweeping down to assist, Jackson claimed to shoot down a Zero, but Crawford then became embroiled in a turning fight with two other Japanese fighters. In this kind of situation, there could only be one outcome, and it did not take long to arrive. The Zeroes repeatedly hit Crawford's Kittyhawk. A hole in the fuel tank caused petrol to spill into the cockpit, and then the control cable to the rudder was severed. A bullet that ripped off his throat microphone seared Crawford's neck. Low down over Moresby harbour, there was no way out for the Australian, except to ditch. At 170 kilometres an hour, this was a difficult task. After a succession of spectacular bounces across the water, Crawford's Kittyhawk came to rest in two metres of water. He emerged shocked, but otherwise unharmed.

Four other Kittyhawks were now airborne, piloted by Arthur Tucker, Bill Cowe and Michael Butler and led by Ozzie Channon, who took the flight up to 8000 metres. On one of the occasions the Australians would gain a height advantage, the results were tragic. Diving to engage the Zeroes, as the Australians swept down from chilly high altitude to the warmer tropical air at 2000 metres, Tucker found himself effectively blinded by a build-up of condensation on the cockpit Perspex. He regained some vision by wiping his windscreen, but after a short burst

One of the best: Ozzie Channon prepares for a mission.

at a fleeting Zero, he climbed up to 3000 metres to open his canopy and clear the fog.

Channon was not so lucky. He turned rather than zoomed for height, and with his windscreen presumably in the same condition as Tucker's, he probably never even saw the Zero that shot him down. Butler witnessed this action, and later the Australians saw smoke rising from Porabada village. It proved to be Channon's machine, and he was still aboard, dead. Channon was much admired by his fellow pilots, and his loss was a heavy blow.

Bill Cowe and Michael Butler were also hard-pressed. Cowe made two firing passes before exiting the fight unharmed, but Butler found a Japanese fighter pursuing him at low altitude. Butler sought refuge in a 'nice cumulus cloud', but unfortunately, it proved not a very big one. Ducking in and out of this scant cover, he evaded one firing pass with a flat turn that threw off the aim of the Japanese pilot and gave him the satisfaction of seeing the 'damned tracers' of the Zero 'going three or four hundred yards in front of me'. He looked to have escaped when another Zero scored hits. 'All hell let loose [and] black smoke started pouring out from behind the spinner'.

By this stage, Butler was down to 200 metres, and the chance of bailing out safely seemed remote. Still far from home with an overheating engine, Butler scanned the terrain below. Ahead he saw a 'great big patch of green', and despite an indicated airspeed of 400 kilometres an hour, he elected to crash-land. Still going very fast, he put the Kittyhawk down on the kunai grass, and by a miracle the fighter kept going straight ahead—had it turned slightly, a fatal cartwheel would surely have occurred, and nor did it hit a log, which would have been equally disastrous.

The Kittyhawk slid to a halt and Butler emerged from the wreckage, and understandably concluded he was 'bloody lucky' to still be alive. The fighter had snapped in half, with the fuselage from just behind the cockpit left 150 metres away. Sighted by a passing American aircraft, and then by Johnny Piper out searching for his comrades, Butler opted to await rescue rather than walk out himself. 'Really completely exhausted', he climbed up on the wing of the crashed fighter and had a sleep in the sun until an army patrol arrived around evening to bring him in. Butler was back in action the next day.

In this one action, 75 Squadron had three Kittyhawks shot down and one pilot killed. The heavy losses were explained by the quality of their opponents. Fifteen Zeroes of Tainan Air Group, piloted by Sakai and Nishizawa among others, swept over Moresby that day, and although their claims were inflated—six Kittyhawks and two bombers shot down—the impact of the combat did not end with the dogfighting. Having cleared 75 Squadron from the air, the Japanese went on to strafe both Seven Mile and the harbour. At the airfield, they set fire to three Kittyhawks and an American B-26, while on the harbour they gutted a Catalina with fire. Nearing the end of its tether, 75 Squadron now vacated Seven Mile and moved inland to a new strip at Bomana, hoping the change of scenery might escape the attention of Japanese raiders, at least for a few days.

As it happened, the Japanese tracked the move almost step by step, taking the opportunity to strafe 75 Squadron personnel making their way to Bomana on 25 April. Kittyhawks flown by Whetters, Cowe, Atherton and Brereton intervened to protect their mates on the ground, and another wild melee followed with the Zeroes of Tainan Air Group, among whose pilots Sakai again figured prominently. Once more, the Japanese interpretation of events was wildly optimistic. They reported shooting down six Kittyhawks, whereas all the Australians escaped, albeit with damage to two machines. Bill Cowe was especially lucky, following up his timely withdrawal from the previous day's heavy fighting by surviving a hit on his tail fin by a 20-millimetre cannon shell. Having once more driven off the Kittyhawks, Sakai and his comrades were able to follow up with strafing runs on Seven Mile. These did not account for the seven aircraft claimed by the Japanese, but the two American bombers they did destroy was loss enough for the Allies, given the dwindling numbers of aircraft available to them.

The patrols put up by 75 Squadron were now down to a handful of aircraft. On the morning of 26 April, four Kittyhawks led by Atherton were at 3500 metres when they came across Zeroes below them, 16 kilometres south-east of Moresby. Atherton led Whetters, Cowe and Butler down to attack, and the Australians made an inconclusive pass on the Japanese. After this, the action broke up into individual fights. The long-suffering Michael Butler found himself pursued by five Japanese fighters in a north-easterly direction, up the New Guinea coast and away from the sanctuary of Moresby. Butler kept going north-east in an attempt to outrun the Japanese, but when that failed he faced the difficult task of making a long slow turn out to sea in an effort to head back to base. As Butler recalled, the Japanese followed him around. Whenever they thought themselves in range, the Zero pilots let fly, and Butler could only hold his breath as the Japanese cannon shells tore up the water close below him. According to Sakai, among Butler's hunters was the ace Nishizawa, who reported chasing a Kittyhawk 'all over the sky', pouring fire into it at every opportunity, only to have his quarry escape.

To stay alive, Butler was forced to push his fighter to the limits, dangerously 'over-boosting' the engine. The risk facing him was that the engine would get so hot that the fuel would detonate before it fully entered the cylinders of the big Allison motor. If he reached that point, Butler would lose power or seize the engine completely, and the game would be up. To keep his machine going, Butler pushed the throttle forward for a time, and then eased off to give the motor some respite. However, when he did so, the Japanese gained on him, so there was no option but to drive the engine hard again. This went on for more than 200 kilometres, with the Japanese splashing shells into the sea close by him, until as they neared the Moresby airfields, the Zeroes pulled away. Butler naturally got down as quickly as he could, 'absolutely stonkered'. When an American

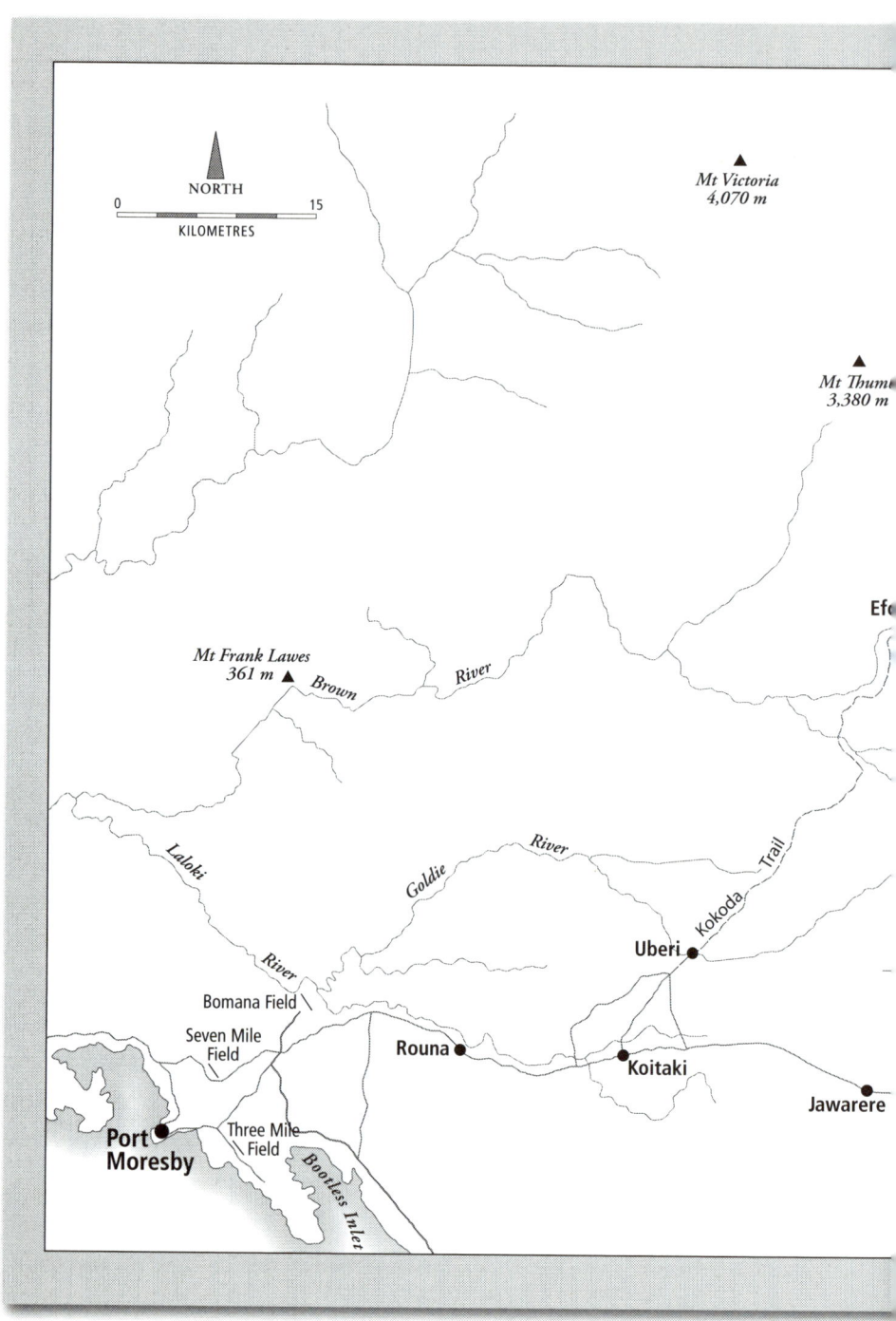

'... I'VE NEVER BEEN SO SCARED IN MY LIFE'

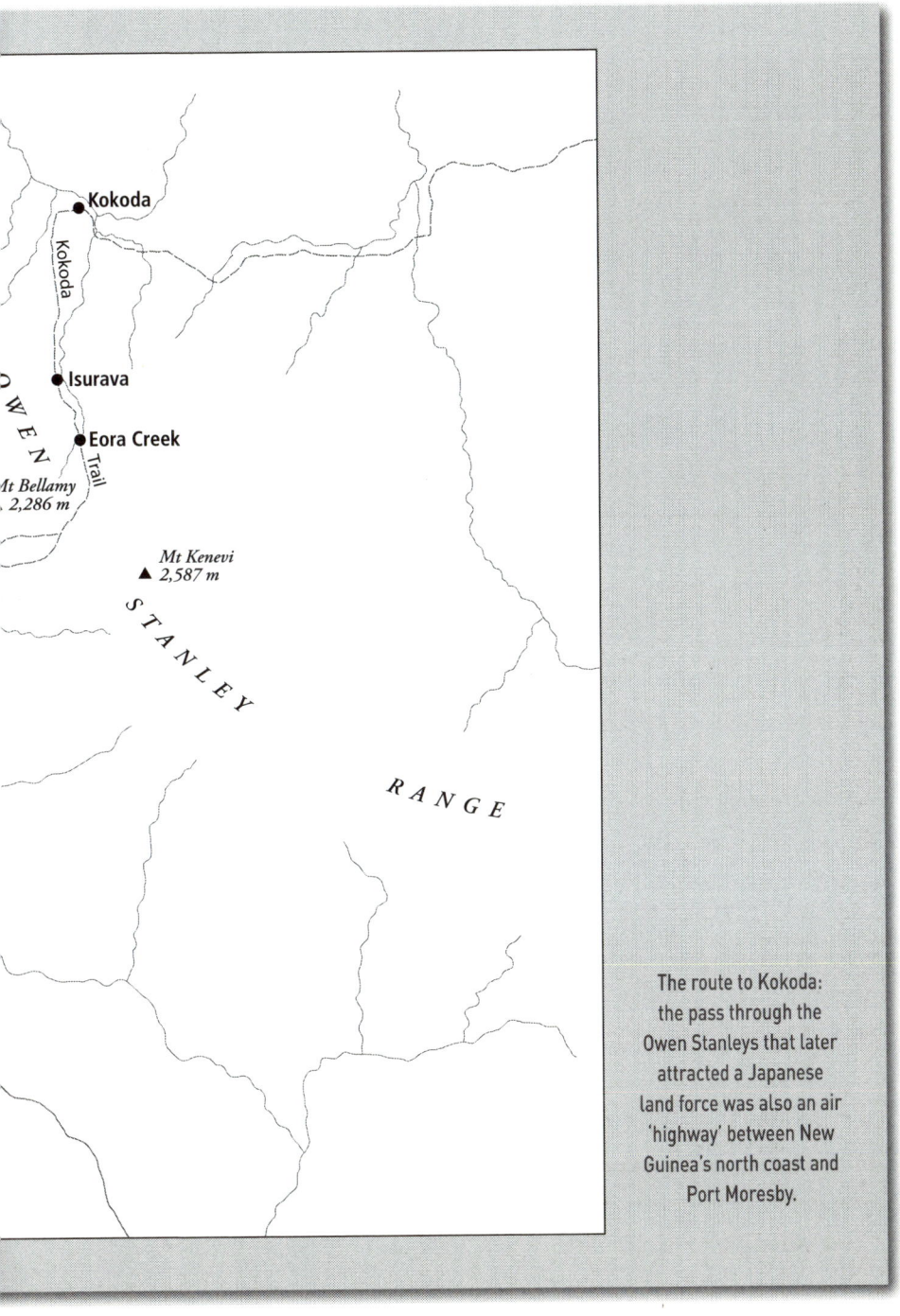

The route to Kokoda: the pass through the Owen Stanleys that later attracted a Japanese land force was also an air 'highway' between New Guinea's north coast and Port Moresby.

Band of brothers: *(left to right)* Geoff Atherton, Alan Whetters, Bob Crawford and Michael Butler.

came up to him as he stood by his steaming Kittyhawk, 'I think I smoked half a packet of cigarettes before I could, you know, be sensible ... I've never been so scared in my life'. The effects of this action on the machine matched the strains on the man flying it. Butler's Kittyhawk had started the action brand new, but when the fight ended, his treatment of the engine was such that it was already 'buggered'.

Butler at least got his steaming aeroplane home. In the same combat, Alan Whetters spent so much of his fuel load jousting with the Zeroes that his Kittyhawk ran low on petrol. Whetters had joined the air force as a boy, and rose from the humble ranks of a cadet to join flight training. The peacetime RAAF was short of aeroplanes (and cash) and young men like Whetters were drilled in the need to look after them. Aware now that 75 Squadron was desperately short of aircraft, he cast about for options and elected to land in a patch of kunai grass, taking the brave decision not to 'pancake', or crash-land on the belly of the plane with the wheels retracted. Instead he lowered his undercarriage and attempted to land in the normal way. This would help get the fighter home more quickly, but in doing so, Whetters took a big personal risk. If the grass concealed rocks and logs, they would surely rip off his undercarriage and send the fighter cartwheeling, something Whetters could scarcely hope to survive.

Whetters' gamble paid off, and the Kittyhawk ran through two-metre-high grass before coming to a halt. He initially set off to walk to the coast, but finding the going difficult, returned to the fighter. Sitting in the cockpit 'just wondering what my next move would be', Whetters' luck doubled when an NGVR patrol not only found him, but cut the grass into something resembling an airstrip, and even located a petrol supply nearby with which to top up the fuel tanks of the fighter. After two attempts, Whetters flew his machine back to Moresby the next day.

In the interim, some of the tensions in the ranks of 75 Squadron now became evident. As Whetters got ready to spend a night in the bush, back at Moresby Les Jackson insisted that Butler, despite his ordeal, should join the next day's flight-line. Butler gently protested, saying 'Oh Les ... do I have to?', and found support from Deane-Butcher, who pointed out to his friend, 'Les, come on, give him a day off, he's deserved that'. Butler got his rest day, but Les Jackson never forgave the young sergeant, and the animosity between the two would dramatically surface in the months to come.

One of the reasons Nishizawa and his comrades might have pulled away from Moresby on the morning of 26 April was that they now faced a much more formidable foe on the ground. Three days previously, the 2/3rd Light Anti Aircraft Battery bolstered the defences of Moresby when its gunners went into action for the first time. Commanded by a rugged and practical artillery officer, Major Patrick Kelso, this new addition to the defences added much-needed firepower to the close protection of key Moresby targets. Equipped with the fearsome 40-millimetre Bofors cannon, the war's premier low-altitude anti-aircraft gun, Kelso's battery soon had Japanese pilots thinking twice about strafing runs over defended targets. After his tour of duty in New Guinea, Kelso wrote a lively and insightful report on the lessons learnt by his battery. From the prosaic—'men without shirts are more conspicuous' than those fully clothed, and 'dark glasses are essential for [gun] layers ... don't come without them'—to the tactical—'the idea of waiting for a kill is very attractive, but remember protection of the Vulnerable Point is the sole object'—Kelso was a fountain of helpful tips for apprentice anti-aircraft gunners. Kelso's command philosophy began with the longstanding presumption that the first duty of an officer lay with the care of his men. Everything he did was built on the comfort and welfare of the men in his charge, from the most effective layout of trenches and gun pits, to the preparation of hot and varied meals—'primus stoves are essential for site cooking'. To keep his men fed at their battle stations, Kelso recommended that every gun pit should have such a stove, and in defiance of army economy—'damn the expense'.

Most importantly, his guns were soon having the desired effect, Kelso noting proudly that 'the deterrent effect of Bofors firing has proved sufficient to turn every attack in which the fire was opened' before the Japanese commenced their firing run. For fighter pilots like Michael Butler, seeking a landing approach free of pursuing Zeroes, the arrival of Kelso and his men confirmed that, piece by piece, the defences of Moresby were strengthening. However, the question remained: could 75 Squadron hang on long enough?

The stresses under which the men were operating were reaching breaking point. On the evening of 26 April, Arthur Tucker and his tent-mate Dave Ellerton sat on their bunks in the soft glow of the kerosene lamp that lit their tent. Ellerton had just turned twenty-three, and had recently married after a tour in Libya with 3 Squadron. He was reading a letter, written on blue paper, the kind used by his new wife. Quite calmly, Ellerton looked up and asked of Tucker, 'Well Friar, I wonder which one of us it'll be tomorrow, you or I?' Tucker by now was reaching a point of exhaustion. After a recent scramble had been aborted, he had attempted to leave his cockpit, only to find when he clambered down from the cockpit that his legs—for no reason—just gave way. No matter how he tried, Tucker could not regain his feet. Young he might have been, but Tucker understood that the psychological loads he was carrying in the face of death or horrible injury were taking their toll. Thus when Ellerton asked his question of awful premonition, it seemed to Tucker a sensible, 'logical kind of question'.

About an hour later, it seemed that the challenge of surviving another day would fall to Tucker, not Ellerton. Les Jackson, looking for a ferry pilot to bring up a spare Kittyhawk from Cooktown, dropped into their tent and decided that Ellerton, after a heavy recent flying schedule, should get the job, while Tucker should remain at Moresby with the other pilots to fight it out with the Japanese as usual.

Tucker's maudlin state of mind did not improve the next day. While Ellerton went south to pick up the replacement fighter, the rest of 75 Squadron's pilots gathered on 27 April to bury Ozzie Channon. The circumstances in which this service was conducted infuriated them. As Tucker recalled, 'we stood there for three quarters of an hour because the station padre wouldn't come out because there'd been an air raid alarm, so we stood beside the grave till he felt it was safe enough to come down and bury the poor bugger'. Understandably, the incident 'really upset us'.

By the end of the day, Tucker and his mates had one more reason to grieve. Dave Ellerton, on what should have been a 'cushy' ferry run, made a tragic if noble miscalculation. Having served in the Middle East, where pilots often landed in the desert to pick up stranded or shot-down comrades, Ellerton opted to land on a beach north of Cooktown when he saw a force-landed American fighter on the sand. Thinking to save the American pilot a long walk home, Ellerton lowered the wheels of his Kittyhawk and came in to land on the beach. The sand proved softer than the baked landscape of Libya. When his wheels dug in, the Kittyhawk flipped over. Trapped inside, and with no one to help him—the American pilot was already presumably walking back to base—Ellerton was drowned by the incoming tide.

After such a melancholy day, on the evening of 27 April, John Jackson called his pilots together. What followed would prove to be the most controversial moment of the battle for the defenders of Port Moresby. Such were the sensitivities of what transpired that in his later report, intelligence officer Stu Collie would only write cryptically that Jackson called his men together, 'tactics were discussed', and 'advice was given ... for the future guidance of the squadron'. Behind this diplomacy, what Jackson really said was more hurtful. According to interviews given later by Arthur Tucker and Michael Butler, Jackson told his men that Gibson and Pearce thought the Kittyhawk pilots were 'not pressing the enemy ... not getting close to them'. Butler even remembered Jackson saying they were 'frightened of them'. The assembled men howled that it was not possible to dogfight the Zeroes; 'you told us *not* to,' said one, at which point 'Old John' calmly told the group, 'Tomorrow I'm going to show you how'.

If there was a conversation between Jackson, Gibson and Pearce in which the senior men laid down the new tactical law to go head to

A terrible way to die: Dave Ellerton's Kittyhawk on a beach north of Cooktown.

head with the Japanese, there are no witnesses to it. However, there is other circumstantial evidence that senior RAAF commanders were riding their men hard at this time. We know, from his commentary on Goff Hemsworth's work as a flying boat captain before the outbreak of the war, that Charles Pearce leapt quickly to acerbic criticism of his subordinates. And thirty years after the battle, David Campbell, the Hudson pilot badly wounded on 6 February, published a poem in the *Sydney Morning Herald* in honour of his friend, Bill Pedrina, who would be killed later in 1942. In a simple but heartfelt lyric, Campbell identified who was responsible for driving men beyond endurance:

Pedro, the day you flew in
With your four Hudsons, Pearce said,
'The bastard's scared'

Whatever happened on the evening of 27 April, Jackson by now was a tired, if not exhausted, man. Journalist Osmar White saw him that fateful night, and although 'his hands and eyes were still and rock steady', 'to see him ... was to look upon a man who was weary in soul' and 'too long in the shadows'. White went on to pen this moving tribute on the eve of battle:

> *I have never seen a man who needed more desperately some kindness to make him feel again, as living men should, that the face of death is terrible and to be feared. He had done more than conquer fear—he had killed it.*

Before dawn on 28 April, the squadron duty officer flashed a torch into the tents of the sleeping pilots. With Kittyhawks now in short supply, only five men were required to go to standby: John Jackson, Barry Cox, Bill Cowe, Cocky Brereton and Peter Masters. The day was wet and windy. While Jackson went about the squadron paperwork, the other four men played poker, and perhaps listened to 'Daddy, I want a diamond ring' for the umpteenth time. The chore of starting up the Kittyhawk engines every hour, to ensure they were warm and ready to go if needed, proved the sole interruption to the fall of the cards. Barry Cox, only recently discharged from hospital after a bout of dysentery, was pale and emaciated. Still, when someone pulled out a camera to take some snaps of life on the flight-line, he found the energy to ham it up, pretending to shave off Stu Collie's moustache. When Jackson joined in, he kept the group amused with anecdotes from his escape from Lae. Jackson's account of his brush with the crocodile during his swim to shore tickled Peter Masters' fancy in particular. Jackson recounted how, weighed down by his clothes, he had hoped to get some help from a piece of driftwood floating nearby, until the 'log' blinked at him, at which point he 'got some new strength for the final dash to the shore'.

This relaxed banter ended at a quarter past eleven, when the telephone hanging from the centre pole of the tent rang. Collie jumped up and answered it, and shouting 'It's on!', he sent the pilots scrambling to their machines. On their way to Moresby were eight Betty bombers of the 4th Air Group, escorted by eleven Zeroes, led in person by the commander of the Tainan Air Group, Commander Masao Yamashita. Dividing his force in two, Yamashita allocated three Zeroes to provide close escort to the bombers, while he led the remaining fighters as top cover. Taking off from Rabaul's Lakunai airfield, the Zeroes refuelled mid-morning at Lae and picked up the Bettys in transit.

Climbing hard, Jackson led his squadron north to engage the incoming raiders, but found, as usual, the Japanese still high above. Brereton and Cowe were flying older Kittyhawks that struggled to keep up, so the Australian formation was ragged even before battle began. Jackson made a firing pass on the eight Betty bombers along with Masters and Cox. Masters wrote that as he closed in on one Japanese machine, 'I could see the face of the side gunner glaring out at me from behind the gun in the blister turret'. At this close range, he opened fire and, before his Kittyhawk stalled and fell away, saw 'holes appear in the underbelly and rear fuselage of the enemy bomber'.

Yamashita led the Zero top cover down on the Australians, and Jackson and Cox were soon isolated. True to his word, Jackson was determined to fight it out, despite the Japanese superiority in numbers and dogfighting ability. Over the radio, Masters heard him 'shouting epithets as only he could do, indicating he was making one hell of a fight of it'.

Down below, Osmar White gave a graphic account of the battle, watching as the 'bombs came away' as the Bettys flew on through anti-aircraft fire to hit their target. 'Over the crest of the hill, dust and smoke rose in massive, fluttered columns. The valley shook and the mountains gave back the snarling rumble of explosions'. As the journalist watched, he could hear, more than see, the dogfight in progress: 'Somewhere, at an

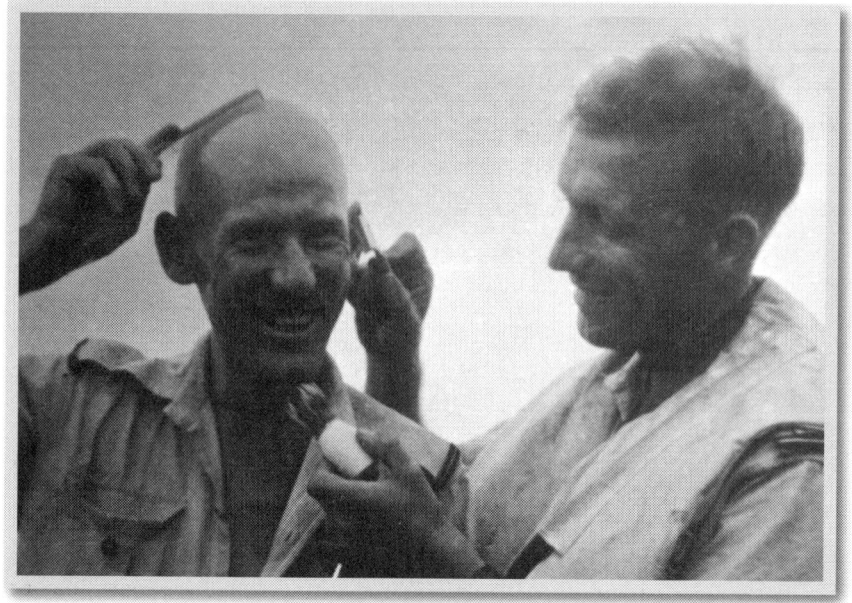

Fateful day: Stu Collie (left) and Barry Cox play up for the camera; Cox was killed in action within an hour of this picture being taken.

altitude one could not see, there was fighting. The guns tapped plainly'. Within seconds, the result would be death for one brave Australian: 'A watcher called beside me, "look, look there!" A little dark cross was drawing a line of white straight down the sky. He was one of ours'.

The machine seen by White was that of John Jackson. It dived at great speed with a smoking engine into the side of Mount Frank Lawes, north-east of Moresby, half way to Kokoda. Such was the force of impact, the Kittyhawk's engine was buried two metres into the soil. The recovery party that found the crash only identified Jackson by his size ten boots and the pistol he carried while on duty. The next day, the leadership team at Seven Mile buried him at the Bomana cemetery, a ceremony attended by his brother Les, Deane-Butcher, the squadron padre, Bill Gibson and Charles Pearce. Ironically given the circumstances of Jackson's death, Pearce conducted the service.

Barry Cox died in Jackson's final combat too, but in what circumstances we have no record. United States army engineers draining a wetland to build yet another airfield finally found his Kittyhawk months later, but left it where it fell. After the war, the Port Moresby golf course took advantage of the American landscaping for the purposes of the course design, and more than sixty years after the event, parts of Cox's fighter were still visible.

For once, the Japanese pilots reported less damage than they actually caused. Only Hideo Izumi claimed to shoot down a Kittyhawk that morning, and given the highly visible way in which Jackson met his fate, Izumi was presumably responsible. Which Zero accounted for Cox we shall never know. Of the Japanese fighters, only that flown by Nishizawa suffered any damage, but this was enough to force him to ditch in the sea off Salamaua on the return flight. Reportedly plucked from the sea by a Japanese patrol boat, Nishizawa was wet, but also furious at the indignity, although he might have been grateful to emerge unharmed. The Tainan Air Group lost a second Zero that afternoon, when Yoshimitsu Maeda made a forced landing 160 kilometres east of Moresby. Maeda was made a prisoner of war, and his Zero, one of the first recovered relatively intact anywhere, was sent to Moresby by barge for examination, where it was photographed by the famous cinematographer Damien Parer as it sat on the main harbour wharf. It wore the serial number V110, and was one of the machines so expertly identified by the NGVR men on the Lae strip five days before.

John Jackson was dead, his squadron exhausted. Such was the toll on the pilots that 75 Squadron rushed newly arrived and inexperienced

205

War prize: Maeda's wrecked Zero on the Moresby waterfront.

reinforcements into battle. On 2 May, Bob Crawford took off on patrol with nineteen-year-old Don Munro flying as his wingman. They had barely taken station when they tangled with six or more Zeroes. Crawford, now an old hand, knew what to do and immediately dived away. Munro, still learning the craft, took too long to follow, and Crawford could only look on in horror as the young sergeant's Kittyhawk, consumed in a fireball, fell by his wingtip.

The weariness of the pilots was matched by the battered condition of the machines they flew. Despite the labours of Bill Matson and his ground staff, squadron pilots were being committed to action in machines that were clearly not combat ready. On 3 May, Tucker scrambled in the company of American Airacobra pilots, only to find his Kittyhawk unable to keep up. He was flying the machine that Michael Butler had force-landed in the kunai grass some days before, and although Matson and his men had done their best, some of the grass remained clogged in the fighter's engine air-intake. Tucker returned to base exasperated, and until his dying day, bitterly resented the way the RAAF's Official History described this episode, believing that he was unfairly criticised for cutting the mission short.

However, the presence of American pilots next to Tucker that day at least showed that reinforcements were at hand, with the arrival of two US Airacobra squadrons. Even so, it seemed the Japanese would prevail. As 75 Squadron made arrangements to head south for rest and re-equipment, a Japanese invasion force and its mighty escort of aircraft carriers and heavy cruisers sailed for Rabaul. Their purpose: to execute Operation MO, the Japanese invasion of Port Moresby, and strike the bases at Townsville and Cooktown, from where the only reinforcements for the beleaguered garrison might come. The most fateful hour in Australian defence history had struck.

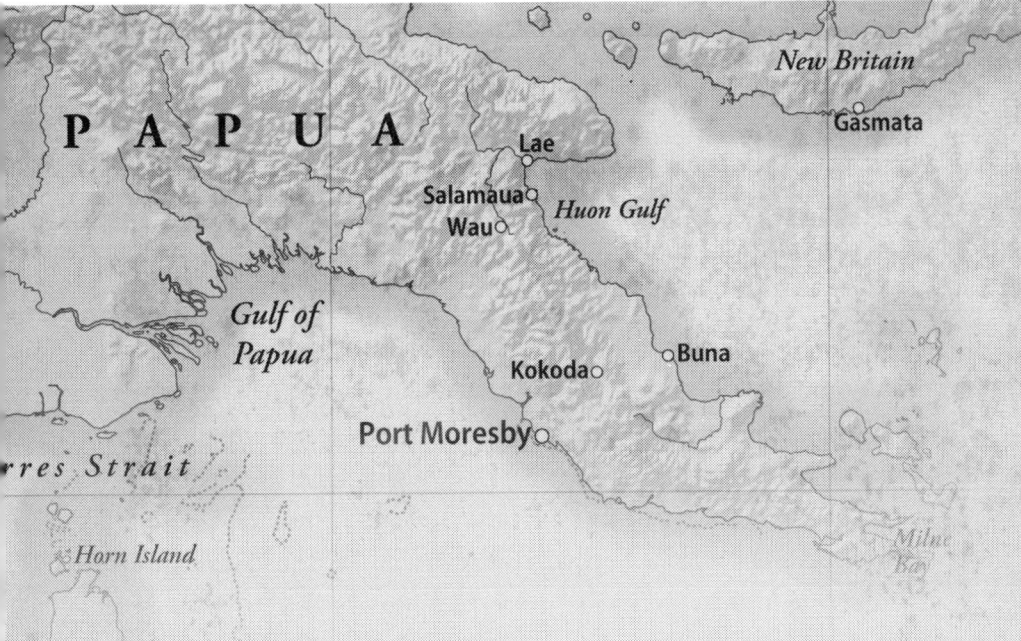

CHAPTER TEN
'... our grief was overwhelming'

On the evening of 7 May 1942, Les Jackson and Bill Deane-Butcher pulled up a pair of deck chairs under a tree overlooking Port Moresby harbour. They were all too aware that they were awaiting a great climax in the affairs of men, and so to while away these fateful hours, the young Australians took a drink of beer and made what small talk they could. Somewhere to the east, a Japanese invasion fleet was manoeuvring for an opening, and the next morning the defenders of Moresby were expecting to face that mighty flotilla in a showdown for control of New Guinea and thus the Coral Sea.

Jackson and Deane-Butcher were part of 75 Squadron's modest contribution to that last stand. The air defence of the base was now in the hands of the American Airacobra squadrons. To mark the handover, 75 Squadron hosted a banquet—if such a term could be applied to the dreary rations available—to greet the newcomers. At least the weary Australians had kept their sense of humour—the menu listed two choices for soup, 'a bowl of hot water', or for the more discerning, 'a bowl of cold water'. Peter Masters did his best to expand the menu by replicating John Pettett's efforts at hand-grenade fishing. He cleared the swimming pool in Port Moresby harbour of bathers, and his detonation certainly produced a collection of multi-coloured fish that might have made an aquarium proud, but unfortunately none was more than a few centimetres in length.

Undaunted by the culinary limitations, the Australians did their best under a large marquee, with trestle tables, beer and a gramophone, this time equipped with a more diverse American record collection. Proceedings were lit with the soft glow of kerosene lanterns, and the tent decorated with flowers. In these congenial surroundings, Stu Collie gave a toast to the fallen, and as the silence fell, the thoughts of many turned to the memory of John Jackson, who had done so much to sustain the defence.

After these festivities, 75 Squadron started packing up, but with three Kittyhawks still fit to fly, the RAAF determined that some among the pilots and ground crew had to stay to fight it out. The squadron pilots literally drew straws to see who would remain to fly these battered fighters and oppose the Japanese invaders. Naturally, as the pilots gathered to take their turn at drawing lots, Arthur Tucker recalled the mood was 'very tense'.

Les Jackson, determined to avenge his brother, insisted on being one of the three pilots to stay behind. Michael Butler and Peter Masters had the honour, or bad luck, of taking the two short straws. A handful of ground crew volunteered to remain to service the Kittyhawks, and Deane-Butcher of course insisted on tending to his charges to the last. With these sombre proceedings completed, the balance of the squadron's personnel trooped down to the Moresby wharf to go aboard the steamer *Taroona*, likely to be the last ship that would get out of the harbour before the Japanese arrived. Arthur Tucker staggered on board, exhausted and emaciated. A tall man, after weeks of diarrhoea and poor diet he weighed less than 63 kilograms, and once on board, promptly set about the ship's stock of biscuits, cheese and apricot jam. Sharing the journey south was the captured Zero pilot Yoshimitsu Maeda, who proved something of a curiosity to the Australian pilots who so recently had sparred with him in the skies above Moresby. Tucker had the grace to observe that the disconsolate air of the Japanese pilot was in stark contrast to his own relief at having survived the battle.

With their comrades under way, all that remained for Jackson, Butler, Masters, Deane-Butcher and the engineering staff was to wait for the passing of events over which they had no control. The Battle of the Coral Sea was already under way, and its course would determine whether Moresby would face invasion. The garrison put in place what preparations they could. With the Japanese almost on the horizon, the army concluded that the forces available were too scant to hold the coast, and moved the defence line 12 kilometres inland, behind the Laloki River. To conform with this redeployment, commander of RAAF Moresby Bill Gibson prepared a line of retreat for air force personnel to the new position, where he established an operations room and signals station to maintain air support for the troops.

211

As Jackson and Deane-Butcher were taking their beer on the Moresby waterfront, the battle had been raging out at sea for five days. The Japanese landed the first blow on 2 May, when their troops took the Australian flying boat base at Tulagi, near the island of Guadalcanal in the southern Solomons. The American aircraft carriers *Yorktown* and *Lexington*, warned by code-breaking intelligence of Japanese moves, hit back on 4 May, smashing the Japanese shipping anchored off Tulagi, just as they had at Lae two months earlier. With the presence of an American carrier force revealed by this intervention, the two sides jockeyed for position for several days, while their reconnaissance crews swept the oceans to find each other.

While Jackson, Butler and Masters got ready for 75 Squadron's last stand, far away in Rabaul, one of their squadron mates was enduring yet another interrogation at the hands of his enemies. The Japanese considered David Brown, the young sergeant captured at Lae on 11 April, such a potentially rich intelligence source that they felt it worth flying him back to Rabaul. In late April, thirty-five-year-old Lieutenant Yataka Fukumara, the supply officer of 25th Air Group, flew to Lae to report on the logistics situation facing the undernourished men of the Tainan Air Group. A Betty bomber was detached for Fukumara's tour, and once he completed his inspection, space was found aboard to carry Brown back to Rabaul for further interrogation. Fukumara's description exactly matched the Australian's physical characteristics, the Japanese staff officer remembering Brown as 'a young man of 23 or 24', of slight build, 'about five feet 3 inches tall', with 'chestnut colour hair'. Fukumara condescendingly thought Brown 'timid', but since the Australian was under armed guard, with his hands and feet tied, his circumstances were hardly conducive to theatrical acts of defiance.

At Rabaul, Brown was held with other allied aircrew, including the two American crewmen Lutz and Reed, who survived the flaming end of

David Stuart Brown.

the B-26 Marauder bomber shot down over Simpson Harbour on 18 April. From a Japanese perspective, these Americans proved particularly talkative, confirming the presence of large numbers of P39 fighters at Townsville. There has been a recent attempt to explain away this security breach, with the explanation that the Americans intended to deceive the Japanese with the intelligence they provided, and their disclosures were in any event 'old news'. The sequence of events suggests otherwise. Apart from a handful of aircraft that visited Moresby in early April, there was nothing to forewarn the Japanese of the arrival of American fighter reinforcements, except what they now gleaned from prisoner interrogations. Their willingness to cooperate probably kept the Americans alive, but at the cost of assisting the Japanese in their planning. Small wonder that Operation MO included plans for carrier strikes on Cooktown and Townsville, where they expected, correctly, to find significant allied air assets.

For the Australian aircrews at Moresby, the Battle of the Coral Sea followed the same course as the invasion of Rabaul four months before, with shocking losses to the Catalinas sent out to find the Japanese flotillas. At 6 am on 4 May, as the American carrier pilots blasted the Tulagi invasion fleet, Flying Officer Allan Norman of 11 Squadron lifted his Catalina off the waters of Moresby harbour and headed north-east, towards Bougainville in the central Solomons. He and his crew flew directly into the path of the Japanese fleet, scheduled to sail from Rabaul and move south to Moresby. Not surprisingly the Japanese were determined to safeguard this airspace. Norman reported coming under attack at 12.17 pm, but thereafter Moresby heard nothing more. Unknown to their mates, Norman and his crew survived the shooting down of their Catalina, and the Japanese picked them up unharmed from the sea. They were shipped off to Rabaul, to join Brown in the growing cage of allied prisoners held there. The families of Norman and his men duly received the dreaded telegram, advising them that their loved ones were missing in action, but it would be another eight emotionally gruelling years before the fate of these men was finally known.

Despite this latest loss, the Moresby flying boat squadrons kept up the pace of operations as the battle gathered pace in the Coral Sea. By 6 May, danger crept closer. To support their final push on Moresby, the Japanese sent the seaplane tender *Kamikawa Maru* to anchor at Deboyne Island, in the middle of the Louisiade Archipelago, the chain of islands that stretches south-east from the tail of New Guinea. From there, they could despatch Mitsubishi F1M floatplanes, code-named 'Pete' by the Allies, to provide close-range reconnaissance around the waters south of Port Moresby. This was an ominous development. The presence of a 'seaplane carrier of 7,000 tons' was reported in these waters on 4 May, probably prematurely, but to clarify the situation, two days later Goff Hemsworth and his crew from 11 Squadron set out to reconnoitre the area.

Theirs was a flight into peril, as the crew must surely have known. A premonition had haunted at least one among them for months past. Returning to duty from leave, nineteen-year-old Bill Parker stood on the platform at Sydney's Central Station in early 1942 and confided to his father, Bill senior, that this would be the last time they would see each other. Bill senior later wrote that the young man 'knew what he was going back to', and rightly concluded 'that takes guts'. The father must have been racked with emotion about his son's foreboding, because Bill junior only joined up in the first place thanks to his intervention. An apprentice electrical fitter, Bill junior might well have remained safe at home in a 'reserve occupation', and indeed his employer wrote to the authorities when he enlisted to point out that their contracts for war goods would be affected if the young man went into the military. The firm's managing director then changed his mind, writing again to the RAAF and dropping his objection to young Bill's enlistment, but only after representations made to him by Bill senior, who was proud to support his son's sense of duty.

The young man was right to fear for the future. Approaching the designated patrol zone on 6 May, his captain Goff Hemsworth reported two Japanese destroyers five kilometres south of Misima Island, and then Moresby received a further message that the Catalina was under attack by enemy aircraft, perhaps 'Pete' floatplanes from the *Kamikawa Maru*, or Zeroes from the small escort carrier *Shoho*. Three months earlier, Hemsworth had kept his men alive in a night-time dice with Japanese fighters, but in vivid daylight over the Louisiades, there was nowhere to hide. A gaggle of Japanese aircraft quickly shot down his Catalina.

On the night of 6 May 1942, Zenji Katayama, the chief steward of the Japanese troopship *Matsu Maru*, awoke from his bed, startled by the sound of a gangway going over the side. His ship was under way, carrying the men of Major General Horii's South Sea Force to the beaches of Port Moresby that they were set to storm in a few days' time. Katayama looked out on deck the next morning, to see nine Australian aircrew sitting there—the men of Hemsworth's Catalina, plucked safely from the ocean after the destruction of their machine the previous day.

For Horii, the prisoners were a godsend, because they offered the prospect of fresh intelligence on the defences his men would face at Port Moresby. The Japanese high command had deliberated long and hard over the best way to crack the Moresby nut. The problem facing them came in two parts, the first being the tricky coral reefs that formed a natural barrier to an amphibious landing force. There were three channels through these reefs. However, the most direct and logical of these—the central route through the Basilisk Passage—would also deliver the invaders straight into the guns of the Australian defence. The Japanese therefore settled for landings on both flanks, through the Liljeblad Passage to the west of Moresby, and Padana Nafua to the east.

As to the Australian defences, the Japanese were less certain. On 29 April, 25th Air Flotilla concluded that the air defence of Moresby was on its last legs, a reasonable analysis given the weariness of 75 Squadron and the fact that the American Airacobra squadrons were yet to complete their move. Japanese estimates of the ground force they might face were less well informed. They concluded the Australians might have 5000 men at Moresby, but the Japanese thought most were base and supply troops, with only about one-fifth of the available men organised for combat. Actually the Australians had more than 6000 troops at Moresby, over 2000 of them fighting infantry soldiers in the 30th Brigade, although admittedly this was a militia unit made up of mostly very young reservists, who were criticised at the time, and later, for lapses in discipline. On the other hand, they were well supported by artillery from 13th Field Regiment, an arm in which the Japanese were weak, and a crack commando unit, 2/5th Independent Company, was available to stiffen the resolve of the militia. Horii might get ashore, but unlike Rabaul, the invasion of Moresby would not be a pushover.

With only this sketchy information to guide him, Horii no doubt looked at Hemsworth and his men as an opportunity to fill in any number of blanks about the state of the Moresby garrison, and he lost no time in questioning the Australians. In the post-war search for Hemsworth and his crew, the Australian authorities left no stone unturned. In the late 1940s, Australian intelligence officers interrogated scores of Japanese soldiers and sailors who were aboard the *Matsu Maru* that day. The interview transcripts are so voluminous they require four archival boxes for storage, but the accounts they offer are so conflicting, we shall probably never know what befell Hemsworth and his men. Some insisted the Australians were well treated, on Horii's express orders. However, one of his men, Shigeaki Okada, who survived the war having been one of the few Japanese to leave the battles of the Kokoda Track alive, conceded that the Japanese whipped at least one of the Australians with a leather strop during these interrogations. Others spoke of Japanese interrogators waving baseball bats about while they questioned their prisoners.

It seems that the nine Australians aboard the *Matsu Maru* did their duty to the end. Some Japanese accounts contend that Horii's men bayoneted the Australians on the night of 6 May and threw their bodies

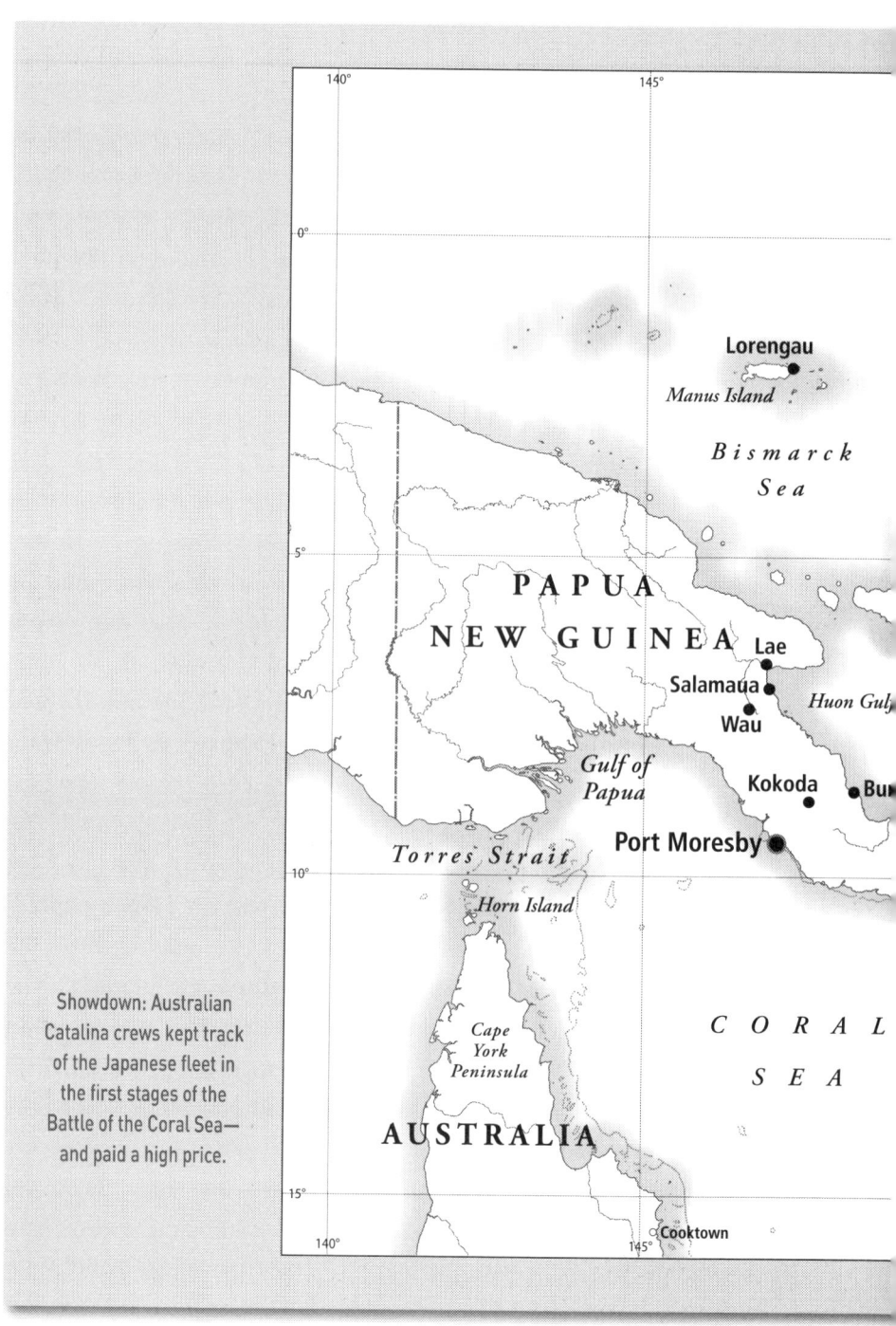

Showdown: Australian Catalina crews kept track of the Japanese fleet in the first stages of the Battle of the Coral Sea— and paid a high price.

'... OUR GRIEF WAS OVERWHELMING'

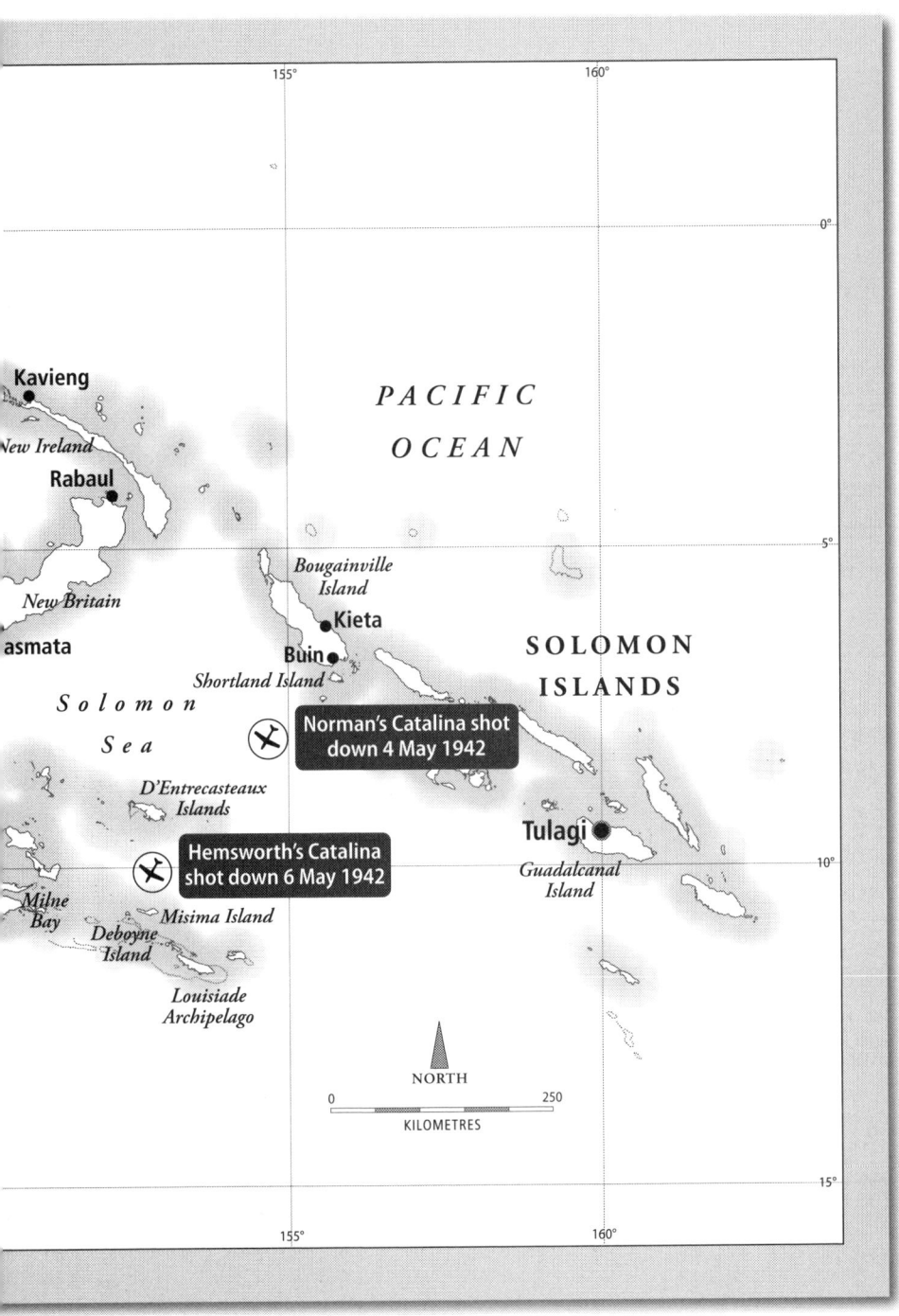

overboard, others that the Catalina crew were offloaded at Rabaul. If they did survive the journey to Rabaul, their subsequent fate remains a mystery.

The Australian Catalina crews were giving their all in the first great climax of the south Pacific war. On 7 May, the shadow-boxing between the rival carrier fleets came to an end in a rain of deadly blows. The Americans thought they located the large Japanese carriers, and attacked hard, only to sink the small escort carrier *Shoho*. At the same time, the Japanese made an equivalent mistake, sending a powerful strike force to hit what they believed were the American carriers, only to sink the supply ship *Neosho* and an escorting destroyer.

The next day, 'Pop' Woods and John Pettett were ferrying Kittyhawks down the Queensland coast, one of the flights needed to reassemble 75 Squadron so that it could regroup, re-equip and retrain. In their headphones, the two veteran pilots could hear, even at a distance, the startled cries of airmen in combat. What they were listening to was the climax of the Battle of the Coral Sea, as the US carriers *Yorktown* and *Lexington* traded hammer-blows with their Japanese counterparts, *Shokaku* and *Zuikaku*.

Both sides inflicted grievous harm on the other. Japanese aircraft sank the *Lexington* and badly damaged the *Yorktown*; the Americans in turn hit the *Shokaku* with three 500-kilogram bombs, wrecking her flight-deck and starting raging petrol fires that took hours to quell. The *Zuikaku*, hidden by tropical rain clouds, escaped direct harm, but the American carrier pilots so badly mauled her air groups that she was unable to continue Operation MO unaided. Without carrier aircraft to force the issue, the Port Moresby garrison and air defences remained unsubdued. Acknowledging military reality, the Japanese cancelled the

'... OUR GRIEF WAS OVERWHELMING'

Supply run: In his Kittyhawk, Arthur Tucker escorts an Empire flying boat transporting men and equipment between Moresby and Townsville, indicating the reason why the north Queensland town was slated for attack by Japanese carriers in the Battle of the Coral Sea.

invasion, together with the supporting air strikes on Townsville and Cooktown, and withdrew their flotillas to Rabaul. New Guinea, and the Australian east coast, were safe.

With the immediate threat to Moresby thrown back, 75 Squadron could complete its withdrawal to the mainland. By the time the salvoes and tumult of the Coral Sea battle died away, only one Kittyhawk remained airworthy. Les Jackson flew this machine out on 9 May. To get home in a hurry, Bill Deane-Butcher agreed to serve as an impromptu rear gunner on an American Dauntless dive-bomber that was heading south the same day. With a brief lesson on how to find the trigger on his machine gun, Deane-Butcher clambered aboard. With a reasonable if pessimistic assessment of his own ability to hold off the prowling Zeroes, the doctor was convinced the Japanese would shoot down the Dauntless. Even if he survived, Deane-Butcher assumed some Japanese warship lurking off shore would take him prisoner. Thus before take-off, to prevent his most treasured possession—his latest letter to his wife—from falling into the hands of the enemy, he tore up the correspondence and stuffed the pieces into his overalls. With his heart in his mouth, Deane-Butcher and his pilot got past a patrol of three Zeroes and made it safely to Cooktown. Once there, the doctor glued his letter back together, and it now forms one of his family's most beloved mementoes of their father.

The Battle of the Coral Sea was a turning point in the war in the Pacific, and the Australian pilots and ground crews who had fought long and hard to hold the Moresby base had more than played their part. Their endurance and sacrifice forced the Japanese to commit their precious aircraft carriers in an effort to force the issue in New Guinea, one that failed when their American counterparts ambushed them on their way to Moresby. Eric Feldt, the Director of Naval Intelligence, succinctly summarised their achievement: Port Moresby formed a flank for the Japanese, and if they could secure it, they would be free to advance, as they planned to do, 'to Noumea and cut off Australia from America for all practical purposes'. The American official historian drew a similar conclusion: 'Moresby was a key point, for if it was useful to the Japanese, to the Allies it was the key to the defense of northern Australia'.

Standing in their way were the men of the Royal Australian Air Force. Notwithstanding the achievement of those who fought it, the air battle for Moresby was still only the first phase in the struggle for New Guinea, one that continued for many more months. Each side continued to jockey for position, the Japanese in the ill-fated attempt to march over

'... OUR GRIEF WAS OVERWHELMING'

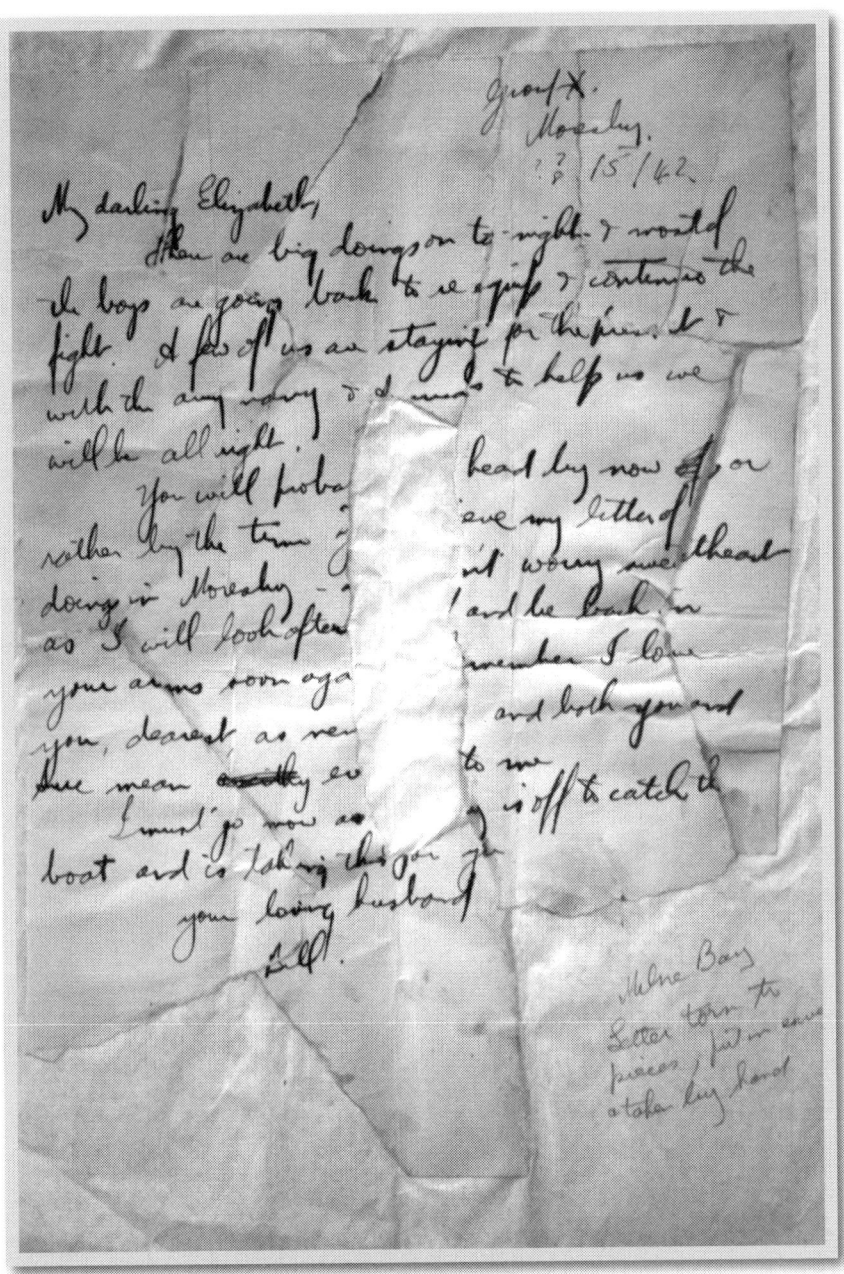

Just in case: Bill Deane-Butcher's final letter from Moresby to his wife, dissected for safe keeping.

223

to Port Moresby from the north coast villages of Buin and Gona, a move that led to the awful battles along the Kokoda Track, and the Allies with the counter-attack landings at Milne Bay and Guadalcanal.

If the early fighting over Gasmata, Lae and Port Moresby cost the RAAF dearly, the later fighting was a funeral pyre for Japanese aviation. Saburo Sakai's close friend Lieutenant Gitaro Miyazaki, judo expert and the strongest arm-wrestler in the Tainan Air Group, who was mistakenly thought by the Australians to have died over Moresby on 17 April, was eventually killed in action with the American Airacobras on 1 June. Eight days later, the Americans also shot down and killed Ensign Satoshi Yoshino, the man responsible for smashing the raid on Gasmata by John Lerew, Bill Pedrina and Graham Gibson on 11 February.

When the American counter-attack on Guadalcanal began in August, the already over-stretched Japanese pilots were trapped in a war of attrition they could never win. On 7 August, in the very first Japanese strike of the Guadalcanal campaign, the indomitable Saburo Sakai escaped death by millimetres. When he dived to attack American bombers, one of the rear gunners put a burst of heavy machine gun shells into his cockpit, smashing instruments and grazing his scalp so severely he eventually lost the sight in one eye. With blood saturating his helmet and flying suit, Sakai used his silk scarf to stem the bleeding, and then flew more than 1000 kilometres back to base at Rabaul. Invalided back to Japan, Sakai spent some time as a flight instructor before returning to action in the hopeless Japanese attempt to repel the American advance to the home islands.

Most of his squadron mates were not so lucky, and never left the Solomons. Lieutenant Jun-ichi Sasai, the man responsible for downing the American B-26 Marauder on 18 April, went on to claim the title of the 'Richthofen of Rabaul', after the legendary German Red Baron. He was shot down and killed in a raid on the American airbase Henderson Field on Guadalcanal on 26 August. Flight Petty Officer Kazushi Uto, nicknamed 'Poppo', or 'sound made by the doves', who claimed his first combat success against 75 Squadron over Moresby on 10 April, was also killed over Guadalcanal, on 13 September. Five weeks later, another of Sakai's close comrades from the days at Lae, Warrant Officer Toshio Ota, was likewise killed in the fighting over Guadalcanal.

Precious few of the Japanese pilots who got to Rabaul survived to see their homeland again. One was Lieutenant Hiroyoshi Nishizawa, Goff Hemsworth's opponent over Rabaul on 3 February. He survived the tour of the Tainan Air Group at Lae, and even the fighting over Guadalcanal that consumed so many of his colleagues. He returned home to endure a spell as a flight instructor, a task he despised, and welcomed the opportunity to go back into combat in the vain Japanese attempt to hold the Philippines. Against the overwhelming odds facing the Japanese air forces when confronted by the might of the American carrier fleet, his luck could scarcely hold. On 26 October 1944, flying aboard a transport aircraft between Japanese airfields to collect replacement fighters, he was shot down and killed, to be given the posthumous honorific *Bukai-in Kohan Giko Kyoshi*, ('In the Ocean of the Military, Reflective of all distinguished pilots, An honoured Buddhist person').

One of the few Japanese airmen who survived the war in the south Pacific unharmed was Nobuo Fujita, the remarkable reconnaissance pilot who so badly exposed Australian defence planning with his flights over Sydney and Melbourne. On the same cruise, Fujita made similar sorties over Hobart and Auckland, New Zealand, before mounting one of the most bizarre bombing raids of the war. Still serving on mother submarine I-25, in September 1942 Fujita tried to knock the United States out of the war single-handedly, by setting fire to the pine forests of the American north-west. He managed the flight as expertly as he had over the cities of Australia, but heavy rain the night before meant his incendiary bombs fizzled out harmlessly on the forest floor. This would be the only time enemy aircraft bombed the American mainland, and it was fitting that the achievement, however madcap, should go to Fujita.

After a more humdrum post-war business career, and several trips to the United States to visit the townsfolk he once tried to envelop in bushfire, Fujita died peacefully in 1997, aged eighty-five.

Just as the war ground on mercilessly for the Japanese, so later fighting thinned the ranks of the Australians who survived the battle of Moresby. Bill Pedrina, the Hudson captain who brought his crew home from the ill-fated raid on Gasmata on 9 February, was killed in combat later in the year. Brian Higgins, who saved his men by plunging his Catalina into the volcanic clouds over Simpson Harbour, was killed in the crash of another flying boat at the Rathmines base north of Newcastle in May 1943. The crash of a Liberator bomber in New Guinea also cost Leigh 'Golden Voice' Vial his life, when it went down during a leaflet-dropping run over the villages of northern New Guinea in April 1943.

Other Hudson and Catalina aircrew were more fortunate, even if their careers after Moresby followed different courses. John Lerew, who led the defence of Rabaul and Port Moresby in the darkest hours of the campaign, unflinchingly and from the front, seemed to reap the consequences of having rubbed too many people in authority the wrong way. Despite his well-earned Distinguished Flying Cross, Lerew never served in combat again. His successor as commander of 32 Squadron had a longer operational career. Deryck Kingwell, after doctors picked most of the glass from his eye in an injury sustained in the long-running battle with the Zeroes over Salamaua, recovered to resume command of the squadron and bring it back from New Guinea after its long tour of duty there. The doctors did well, considering they had to leave two glass fragments behind in his eye, but as Kingwell cheerfully explained, these relics of the battle never seemed to do him much harm. By war's end, Kingwell had formed and led a wing (three squadrons) of heavy bombers, and deployed it successfully to support the series of Australian landings along the Borneo coast in 1945. He went on to a varied and distinguished post-war career in the RAAF, rising to the rank of air commodore.

Julius Cohen's career proved equally distinguished, if less combative. Having flown on operations since the northern summer of 1940, by the time his tenure in command of 11 Squadron finished in mid-1942, the RAAF found it could make good use of his skills in training and staff roles. By the end of the war, Cohen was the RAAF's Senior Intelligence Officer; he changed his name by deed poll to Richard Kingsland in 1947. The following year, Kingsland left the RAAF to begin a stellar career in the Australian public service that took him to the very top of the bureaucratic hierarchy. He was knighted in 1978.

In fits and starts, ending with Bill Deane-Butcher's dramatic departure from Moresby, 75 Squadron went south to Kingaroy, in southern Queensland, to regroup and let off steam. To commemorate the unit's experience at Seven Mile airfield, Deane-Butcher put together a bar-room ballad, 'The Moresby Song', and a selection of the verses confirms the pride the Kittyhawk men took in their first New Guinea combat tour:

So we grabbed some P40s and went to the fight
But soon found the Japs had a nice little kite
It's bright shining silver and Zero by name
But a bloody good show as it comes down in flames
Down in flames, down in flames

Now the bombs dropped around us as we joined in the fray
And we saw quite a lot of the Japs every day
But he soon turned for home when he found what it means

To annoy a poor bloke who'd been fed on tinned beans
On tinned beans, on tinned beans

Now the newspapers tell of the squadron's success
And Nippon has now many aeroplanes less
But the newspapers don't tell how the hell it was done
Without our replacements the odds are seven to one
Yes to one, yes to one

And then we went home for a beer and a rest
And we stood in the pubs where the drink was the best
But now we're up north just to pay off some debts
And to make bloody sure the Rising Sun sets
That it sets, that it sets

Relations within the unit were actually a good deal more strained than the camaraderie of the squadron's drinking song would suggest. Pilots posted in to 75 Squadron as reinforcements at Kingaroy soon found a sharp distinction drawn between them and the New Guinea veterans. Through no fault of their own, these new arrivals had been overseas at the time Japan entered the war, but the pilots who survived the first tour at Moresby were not about to let them forget who had held the line against all odds. Bruce Brown was one of the replacement pilots. He recalled arriving at Kingaroy on a bitterly cold morning, and the hot coffee he received was the only part of the welcome that held any warmth. According to Brown, as he was introduced to the New Guinea veterans somebody remarked, 'Just because you guys have been over in England, don't think you can come back here telling us how to fight this war'. The accusation took Brown aback—he may have been overseas, but he was still to fly in combat, and was happy to learn from those who had. As he protested, 'We had no intention of telling anybody but we expected them to tell us'. It soon became obvious the 'new chums' would be forced to learn the trade as those who first went to Moresby had—the hard way. As Brown ruefully concluded, 'We expected them ... to be full bottle on tactics, both with offensive formations to fly, and defensive formations, but in fact, we were told nothing in that regards. And if we opened our mouth about it we were told, "well, you'll find out later on"'.

The factionalism that divided 75 Squadron went so deep that even Moresby veterans could find themselves on the outer. The enmity that Les Jackson felt for Michael Butler after the young sergeant asked for a day's rest at the end of April was ferocious. Many of his comrades found Jackson a handful on the drink, and Butler more than most. After one heavy session, Jackson flatly declared, 'Butler, I hate you', and proceeded to chase his erstwhile squadron-mate around the base, firing a Thompson sub-machine gun in the air. When 75 Squadron went back into action later in 1942, Butler was mysteriously posted to a training school, and never flew on combat operations again, for reasons never explained to him.

Butler was not alone in leaving the squadron to work as an instructor. Alan Boyd, who arrived in Moresby in early April, went back to an operational training unit. Having survived a combat tour in Libya, Boyd was probably owed a longer rest before being sent back into action with 75 Squadron, and his experience at Moresby clearly left an impression. When he arrived at his new training school to begin work as an instructor, he was put through a flight test, followed by a medical examination. Boyd's bravura impressed the officer reviewing his flying skills, but this bordered on 'a tendency to be impulsive'. His assessor went on, noting Boyd would 'take a risk and try something he has never tried before ... he is also inclined to cut things very fine, instead of giving himself plenty of room and time, and go at it like a "bull at a gate"'. As Boyd's examiner concluded, 'this type of flying is brought on by operational experience, where the pilot has to cut things fine and do everything in a hurry, if he cannot he will not live to tell the tale ... a very sound pilot'.

The doctor's account of Boyd's demeanour told a different story. He was less impressed with dashing piloting skills, and found instead signs of what we would now call post-traumatic stress syndrome: 'This officer is now very disinterested in his work and has no inclination to any flying. He is unable to sleep at night and states he feels very fatigued at times. His appetite is good, although he has lost over 1.5 stone in weight in the past two months. At the moment he thinks he is putting on weight. He is inclined to be nervous—for example when speaking to him a phone rang and he gave quite a start. Comparing this officer's present state with when he was here some months ago there is quite a noticeable difference ...'

Boyd recovered to continue a productive air force career, but many of his squadron-mates were less fortunate. One was Peter Turnbull, who commanded the squadron in John Jackson's absence in mid-April. He was killed in the fighting at Milne Bay later in the year, when his Kittyhawk flipped over at 'zero feet' and crashed, probably brought down by a freak shot from an unknown Japanese rifleman.

John Piper survived that second tour to Milne Bay in late 1942, only to have his flying career brought to a spectacular end a year later. Helping to train American patrol boat gunners, Piper swept in at low level in a mock attack, but got too close to the sea. When a wingtip hit the water, his Kittyhawk cartwheeled in a crash that left the American sailors awestruck, and him injured badly enough to confine his career to staff postings for the rest of the war. Other 75 Squadron pilots to get through the war included Bob Crawford and Alan Whetters, although both had further narrow scrapes. At Milne Bay, Whetters ditched his Kittyhawk in shallow water under the noses of the Japanese, and lived to tell the tale. Still determined to honour his peacetime air force training and bring his aeroplane home come what may, Whetters attempted to float his Kittyhawk back to base on an improvised raft, but gave up the attempt when his ramshackle craft drifted under the guns of a Japanese artillery position. Crawford, having had a throat microphone shot off his neck at Moresby, followed up by surviving a hit from a Japanese anti-aircraft shell in March 1945, which passed through the canopy of his Kittyhawk centimetres from his head.

Likewise, Les Jackson survived the war, giving further valiant service at Milne Bay and rising to command a wing of Kittyhawks before Japan finally surrendered. The squadron 'wild child' returned to civilian life in Queensland, buying out his brother's car dealership and going on to a successful business career. He died in the early 1980s. The family name lives on in New Guinea—Port Moresby's airport is named Jacksons International Airport in honour of John.

Les Jackson's mate at Moresby, Bill Deane-Butcher, went on to the glittering medical career to which he was destined. He went to Milne Bay along with the rest of 75 Squadron, and then to various other air force postings, rising to the rank of wing commander. After the war, he took a postgraduate diploma in ophthalmology and then helped establish the ophthalmology program at the University of Sydney. Deane-Butcher was born to be a surgeon. The long, elegant but rock-steady fingers that stitched the wounded back together at Moresby proved ideal for the intricacies of eye surgery. Deane-Butcher pioneered corneal transplants at Sydney Eye Hospital, and contributed to or chaired medical-related charities too many to mention. One exception should suffice, since it speaks for the interest Deane-Butcher retained in the people of the south Pacific: in 1978, he established the ophthalmic service in the New Hebrides (Vanuatu). Just to show there was life left in an old-timer, Deane-Butcher climbed the Sydney Harbour Bridge to celebrate his ninetieth birthday. He died in 2006.

Deane-Butcher was joined in the medical profession by Arthur Tucker. After service at Milne Bay, Tucker survived another combat tour in western New Guinea, where in September 1943 he had further combat success against Japanese aircraft. He entered medical school after the war, and went on to a notable post-war career as a doctor. Working in

Cooma, New South Wales, for many years, Tucker was among the most outspoken of the former 75 Squadron pilots, and gave his account of life at Seven Mile without fear or favour.

The final medical figure in our story, Esther Stock, the nurse who distinguished herself in the evacuation of Salamaua, honoured her pledge to return to New Guinea. When the war was over, she applied successfully to return, and gave great service before retiring in 1958 as matron of Lae Hospital.

Wilbur Wackett, who played a leading role in 75 Squadron's very first action over Morseby, and then became the first of the Australians to walk back to Moresby after a crash-landing on the north coast, recovered his health and went on to test-pilot duties. At the instigation of his famous father, aircraft designer Lawrence Wackett, Wilbur's adventures were used for wartime propaganda purposes, including a graphic account of his trek through the jungle, which was published in 1944 in *The Boy's RAAF Book*. Promoted to squadron leader at the age of just twenty-two, newly married to Peggy Stephenson, and recently blessed by the arrival of his baby daughter Rahna, Wilbur returned to combat service, flying twin-engined Beaufighters against Japanese bases north of Darwin.

Tragically, Wackett was killed in September 1944 when, lost and disoriented in the smoke haze of bushfires sweeping the Top End, he and his crewmate parachuted from their aircraft when it ran out of fuel. A prospector found the wrecked machine six months later; no trace of Wackett and his crewman was ever found.

The blow to Lawrence Wackett and his wife Letty was prodigious, but worse was to follow. Nine months later, they received a phone call from Peggy's father telling them baby Rahna was ill. The Wacketts 'lay awake for hours, thinking of our dead son and now his sick baby'. The dawn brought the dreadful news that Rahna had died in the night, at which point time became a blur for the Wacketts; 'I cannot recall how we passed the next few hours for our grief was overwhelming'. Travelling to the funeral, the grieving grandparents endured the cheering throngs of crowds celebrating VJ-Day, the end of the war against Japan, in which father and son had given so much. The juxtaposition could not have been harder to bear, as the family struggled through the funeral service, in which Wackett supported his wife with one arm, and with the other held up Peggy, 'who had lost in a little over a year both husband and child'.

For some lucky families, the end of the war became a fairytale come true. In late September 1945, Mrs Kit Metzler received a stunning telegram, advising her that her husband Paul would return to Australia the next day, aboard a British warship that carried him home from a prisoner of war camp in Japan.

Only then did the full details of Paul's miraculous survival emerge. Of course his adventures began long before, in January 1942, at the very outset of the battle for New Guinea. High above the Bismarck Sea on that fateful morning, Metzler was at the controls of the Catalina when he saw what looked like a 'number of grey logs smudging the surface of the ocean'. While captain Bob Thompson whipped off a warning message to Moresby, Metzler climbed for the available cloud cover, noting as he did so, that Zero fighters were scrambling off the deck of the nearest Japanese aircraft carrier.

The Australians did not immediately retreat, but bravely followed their orders to shadow the Japanese fleet, ducking in and out of cloud to catch glimpses of the enemy warships. Four Zeroes put an end to this game of hide-and-seek when the Japanese fighters pounced on the slow flying boat between cloud banks, and battle was joined. The Japanese fighters lined up for firing passes from astern, but as they swept by his cockpit, Metzler could make out the fine detail of his adversaries: the Zeroes were 'dark olive-green with large dull-red "rising suns" on wings and fuselage, flown by dark-helmeted hunched-up-looking pilots'.

The Catalina crew soon found their equipment letting them down. The decrepit Lewis guns, the hand-me-downs left over from World

War I that served as the defensive armament for the flying boats, performed in their 'normal shocking fashion'. After the first few bursts, each broke down in turn, forcing the infuriated gunners to clear stoppages in the heat of battle.

As a result, the Catalina never stood a chance. Soon, the gunners were killed or wounded. Metzler had an awful, front-row view of the carnage all around him. 'Tracer bullets, looking like heavy slanting rain', hissed past. The Japanese cannon shells were particularly frightening: these were like 'blurred oranges going past at what seemed about two yards from my ear'. Metzler was briefly puzzled by the sound of what appeared to be gravel being thrown against a windowpane. What he could hear, in fact, were Japanese bullets smacking through the fuselage and skinning and striking the bulkhead behind him.

Metzler later wrote that up until this point, in some psychological act of detachment, he had 'quite enjoyed' himself. When the Catalina caught fire, reality caught up with him. The big flying boat had aboard 1500 gallons of high-octane fuel, stored in fuel tanks that ran virtually the length of its wing. When this load caught fire, there was no stopping it. As the Catalina fell away to the sea, 'we were like a great bonfire coloured red and black.' The machine might have been an engineering marvel of the age, precisely crafted from the latest duralumin alloy, but its control surfaces were old-fashioned linen. These burnt away in an instant, leaving Thompson struggling vainly for control, with the rudder, elevators and ailerons nothing more than metal ribs melting in the blaze. While he hauled on the control column as best he could, Metzler juggled the throttles, doing what he could to alter the engine power and keep the flying boat's nose up.

Even with their best efforts, the Catalina hit the water with a mighty thud, bouncing fully 200 metres on impact. It then skipped like a stone on a pond for a further, seemingly interminable distance. Having got this far, the surviving crew needed no second invitation to abandon ship, and got out while the boat was still in motion. Indeed, the Catalina was now a demon possessed, and while Thompson, Metzler and their crewmates regained their composure and their breath treading water, the flying boat 'careered around us several times burning and crackling like a bushfire'. Its mechanical torture was not yet over, and the Catalina only came to a stop as its multi-coloured load of flares 'exploded like fireworks, one after another'. As the Australians looked on, the fire burnt out the aircraft's hull, so that with 'the nose and the tail tilting up', its carcass finally disappeared with a 'terrific hiss of salt water on hot metal'.

The Australians struck out for the nearest land, a distant island, but made only modest progress when a Japanese cruiser came by. As they attempted to ignore the ropes slung over the side and instructions in Japanese to come aboard, the sudden arrival of a school of sharks, which began biting the driftwood on which one of the men was keeping himself afloat, changed their minds about the enemy's offer. Clambering aboard, the ship's captain treated them to an unusually pacific interrogation by Japanese wartime standards, before sending them below for medical treatment.

There, a Dr Hosogi Daisabura treated the Australians with great kindness and diligence. His consideration made a deep impression on the Catalina crew, who were expecting slightly different treatment. To record this unusual outbreak of camaraderie, Daisabura asked each of the Australians to inscribe some words in his small notebook, which each of them did.

Under his care, the Australians were safely delivered to Japan, where Metzler was incarcerated for three and a half years at the Zentsuji camp. To keep himself busy amid the tedium of prison life, he co-wrote a book on aerodynamic theory with a Dutch POW, Captain C. W. A. Oyens. A copy of this manuscript is now in the care of the Australian War Memorial: in battered scrapbooks, the interested reader can find in meticulous hand-written copperplate, complete with carefully drawn diagrams and scientific graphs, a detailed study of the then state of aerodynamics. Metzler was content simply to have kept his mind occupied in captivity; Oyens had his copy published in The Netherlands after the war.

Returning home to his beloved wife Kit, Metzler raised a family and rejoined the RAAF, making modest career progress before transferring to the reserve in 1959. One final twist in Metzler's remarkable war remained. In 1963, War Memorial historian Bill Sweeting contacted him on behalf of an Australian diplomat who had come across Daisabura in a remote Japanese fishing village. Daisabura still had his notebook, and Sweeting set about contacting the Australians who had scribbled their remarks of gratitude in it more than twenty years before. When Sweeting found Metzler in suburban Canberra, the amazing, small-world coincidence of the whole episode prompted the former Catalina man to write about his experiences for the first time, thus giving posterity the chance to remember him, and those with whom he served.

For other families, peace brought no end to the anxiety clouding their lives since 1942. The Australian government devoted considerable resources to search parties that scoured the south Pacific for missing aircrew.

One of these teams was led by Squadron Leader Keith Rundle. A severe asthmatic, Rundle bluffed his way into the RAAF in July 1940, but then found himself confined to a succession of desk jobs for the balance of the conflict. When peace brought the opportunity to get into the field to find Australia's missing airmen Rundle jumped at the chance, having worked in casualty records, and he devoted the rest of his life to the task.

One of his earliest successes came in December 1945. Acting on information from local villagers, Rundle and his team found the Hudson bomber flown by Arthur Nicolay in just over a metre of water on a reef 700 metres from Gasmata. Missing since 3 March 1942, Nicolay and his men had long been thought to have perished at the hands of the storm that beleaguered Australian air operations that night. In fact Nicolay and his three crew—Sergeants Mark Korbosky, Ian Cass and Bill Coppin—beat the weather, bombing their target only to fall victim to the Japanese defences. Rundle successfully identified the wreckage of their machine, but of Nicolay and his men there was no sign. In March 1946, they were officially presumed to have been killed in action. From this, their families took some solace, Korbosky's widow writing to the air force that the news brought an end to a 'long anxious time of waiting'.

Having found Nicolay's Hudson, on the same expedition Rundle located the bomber of Ken Erwin, who had also been missing with his three mates since 3 March 1942. In this case, the news was even more distressing. Erwin's bomber hit the shallow water near Urai Island, three kilometres south-south-west of Gasmata, so hard it exploded, showering the waterfront with pieces of wreckage. Three of the crew—Pilot Officer E. L. McLauchlan, and Sergeants J. W. Simpson and Ian Barwick—were killed on impact. Horrible though their fate was, they were the lucky ones.

The shot-down Hudsons provided the Japanese with valuable intelligence. It was a map recovered from one of the bombers—presumably that of Nicolay, given that it came down relatively intact—which revealed the Horn Island base to the Japanese. To support their search and collection efforts around the downed bombers, they enlisted neighbouring villagers. It was these locals who found Erwin, alive but badly hurt with a broken leg. They shamefully mistreated Erwin, bashing him with a rifle butt amid a welter of punches. When the Japanese finally took charge, they interrogated Erwin, and then shot him dead, dumping his body in the lagoon.

The only comfort to take from news like this was finality, and unfortunately for some families, there would be no closure for year after lonely year.

Not surprisingly, as time dragged on many grasped at any faint hope they could find. Having received a rumour that their son David Brown was seen in a prisoner of war camp in Japan, his parents mounted their own enquiries, alongside the official search teams. In July 1946, they wrote to the authorities, convinced that a photograph published in the American magazine *National Geographic*, of POWs at the time of the Japanese surrender, included a shot of young David. Mrs Brown in particular was certain that the man was her son, and must have been crushed when Australian officials found an Australian army officer held captive at the camp, who confirmed that Brown had never been seen there. Still, neither the authorities nor the Brown family gave up. The Australian Air Board, hearing that the American airmen Lutz and Reed, shot down over Rabaul on 18 April, had seen Brown at Simpson Harbour in late May 1942, wrote to them in 1947. Reed took the trouble to reply and gave such personal details, including the name and address of Brown's father Leslie, that it was clear the Americans had been held with the young sergeant. Reed reported that he and Lutz were shipped to Japan on 26 May; they last saw Brown left behind on the wharf at Simpson Harbour. After this tantalising news, the search went cold, and the authorities advised the Brown family in May 1947 that David was by then presumed dead.

On Saturday 25 July 1950, Bill Parker senior opened his copy of the *Sydney Morning Herald* at his home in the Sydney suburb of West Ryde to find, under a headline 'Bodies Found of 15 RAAF Men', the name of his son listed among those executed by the Japanese eight long years before. The shock was profound and understandable. As he explained in a letter of protest to the RAAF, this was the first definitive news he had had of young Bill's fate, 'and Sir, I think you will admit,' it was a 'rather brutal way of being informed'.

The remains of Allan Norman's crew were found thanks to yet more tireless work by Keith Rundle. In mid-1950, assisted by local men, he uncovered a mass grave in the shadows of Matupi volcano, alongside Simpson Harbour, Rabaul. The Australian recovery party found fifteen Australians, twelve Americans and an unidentified civilian. They included the nine crew of the Catalina piloted by Allan Norman—and David Brown, missing since last being seen by the Americans on the wharf at Simpson Harbour on 26 May 1942. Rundle identified the remains from service discs ('dog tags') and dental records. The men had been buried with personal possessions such as kitchen utensils, suggesting that the Japanese had led them to believe they were being transported to another camp, before a last, fatal detour.

The RAAF's overall search effort was co-ordinated back in Melbourne by Flight Lieutenant Deste Kibble, who, like Rundle, was a man on a mission. Kibble angrily told the Australian press that the Japanese commander responsible for the massacre, Captain Mizusaki, was 'hale and hearty', walking the streets of Tokyo a free man.

After Rundle's discovery, Australian officials interrogated a raft of Japanese personnel in an attempt to establish what occurred. This prodigious effort allows us to know that the Japanese executed Norman and his compatriots, decapitating them with a single sword strike as they knelt next to the open grave. At the time of their deaths, a number of the Australians lay injured and wounded on stretchers. The Japanese killed them where they lay. The Japanese officers responsible reportedly spoke later to their men, suggesting that were they in a similar situation, they should go to their deaths with the valour shown by the Australians.

On 18 July 1950, the victims of Matupi were reburied with full military honours, following a service at the Rabaul cricket ground. 'Out of a cloudless sky, the tropical sun shone down', as the various clergymen went about the funeral rites. Father Virgil Copas wrote later that after twenty-three years as a Catholic priest, the service made a deeper impression on him than any he had conducted: 'the passing of the years has not obscured the sadness—or the triumph—of that funeral'.

The shocking news from Rabaul allowed the Australian authorities to clarify the fate of the men, finally declaring them killed while on active service. Ironically, the man responsible for making that declaration was Bill Bolitho, another of the flying boat captains at Moresby in 1942. Eight years after his mate Allan Norman went missing, it fell to Bolitho in his post-war capacity as RAAF Director of Personnel to update the service records for each member of Norman's crew. One can imagine Bolitho's feelings as he went through this task. The plot numbers of the gravesites were included in the advice provided to the next of kin, together with an assurance that the Imperial War Graves Commission would tend to them 'in perpetuity'. This advice to his family forms the last item in the file on David Brown.

In cases of atrocities, the authorities first sent news to relatives by way of a visit from a clergyman of the relevant denomination, and then followed up with written confirmation. For whatever reason, this arrangement fell down in the case of Bill Parker senior, hence his shock when he opened his newspaper that winter's day in West Ryde.

Understandably, Bill senior peppered officialdom with letters of protest. In the first of these, he recounted how he had stood on the platform of Sydney's Central Station in early 1942, while his boy made the haunting, final farewell in which he predicted his own doom. From this recollection, Parker took some solace, because if his son could go back to the front knowing his own likely fate, 'one thing I am convinced of, my lad met his death as I hoped he would meet it, fearlessly'.

Parker went on to ask the Secretary of the Australian Air Board for an explanation of how the mix-up in notifying him could have occurred. His grief was fuelled in part by this regrettable, insensitive official blunder, but perhaps too the pain and anger in Bill Parker's final words spoke for all those families bereaved by the air battle for New Guinea: 'Well sir', he wrote in protest, 'I will leave it to you. I feel pretty wild about it all ...'

References

PRIMARY SOURCES
AWM: Australian War Memorial
AWM 52 8/4/18 New Guinea Volunteer Rifles
AWM 54 31/2/19 Report from Major P. Kelso, Commanding Officer, Australia Light Anti-Aircraft Regiment, AIF, New Guinea Force
AWM 54 253/5/7 Allied translator and interpreter section. Captured documents Nos 58 and 74, Diaries of members of Kure No 3 Special Landing Party
AWM 54 419/4/1 Report on New Guinea Rifles
AWM 54 425/18/2 History of New Guinea Air Warning Wireless Company
AWM 54 779/3/3 HQ Allied Air Forces, SWPA—Directorate of Intelligence Nos 2 to 6—Interrogation Reports, Moresby and Milne Bay Areas, 1942
AWM 65 752 Cohen, Julius Allen 117
AWM 66 9/2/1 RAAF Intelligence Summary Serial No. 76 18 June 1941
AWM MSS 696 Battle for Port Moresby, P.A. Masters
AWM MSS 723 Peter Masters
AWM MSS 734 P.A. Masters, Shooting down Zeroes
AWM MSS 1420 Raymond Neal, Paga Battery
AWM S00515 (O211029/403372) Pettett, John Henry Stephen (Flight Lieutenant)
AWM S00577 (250828) Piper, John Walter Wedgwood (Flight Lieutenant)
AWM S00583 Bruce, Edward 'Buster' Brown (Squadron Leader)
AWM S00592 Whetters, William Alan (Flight Lieutenant)
AWM S00701 (405432) Tucker, Arthur Douglas (Flight Lieutenant)
AWM S00738 (407220) Butler, Michael Seymour (Flying Officer)
PR03185 Bates, Albert (Warrant Officer), DFM
PR91/073 Yeowart, Robert Alfred, Squadron Leader, b: 1915 d: 1980

NAA: National Archives of Australia
A452 1965/1063 Miss Esther C Stock
A705 163/34/157 Gibson Graham Ian (Flying Officer)
A705 163/36/142 Hutchinson G.L. (Lieutenant)
A705 163/55/159 Rowe Thomas Nicoll (Flying Officer)
A705 163/90/240 Barwick Ian Munro
A705 163/134/15 Korbosky Mark Richard (Sergeant)
A705 163/149/187 Parker William Murdoch (Leading Aircraftman)
A705 163/150/132 Perrett John (Corporal)
A705 166/6/845 Brown, David Stuart (Sergeant)
A705 166/27/711 Metzler, Paul Maxwell (Flight Lieutenant)
A2670/1 85/1940 War Cabinet Agendum—Substitution of GR Squadron for No 7 Fighter Squadron
A2670 116/1942 War Cabinet Agendum— No 116/1942—Japanese air raids on Darwin
A4181 Vol 15 Supply of Lockheed B.14 (Hudson) Aircraft, Air Board Agenda No. 2377, 20/12/38
A9186 13 Operations Record Book— Number 5 Squadron Jan 41–Feb 46
A9186 30 Operations Record Book— Number 11 Squadron
A9186 95 Operations Record Book— 75 Squadron
A9300 Boyd A
A9300 Campbell D.W.I.

A9300 Hemsworth G.E.
A9300 O'Connor R.K.C.
A9301 20343 Parker William Murdoch: Service Number—20343
A9695 336 Unidentified aircraft over Laverton
A9695 475 Notes on Visit to Darwin, Chief of Air Staff
A9695 560 Catalina Attacks on Rabaul in Feb 1942—interview with Sergeant Douglas Frederick Dick
A9695 902 No 75 Squadron at Moresby and Milne Bay
A11083 7/82/Air, North Eastern Area Headquarters—Fighter aircraft for North Eastern Operational Units
A11083 8/3/Air North Eastern Area Headquarters—Reports—Air raids—Thursday Island sector
A11083 19/18 Part 2, North Eastern Area Headquarters—Visits and Inspections
A11083 906/34/P1 North Eastern Area Headquarters—Court of Inquiry—Catalina aircraft A24/15—Port Moresby—8/12/1941
B3476 336/1/1618 Fate of Catalina A24/20
SP109 3/302/09 First Darwin Air Raids
SP109 381/17 Sydney Sun Air Raid Precautions

NLA: National Library of Australia
Audio Bib ID 733496 Interview with Deryck Kingwell
Audio ID 2350320 Bob Crawford interviewed by Fred Morton
Audio Bib ID 4609052 Jackson, Les
Audio Bib ID 4649904 John Piper interviewed by Fred Morton

Private collections
Richard Deane-Butcher
Peter Tucker
Robert Whetters

SECONDARY SOURCES
Alexander, K. *Clive Caldwell: Air Ace*, Allen & Unwin, 2006
Birkett, G. 'The Magpie's First Strike' in *Flightpath*, Vol. 22, No. 1
Bullard, S. *Japanese Army Operations in the South Pacific Area: New Britain and Papua Campaigns 1942–43*, Australian War Memorial, 2007
Church, T. *They Flew Alone*, Magpie Books, 1947
Claringbould, M. 'Who shot down John Jackson?' in *Flightpath*, Volume 16, No. 2 Nov 2004–Jan 2005
Cooper, R. *Crash of the Kittyhawk*, Wauchope District Historical Society, 2002
Craven, W. F. and Cate, C. L. (eds) *The Army Air Forces in World War II, Plans and Early Operations, January 1939 to August 1942*, Volume 1, University of Chicago Press, 1948–58
Day, G. *Eight Hundred Million Candlepower: Journals of the 67AASL 1942–1945*, Prominent Press, 1999
Deane-Butcher, W. *Fighter Squadron Doctor*, self-published, 1992
Downs, I. *The New Guinea Volunteer Rifles 1939–1945: A History*, Pacific Press, 1999
Eames, J. *The Searchers: And Their Endless Quest for Lost Aircrew in the Southwest Pacific*, University of Queensland Press, 1999
Ewer, P. *Wounded Eagle: The Bombing of Darwin and the Scandal of Australian Air Defence*, New Holland, 2009
Feldt, E. *The Coast Watchers*, Currey O'Neil, 1981
Francillon, R. *Lockheed Aircraft Since 1913*, London: Putnam, first published 1982
Fuchida, M. and Okumiya, M. *Midway: The Battle That Doomed Japan*, Naval Institute, 1955

Gamble, B. *Fortress Rabaul: The Battle for the SouthWest Pacific January 1942–April 1943*, Zenith Press, 2010

Gillison, D. *Royal Australian Air Force 1939–1942*, Australian War Memorial, 1962

Grant, J. R. 'Corrugated masterpieces: Junkers types in Australia and Papua-New Guinea' in *Air Enthusiast*, Issue 77, Sept–Oct 1998

Hatch, A. *Glenn Curtiss: Pioneer of Aviation*, The Lyons Press, 2007

Horikoshi, J. *Eagles of Mitsubishi: The Story of the Zero Fighter*, University of Washington Press, 1981

Huxley, J. *New Guinea Experience: Gold, War and Peace*, Australian Military Publications, 2007

Jackson, P. and Jackson, A. *A Lot to Fight For: The War Diaries of Squadron Leader J.F. Jackson DFC*, self-published, 2001

Jenkins, D. *Battle Surface: Japan's Submarine War Against Australia 1942–44*, Random House, 1992

Kingsland, R. 'Courageous cats pitted against enemy lions' in A. E. Minty, *Black Cats: The Real Story of Australia's Long Range Catalina Strike Force in the Pacific*, RAAF Museum, 1994

McCarthy, D. *South West Pacific: First Year, Kokoda to War*, Australian War Memorial, 1959

Metzler, P. 'Early days' in A. E. Minty, *Black Cats: The Real Story of Australia's Long Range Catalina Strike Force in the Pacific*, RAAF Museum, 1994

——'Recollections of a Catalina pilot', *Stand-To*, Journal of the ACT RSL (July–August 1963)

——'Biographical note' in *Stand-To*, Journal of the ACT RSL (March–October 1964)

Royal Australian Air Force (RAAF), *The Boy's RAAF Book* (Directorate of Public Relations, RAAF, 1944)

Sakai, S. *Samurai!*, Nelson Doubleday, 1957

Sakaida, H. *Imperial Japanese Navy Aces 1937–1945*, Osprey, 1998

Seekee, V. *Horn Island: In Their Steps 1939–1945*, self-published, 2002

Stanley, P. 'Dramatic myth and dull truth: invasion by Japan in 1942', in Stockings, C. (ed), *Zombie Myths of Australian Military History*, University of New South Wales Press, 2010

Stevens, D. 'Australia's Thermopylae? The Kokoda Trail' in Stockings, C. (ed), *Zombie Myths of Australian Military History*, University of New South Wales Press, 2010

Tagoya, O. *Mitsubishi Type 1 Rikko 'Betty' Units of World War 2*, Osprey, 2001

Vincent, D. *The RAAF Hudson Story*, Book One, self-published, 1999

Wackett, L. *Aircraft Pioneer: An Autobiography*, Angus and Robertson, 1972

White, O. *Green Armour*, Penguin, 1991

Wigmore, L. *The Japanese Thrust*, Australian War Memorial, 1957

Wilson, D. *Seek and Strike: 75 Squadron RAAF 1942–2002*, Banner Books, 2002

Notes

Abbreviations
AWM: Australian War Memorial
NAA: National Archives of Australia
NLA: National Library of Australia

CHAPTER ONE

Pages 7–8 For Keen's dramatic account of the Catalina skippered by the American Lieutenant Hutchinson, see NAA A705 163/36/142. Details of Tom Rowe's service record are at NAA A705 163/55/159.

Page 11 The RAAF Official History's description of Keen is at Gillison, *Royal Australian Air Force 1939–1942*, p. 364.

Pages 12–15 The account of pre-war RAAF planning, including the prescient strategic planning of Richard Williams, his demise and the feeble work of his successor Charles Burnett, is based on Ewer, *Wounded Eagle*.

Page 15 Burnett's justification for cancelling the formation of an Australian fighter force is at NAA A2670/1 85/1940.

Page 16 The avoidable loss of the Catalina flown by Lincoln Sloan and his crew on 8 December 1941 is revealed at NAA A11083 906/34/P1.

Page 17 For the loss in action of the Catalina flown by Bob Thompson and Paul Metzler on 21 January 1942, see NAA A9186 30.

Pages 21–2 The use of the various Junkers aircraft in New Guinea is reviewed by Grant, 'Corrugated Masterpieces'.

Page 23 The environmental legacy of New Guinea gold mining is at Downs, *The New Guinea Volunteer Rifles 1939–1945: A History*, p. 157.

Pages 23–6 For life in Salamaua and Bulolo in the 1930s, see Huxley, *New Guinea Experience: Gold, War and Peace*.

Pages 27–8 For the Japanese attack on Wau, and the resistance to it led by Sergeant Vandenburg, see ibid., pp. 43–4. For a general history of the NGVR, see Downs, op. cit.

Pages 29–31 Bob Yeowart's dramatic account of his sortie over Japanese-held Rabaul is at AWM PR91/073.

Pages 31–4 The press coverage of Esther Stock's adventures includes the *Sydney Morning Herald*, 16 February 1942, and the *Courier Mail*, 17 February 1942; details of her career can be found at NAA A452 1965/1063.

Pages 34–5 Burnett's plans to construct a defence line through New Britain, after the fall of Rabaul, are in Ewer, op. cit., p. 209.

Page 35 The efforts of Burnett's staff to obtain Kittyhawks for Port Moresby, and the intervention of the allied high command to prevent their movement, are at NAA A11083 7/82/Air.

Pages 35–6 For Reverend Hardie's blundering correspondence to Kit Metzler, see NAA A705 166/27/711.

CHAPTER TWO

Pages 38–9 For Doug Dick's part in the air battle over Rabaul on 3 February, see NAA A9695 560. For a general account of the action, including the roles of Higgins and Hemsworth, see Gillison, op. cit., pp. 448–9. Nishizawa's part in the action is described by Sakaida, *Imperial Japanese Navy Aces*.

NOTES

Pages 39–40 The RAAF's pre-war assessment of Japanese aircrew is at AWM 66 9/2/1.

Page 42 Pearce's cynicism about Hemsworth's motives is at NAA A9300 Hemsworth G.E.

Page 44 Julius Cohen's adventures in Rabat are described in AWM 65 752.

Page 45 The circumstances around David Campbell's well-earned Distinguished Flying Cross are at NAA A9300 Campbell D.W.I.

Page 47 John Lerew's use of Latin for dramatic effect in his messages to RAAF high command is recounted in the *Canberra Times*, 18 January 1992.

Page 48 Graham Gibson's service record is at NAA A705 163/34/157.

Pages 48–9 The work of Richard Williams to give the RAAF the very best Hudson aircraft can be reviewed at NAA A4181 Vol. 15. The performance advantage that Williams obtained for Australian aircrew is described by Francillon, *Lockheed Aircraft since 1913*.

Pages 50–4 The accounts of John Lerew and Bill Pedrina in the bitter action over Gasmata are held at NAA A705 163/34/157. The combat career of their opponent Satoshi Yoshino is reviewed by Sakaida, op. cit. The subsequent misleading press coverage of that battle is typified by the *Courier Mail*, 13 February 1942. The RAAF staff assessment of Lerew's crews at this time is at NAA A11083 19/18 Part 2.

Page 55 See *Courier Mail*, 18 February 1942, for the panic over school enrolments. Osmar White's description of his perspiring arrival at Port Moresby, and later observations on life in the town, are from White, *Green Armour*, pp. 40 and 51. See the *Courier Mail*, 18 February 1942 for the importance of Port Moresby.

Page 56 Kingwell recounts the use of infantry helmets by his aircrew at NLA Audio Bib ID 733496.

Pages 57–8 Nobuo Fujita's amazing reconnaissance flights over Sydney and Melbourne are recounted in Jenkins, *Battle Surface*. The *Sydney Morning Herald* editorial on the fall of Singapore ran on 17 February 1942; on the same day, Melbourne's *Argus*, among others, covered John Curtin's declaration that the 'Battle of Australia' had begun.

Pages 58–9 The lack of air raid precautions in Sydney is in the *Sydney Sun*, 17 and 18 February 1942, and the censor's efforts to keep the true state of affairs from the public are at NAA SP109 381/17.

Page 59 The post-war research of David Jenkins finally revealed details of Fujita's flights over Australian targets in 1942; his interview with the Japanese ace is riveting reading. See Jenkins, op. cit.

Pages 59–60 Michael Butler discusses his service at Darwin in an interview, AWM S00738. Likewise, Bob Crawford recalls his flight over Bathurst Island at NLA Audio ID 2350320. Mitsuo Fuchida's contempt for the Australian defence effort is at Fuchida and Okumiya, *Midway*, p. 40.

Pages 60–2 The work of the censor to suppress details of the raid, and subsequent embarrassment when the American press told the story, are at NAA SP109 3/302/09; the government's part in the cover-up is at NAA A2670 116/1942; and Burnett's gratuitous speech to the men at the RAAF base is described at NAA A9695 475.

CHAPTER THREE

Page 64 The latter-day indifference to the gravity of the fighting in 1942 is typified by Peter Stanley, 'Dramatic myth and dull truth: invasion by Japan in 1942', and David Stevens, 'Australia's Thermopylae? The Kokoda Trail', both in Stockings (ed), *Zombie Myths of Australian Military History*.

Pages 64–5 The contemporary, and more strategically accurate, analysis of General Sturdee is in Wigmore, *The Japanese Thrust*, see Appendix 5. The American intelligence appreciation of the threat can be found in Craven and Cate (eds), *The Army Air Forces in World War II, Plans and Early Operations*, see especially pp. 430–6.

Pages 65–6 For Japanese planning, see Bullard, *Japanese Army Operations*, pp. 31 and 69.

Pages 67–8 The Australian involvement in the first US raid on Rabaul is told by Gamble, *Fortress Rabaul*, pp. 97–100.

Pages 69 Bill Bolitho's attack on the same target is outlined in Gillison, op cit., pp. 453–4.

Pages 69–70 The *Sydney Morning Herald* invoked the spirit of the laconic Aussie under fire in its edition on 25 February 1942. Gillison, op.cit. also describes the impact of the Japanese raid on Moresby on 24 February on the equipment and personnel of 32 Squadron, while Ted Church gave a more personal account of the destruction of the long-promised permanent barracks in his post-war monograph, *They Flew Alone*, p. 48. See also White, op. cit., p. 48.

Pages 70–1 For Cohen's dive-bombing of Rabaul, see Gamble, op. cit., p. 101–2. Cohen's observations regarding Charles Burnett are at Kingsland, 'Courageous cats pitted against the enemy lions', p. 7.

Page 72 The *Argus* provided Melbourne with its succinct summary of the war on 26 February 1942. The ineffectual Australian response to the Japanese reconnaissance over Melbourne is at NAA A9695 336. The war diary of 5 Squadron, based at Laverton on 26 February, shows how the defenders sent their strike force in the opposite direction to Fujita's course, see NAA A9186 13.

Pages 73–7 Bert Bates' graphic account of the Japanese raid on 28 February is at AWM PR 03185; see also White, op. cit., p. 70. The interrogation reports of Katsuaki Nagatomo are contained in AWM 54 779/3/3.

Page 78 Kingwell's report on the fate of his aircrews on 3 March is at NAA A705 163/134/15. The details regarding Ken Erwin's flying experience are from Vincent, *The RAAF Hudson Story*, p. 296, and Gillison, op. cit., p. 269.

Page 79 The heart-rending confusion between the Air Board and the family of John 'Jackie' Perrett are contained in the exchanges held at NAA A705 163/150/132.

CHAPTER FOUR

Pages 81–2 The work of the NGVR at Salamaua during the Japanese invasion is described by Downs, op cit., pp. 169–70.

Pages 82–3 See Bullard, op. cit. for the effect of RAAF operations against the Japanese at Salamaua.

NOTES

Page 86 Craven and Cate, op. cit., p. 436.
Pages 86–90 The bombing of Horn Island is detailed by Seekee, *Horn Island*, including the experiences of local construction worker Daniel McGrath at p. 35 and the pilots of the US 49th Fighter Squadron at pp. 16–18. The appropriation of the American pilots as 'ours' is typified by the Sydney *Sun*, 17 February 1942.
Page 87 For Japanese use of intelligence gathered from the Hudsons shot down on 3 March, see Bullard, op. cit., p. 46.
Pages 90–1 The account of the raid by Colonel Rupert Hurst, and the efforts of Major Tom Sherman to defuse the unexploded Japanese bomb are at NAA A11083 8/3/AIR.
Pages 93–4 The diet of the searchlight crews on the way to Moresby, and on arrival, is drawn from Day, *Eight Hundred Million Candlepower*.
Pages 94–5 The construction of the '30 mile ring' of observer posts in March 1942 is recorded at AWM 54 425/18/2.

CHAPTER FIVE

Page 97 The story of the reconnaissance flight of Heihachi Kawai over Port Moresby on 21 March is based on Tagoya, *Mitsubishi Type 1 Rikko 'Betty' Units*, and Ray Neal's account is at AWM MSS 1420. See also White, op. cit., p. 72.
Pages 98–9 Arthur Tucker tells his wartime story at AWM S00701.
Page 99 Likewise, John Piper recounts his training and service with 75 Squadron at AWM S00577, and also NLA Audio Bib ID 4649904.
Pages 99–102 John Pettett's equivalent account is at AWM S00515. The newspaper report on his Tiger Moth crash while in training can be found in the *Sydney Morning Herald*, 7 June 1941.

Page 103 Piper's fighter training is at AWM S00577.
Page 105 Tucker's first experience with the Kittyhawk is at AWM S00701.
Page 106 American aviation pioneer Glenn Curtiss has had several biographers, among the most recent of whom is Hatch, *Glenn Curtiss*.
Page 109 Clive Caldwell's pithy summary of the diving characteristics of the P40 Kittyhawk can be found in Alexander, *Clive Caldwell*.
Pages 109–13 Arthur Tucker's account of his bumping landing, and the terrifying ferry flight to Archerfield is at AWM S00701. The view from the ground, including the efforts of Albert and Essie Freeman to save the life of pilot Jim Norton, is told by Cooper, *Crash of the Kittyhawk*.
Page 115 Bill Deane-Butcher's early medical career is in his autobiography *Fighter Squadron Doctor*. The testimonial by the Chief Medical Superintendent of Sydney's Prince Henry Hospital is from a letter by C. J. M. Waters, dated 10 July 1940; private collection of Richard Deane-Butcher.
Pages 116–18 John Jackson's insights into life and flying in North Africa in 1940–41 are drawn from his letters, chronicled by Jackson and Jackson, *A Lot to Fight For*, see pp. 28–37.

CHAPTER SIX

Page 122 Deane-Butcher, op. cit., pp 17–19.
Page 123 Piper, NLA Audio Bib ID 4649904 for his view of the crash on 22 March. Church, op. cit., p. 54 describes his efforts with Deane-Butcher in rescuing Brereton.
Page 124 A good overview of the attack on Lae on 22 March is Birkett, 'The Magpie's First Strike'. Pettett recollects

247

his combat with the Zeroes in this action in AWM S00515.

Pages 125–6 Wilbur Wackett wrote of his tale of survival in RAAF, *The Boy's RAAF Book*.

Page 126 Piper, NLA Audio Bib ID 4649904 for his scrape with a parked Japanese bomber.

Page 129 Church, op. cit., p. 60 paid tribute to Bill Matson's miraculous powers in keeping Kittyhawks in the air.

Pages 132–3 Church, op. cit., pp. 61–3 wrote that the raid in which the Zero crashed on the hill above him and Jock Russell occurred on 6 April. His account of this action in *They Flew Alone* is graphic, but in error as to the date: the circumstances of the raid he recounts clearly refer to the combats on 23 March.

Page 132 Deane-Butcher, op. cit., p. 24 for the doctor's first experience of battle.

Pages 134–5 Bill Matson gave an interview late in the war describing his routines at Seven Mile, which can be found at NAA A9695 902.

Page 135 Tucker's recollections of the Seven Mile diet are at AWM S00701. The standard invitation to breakfast by the 75 Squadron cook is a recollection by Richard Deane-Butcher of his father's account of the speech.

Page 136 Les Jackson recounted the pre-flight nerves that cost him his breakfast at NLA Audio Bib ID 4609052. For the work to clean up Seven Mile, see Deane-Butcher, op. cit., pp. 39–40.

Page 137 The Australian intelligence transcript of Paul Metzler's radio broadcast from Japan is held at NAA A705 166/27/711.

CHAPTER SEVEN

Page 140 For the work of supplying Vial, see Downs, op. cit., pp. 172–3.

Page 145 The sad story of Ron O'Connor's will is at NAA A9300 O'Connor R. K. C.

Pages 145–8 The story of the Zero's design and development is told by Horikoshi, *Eagles of Mitsubishi*.

Page 152 Deane-Butcher told the story of Les Jackson's hijinks at Stu Collie's expense, op. cit., p. 25.

Pages 154–5 The horrific experiences of Deryck Kingwell and his crew in their combat over Salamaua are told in Gillison, op. cit., pp. 462–3, and Church, op. cit., pp. 63–4.

Pages 156–7 For the experience of the American Airacobra pilots at Seven Mile in early April, see Wilson, *Seek and Strike*. Les Jackson's method of liberating beer from the American pilots is told by Deane-Butcher, op. cit., p. 76.

Pages 158–60 Sakai's account of the journey to Lae comes from his autobiography *Samurai!*, p. 92.

CHAPTER EIGHT

Page 163 Piper, NLA Audio Bib ID 4649904.

Page 164 The various efforts made by 75 Squadron to find John Jackson are detailed by Wilson, op. cit., p. 30.

Page 165 John Jackson's remarkable letter to his family describing his escape from Salamaua is reproduced by Jackson and Jackson, op. cit., pp. 235–40.

Page 166 Sakai, op. cit., p. 100 for Japanese morale.

Page 168 Peter Masters' description of the combat over Lae is at AWM MSS 734.

Page 169 The Japanese account of the capture of David Brown on 11 April is at NAA A705 166/6/845.

NOTES

Page 174 Blakey's observations of John Jackson are at Downs, op. cit. The NGVR war diary describing the death of Barney Creswell is at AWM 52 8/4/18.

Page 175 Sakai, op. cit., pp. 107–8 for the accuracy of Australian anti-aircraft fire over Moresby. Sergeant Brumby's account of the 'daisy cutter' raid on Seven Mile is told by Wilson, op. cit., p. 33, and Deane-Butcher, op. cit., pp. 48–50 recounts his terrible ambulance journey attempting to save the lives of the two army men.

Page 177 Peter Masters' recollections of the combat on 17 April are at AWM MSS 696.

Pages 180–82 The bombing raid on Rabaul on 18 April is described by Gamble, op. cit., pp. 144–6. The transcripts of Hineo Inetsugu's diary are at AWM 54 253/5/7.

Page 183 Deane-Butcher, op. cit., p. 72 tells the story of his inglorious role in the welcoming party for John Jackson on 23 April; Jackson's moving letter to his family thanking them for their support is in Jackson and Jackson, op. cit., p. 241.

Page 184 The account of the NGVR patrol that penetrated the Japanese defences to report on the work habits of the Tainan Air Group and the defences of the Lae aerodrome is at AWM 54 419/4/1.

Page 185 Paul Metzler's letter home is at NAA A705 166/27/711. Although drafted in April, the letter did not reach Australia until the following November.

CHAPTER NINE

Page 187 75 Squadron noted the visit of Charles Burnett in the unit war diary, see NAA A9186 95.

Page 188 Sakai, op. cit., pp. 119–23.

Pages 189–92 The account of Crawford's part in the action on 24 April is based on NLA Audio ID 2350320. Butler's account of the same combat is at AWM S00738.

Pages 193–6 The action on 26 April is described by Butler, ibid, and Whetters, AWM S00592.

Pages 197–8 Major Patrick Kelso's report on the life of an anti-aircraft gunner at Seven Mile is at AWM 54 31/2/19.

Page 198 Tucker recounted his melancholy talk with Dave Ellerton, and revealed his bitterness regarding the circumstances surrounding the burial of Ozzie Channon, in the interview held at AWM S00701.

Pages 200–1 Ibid for Tucker's account of the squadron meeting held on the evening of 27 April; Butler's recollections of the meeting are at AWM S00738. Stu Collie's more circumspect but still significant record of the meeting is in an unpublished collection of papers in the collection of Richard Deane-Butcher, titled 'Record of 75 Squadron at Port Moresby 1942—as compiled by Fl. Lt Stuart Collie'. David Campbell's poem critical of Charles Pearce was published by the *Sydney Morning Herald* on 10 August 1974.

Page 202 White, op. cit., p. 72. Events on 28 April were recorded by Peter Masters, see AWM MSS 723.

Page 203 White, op. cit., p. 73.

Page 205 An outstanding forensic analysis of the combat in which Jackson and Cox were killed was written by Claringbould, 'Who shot down John Jackson?'.

249

Page 208 For Munro's death, see Crawford NLA Audio ID 2350320, and Tucker AWM S00701.

CHAPTER TEN

Page 210 The story of Les Jackson and Deane-Butcher's beer on the Moresby waterfront on the eve of the Battle of the Coral Sea can be found in Deane-Butcher, op. cit., p. 79. The details of the 'banquet' to mark the handover between 75 Squadron and the American fighter units are based on Stuart Collie's unpublished collection of papers held by Richard Deane-Butcher.

Page 213 Gamble unconvincingly argues that the American B-26 aircrew gave up nothing of value during their interrogations, op. cit., pp. 181–2.

Page 215 The emotional story of Bill Parker senior farewelling his son Bill junior is at NAA A705 163/149/187. The details regarding the father's intervention to allow his son to enlist are on Bill junior's service record, NAA A9301 20343.

Page 216 For details of Hemsworth's last flight, see Gillison, op. cit., p. 519.

Page 217 Details of the strength of the Australian garrison at Port Moresby are from McCarthy, *South West Pacific: First Year, Kokoda to Wau*.

Pages 217–20 The post-war interrogations of Japanese servicemen involved in the deaths of the Hemsworth and Norman crews are at NAA B3476 336/1/1618.

Page 220 John Pettett recounts the ferry flight with 'Pop' Woods in which they heard the Battle of the Coral Sea unfold, see AWM S00515.

Page 222 See Deane-Butcher, op. cit., p. 85 for his flight out of Moresby on 9 May. Eric Feldt's estimate of the importance of Moresby can be found in his autobiographical history *The Coast Watchers*, p. 53. The American conclusion to the same effect is in Craven and Cate, *The Army Air Forces in World War II*, p. 447.

Pages 227–8 Lyrics to 'The Moresby Song' are held by Richard Deane-Butcher.

Page 229 Bruce Brown's recollections about the frosty reception he received on joining 75 Squadron at Kingaroy can be found at AWM S00583. See also Butler, AWM S00738.

Pages 229–30 The official assessments of Alan Boyd's health after the battle are on his service record, see NAA A9300 BOYD A.

Pages 232–3 The grievous experiences of the Wackett family in 1944 are drawn from Lawrence Wackett's autobiography *Aircraft Pioneer*, pp. 206–9.

Pages 233–4 The marvellous adventures of Paul Metzler are based on two articles he wrote for *Stand-To*, July–August 1963 and March–October 1964.

Pages 236–7 Rundle's work to locate the bombers flown by Erwin and Nicolay is at NAA A705 163/90/240 and NAA A705 163/134/15.

Page 237 See NAA A705 163/90/240 and NAA A705 163/134/15 for the experiences of the Hudson crews shot down on 3 March 1942.

Page 240 Scenes from the funeral in July 1950 are from Eames, *The Searchers*, pp. 50–1. Bill Parker's battle with the bureaucracy over the notice he received regarding the death of his son is at NAA A705 163/149/187.

Text credits

425/18/2 *History of New Guinea Air Warning Wireless Company*, Reproduced courtesy of the Australian Army.

779/3/3 HQ Allied Air Forces, SWPA– Directorate of Intelligence nos 2 to 6–Interrogation Reports, Moresby and Milne Bay Areas, 1942.

Bates, Bert. PR03185, Australian War Memorial Collection.

Brown, Bruce. (Transcript of Oral recording), Keith Murdoch Sound Archive, Australian War Memorial, S00583.

Bullard, Steven. *Japanese Army Operations in the South Pacific Area: New Britain and Papua Campaigns 1942–43* © Australian War Memorial, 2007.

Butler, Michael Seymour. (Transcript of Oral recording), Keith Murdoch Sound Archive, Australian War Memorial, S00738.

Deane-Butcher, Doctor William. Records from the Deane-Butcher Collection.

Downs, Ian. 'The New Guinea Volunteer Rifles 1939-1945: A History' © Pacific Press, 1999.

Eames, Jim. *The Searchers: and their endless quest for lost aircrew in the Southwest Pacific* © University of Queensland Press, 1999.

Huxley, Jim. 'New Guinea Experience: Gold, War and Peace' © Australian Military Publications, 2007.

Inetsugu, Hineo. 253/5/7 Captured documents Nos 58 and 74, Diaries of members of Kure No 3 Special Landing Party, Australian War Memorial Collection. Reproduced courtesy of the Australian Army.

Jackson, John. 'A Lot to Fight For' Ed. Patricia and Arthur Jackson.

Kelso, Major P. Report 54 31/12/19, Australian War Memorial Collection. Reproduced courtesy of the Australian Army.

Masters, P.A. *Shooting Down Zeroes*, MSS 734, Australian War Memorial Collection.

Metzler, Paul. 'Early Days' in A.E Minty, 'Black Cats: the real storys of Australia's long range Catalina strike force in the Pacific' © RAAF Museum, 1994.

Metzler, Paul. 'Recollections of A Catalina Pilot', Stand-To, Journal of the ACT RSL (July–August 1963).

National Archives of Australia, A705 163/150/132 Perrett, John A9301 20343 William Murdoch Parker, A9300, Boyd A, A705 166/27/711 Metzler, Paul.

Pettett, John Henry Stephen. (Transcript of Oral recording Flight Lieutenant), Keith Murdoch Sound Archive, Australian War Memorial, S00515.

Piper, John. Interviewed by Fred Morton, Fred Morton Collection, National Library of Australia.

RAAF Intelligence Summary Serial No. 76, 18th June, 1941.

Samurai! by Saburo Sakai, with Martin Caidin and Fred Saito © 1957. Reproduced with permission of Jeffrey Mackler.

Seekee, Vanessa. *Horn Island, In Their Steps* © 2001.

Tucker, Arthur Douglas. (Transcript of Oral recording Flight Lieutenant), Keith Murdoch Sound Archive, S00701.

Whackett, Sir Lawrence James.
Aircraft Pioneer: An autobiography © Angus and Robertson, 1972. White, Osmar. Green Armour © Penguin, 1991.

Wilson, David. *Seek and Strike: 75 Squadron RAAF 1942–2002* © Banner Books, 2002.

Yeowart, Robert Alfred. PR91/073, Australian War Memorial Collection.

Acknowledgments

This book would not have been completed without the generosity of others. Maurice Austin and Phil Vabre of the Civil Aviation Historical Society gave their time and resources freely. Michael Ewer and Meg Smith were meticulous copy-editors, before Janine Flew took a keen eye and a red pen to the final copy. The families of Australian aircrew involved in this story were especially kind and supportive, particularly Peter Tucker, Richard Deane-Butcher and Robert Whetters. Murdoch's Diana Hill believed in the project with enthusiasm from the start, and my agent Margaret Gee was, as always, a great advocate.

To each of them, many thanks. Finally, a quick review of the sources used for this book shows the unfortunate regularity with which families and enthusiasts have found it necessary to spend their own money publishing books and monographs to commemorate those who served in the air battle for New Guinea. To them, students of Australian history are indebted, and the author is grateful to those who gave permission to quote from their work. In particular, Patricia and Arthur Jackson provided permission to use copyright material from *A Lot to Fight For: The War Diaries of Squadron Leader J.F. Jackson DFC*.

Image credits

Australian War Memorial: p. 9 (AWM 009103), p. 43 (SUK 15175), Front cover and p. 51 (OG 0267), pp. 74–75 (P01797002), p. 117 (AWM 010176), Front cover and p. 118 (AWM 012737), p. 141 top left (AWM 127962), p. 141 (P00849_001), p. 153 (AWM 026642), p. 159 (P02865_002), pp. 206–207 (AWM 012720)

Maurice Austin: p. 40, pp. 84–85

National Archives of Australia: p. 25 NAA 7600544

Richard Deane-Butcher: p. 4, p. 89, p. 103 middle and right, p. 114, p. 130, p. 156, p. 190, p. 201, p. 204, p. 213, p. 223

Robert Whetters: Front cover and p. 196

Peter Tucker: p. 103 left, p. 176, p. 221 2/3rd Light Anti Aircraft Battery 197–8

Index

2/3rd Light Anti Aircraft Battery 197–8
2/5th Independent Company 217
2/22 Infantry Battalion 28
13th Field Regiment 217
23rd Heavy Anti Aircraft Battery 175
29 Radar Station 94, 139
30th Brigade 217
67 AASL Unit 93–4
75 Squadron: ability to scramble 139–40; assembly 105, 110, 113, 115–6; Bomana airfield 192; disease and hygiene 135–6; dogfighting tactics 187, 200–1; enlistments 99–102; entertainment 150–1, *156*; fishing 152, 210; formation flying *118*, 119; handover to Americans 210–1; Kingaroy 227–9; Kokoda action 163; Lae, attacks on 122, 123–7, 155, 167–8, 171–2; Port Moresby air battles. *see* Port Moresby; reconnaissance 139, 155, 161; reinforcement aircraft 142–3, 156; standing patrols 143–5, 189; training for Kittyhawks 105–6, 109, 110–1

A

aerodynamic theory 235–6
AIF, recall of 64–5
air raid planning 58–9
air raid shelters 54–5
Airacobras 156–7, 208
Anderson, Bruce 124
anti aircraft gunners 197–8
Archerfield airfield 113
Aritomo, Goto 17
Asanagi 83
Atherton, Geoff 122, 163, 192, 193, *196*
Australia 14–6, 66
Australian Air Board 78–9, 136–7, 145, 238, 240

Australian Army 13, 26, 28
Australian Army Medical Corps 91
Australian War Cabinet 34

B

Bailey, Ron 139, 149–50
Bankstown aerodrome 105–6, 110
Barwick, Ian 237
Bates, Bert 73, 76
Bathurst Island 60–1
Battle of Britain 11, 94, 139
Battle of Moresby 56
Battle of the Coral Sea 11, 211–2, 214–6, *218–9*, 220–1
Beaumont, Ern 70
Bell, Alexander Graham 107
Bensley, Nev 184
BHP 15, 22, 49
Birrell, Jim 81–2
Bismarck Sea 158, 233
Blakey, Ted 174
Boeing B-17 bombers 67–8
Bolitho, Bill 69, 70, 76, 240
bomb disposal 91–2
Bougainville 152, 158
Bower, H. C. M. 70
Boyd, Alan 182, 229–30
Brandon, Harry 68
Brannelly, Tom 82
Brereton, Guy 123, 178, 192, 202, 203
Brereton, Lewis 35
Brisbane airbase 67
Brown, Bruce 228–9
Brown, David Stuart 167, 168–9, 212–4, 238–40
Brumby, Harry 175
Bulolo Gold Dredging 22–6
Burnett, Charles 15, 16, 34–5, 47, 62, 71, 187
Butler, Michael 59–61, 105, 109, 189–96, 200, 208, 211, 229

C

Caldwell, Clive 109
Campbell, David 45–6, 201

Carmichael, Richard 68
Caroline Islands 13–4
Cass, Ian 237
Catalina flying boats 7, *9*, 234; Catalina A24-8 16–7, 35–6; destroyed in Port Moresby 73–6; training program 16
censorship 61–2
Channon, Oswald 171, 189–91, 199
Cherry, Bob 102
Chinese traders 22
Church, Ted 116, 119, 123, 131–4, 155
Churchill, Winston 11, 107
coastwatchers 140
Cohen, Julius (later Kingsland) 42–5, 68, 70–1, 227
Collie, Stu 129, 151–2, 200, 202–4, 210
Commonwealth Aircraft Corporation 22, 49, 120, 128
Cooktown 214
Cooper, Duff 44
Coote, Doug 9–10
Copas, Father Virgil 239–40
Coppin, Bill 237
Cowe, Bill 178, 189–93, 202, 203
Cowe, Bob 131
Cox, Barry 119, 120, 142–3, 155, 164, 202–5
Craigie, John 8–10
Crawford, Bob 60–1, 105, 109, 189, *196*, 208, 230–1
Creswell, Barney 174
Curtin, John 58, 64
Curtiss, Glenn 106–9
Curtiss P36 108

D

Daisabura, Dr Hosogi 235, 236
Darwin 60–2
Dauntless dive-bombers 158, 164, 171

253

Davenport, J. 102
Davies, Ally 110, 151, 171–2
Deane-Butcher, Bill: as 75 Squadron medical officer 132–3, 155, 175, 178–9, 183, 204; arrives in Port Moresby 122, 123; background 113–5; conditions at Port Moresby 135–6; later medical career 231; Les Jackson 197, 210; remains in Port Moresby 211; returns to Australia 221–2, 223; songs 150, 227–8
Dick, Doug 38–41
Don Isidro 60–1

E

Edwards, Bill 30–1
Elementary Flight Training School 113
Ellerton, Dave 198–200
Empire Air Training Scheme 103, 105, 174
Empire flying boats 11–2, 41
Erwin, Ken 78, 237
European plantation owners 52–3

F

Faletta, Charles 156–7
Feldt, Eric 53, 140, 222
flying boat invention 107
Fraser-Fraser, Stuart 173–4
Freeman, Albert and Essie 112–3
French Morocco 44
Fuchida, Mitsuo 61
Fujita, Nobuo 57, 59, 71–2, 225–6
Fukumara, Yataka 212

G

Gasmata 46, 50–2, 54, 77–8, 87
German Empire 13–4
German U-boats 44–5, 66, 187
Gibson, Bill 45, 187, 200, 204, 211
Gibson, Graham 48, 50, 51–2
Goad, Malcolm 27

Gort, General Lord 44
Granville, Richard 182
Green, Bob 154–5
Guadalcanal 212, 214, 224–5
Guinea Airways 21–3
Gunther, Carl 26

H

Hammond Island 91
Hardie, William 35–6, 79, 185
Havard, Stan 131, 142
Heath, Bert 26–7
Hemsworth, Godfrey 38–42, 201, 215–20
Higgins, Brian 38, 226
Hodge, Tom 102
Holliday, Lloyd 113
Holt, Jack 102
Horii, Major General 216–20
Horikoshi, Jiro 145–8
Horn Island 86–92, 119, 143, 237
House, A. T. 88–9, 90
Hudson bombers *see* Lockheed Hudsons
Hughes, Billy 13–4
Hurst, Rupert 90–1
Hutchinson, Lieutenant G. 7–10
Huxley, Jim 23–6

I

Imperial War Graves Commission 240
Inetsugu, Hineo 180–2
Iwasaki, Nobuhiro 88
Izumi, Hideo 205

J

Jackson, John: as 75 Squadron commander 116, 119, 122, 123–7, 143, 187; aided by Edmund and Arthur 166–7, 170, 172; Americans 157; background 116–8; film-maker 152; final combat 200–4; NGVR rescue 173–4; posted missing 163–5; returns to base 182–4; solo flights 139, 155, 161
Jackson, Les 153; as 75 Squadron flight commander 116, 136, 139, 155, 175, 178, 189, 199, 210; Butler 197, 229; crash-landing 157; John Jackson 170–1, 204; later career 231; remains in Port Moresby 211; returns to Australia 221; as 'wild child' 151–2
Japan: Australia, plans for 64–7, 86, 222; Australian reconnaissance 57, 59, 71–2; Greater Co-prosperity Sphere 160; intelligence 212–4, 216–7, 237; invasion fleet 208, 210; island-hopping campaign 65, 66; Japanese Naval Air Force 39; Tainan Air Group 158–61, 165–6, 184, 192; World War I 13–4
Jeffery, Pete 104, 105, 110, 113, 115, 119, 133
Jeffery, Rod 113
JN4 Jenny 107
June Bug 107
Junkers, Professor Hugo 21
Junkers aircraft 21–2
Junkers G31 22–3, 24–5

K

Kamikawa Maru 215
Katayama, Zenji 216
Kawai, Heihachi 97, 119
Kawai, Shiro 88
Kawanishi flying boats 46
Keen, Tom 7–11, 16
Keenan, Jim 81–2
Kelso, Patrick 197–8
Kerr, George 173–4
Kibble, Deste 239
Kikuchi, Keiji 127
Kingaroy airbase 227–9
Kingsford Smith, Charles 12
Kingsland, Richard 227 *see also* Cohen, Julius (later Kingsland)
Kingwell, Deryck 56, 77, 78, 82–3, 154–5, 226–7
Kittyhawks: diverted to Java 34–5, 64; as Hawker Hurricanes 90, 127;

INDEX

nicknames for 98; P40 design 108–9, 125, 148–9, 163; training program 105–6, 109, 110–1
Koch, Harold 53–4
Kokoda Track 11, 163, 217, 224
Komaki Maru 180–2
Korbosky, Mark 237
Koy, John 183

L

Lae 20, 69; 75 Squadron attacks on 122, 123–7, 155, 167–8, 171–2; 76 Squardron reconnaissance of 174; condition of base 158–9, 165–6; evacuation of 30–1; Japanese caste system 188; Japanese invasion of 81, 83, 86; NGVR reconnaissance of 183–4
Langslow, M. C. 79
Lauder, John 45
Laverton airbase 72
League of Nations 13, 14
Lerew, John Maynard 47–8, 49–54, 56, 78, 226
Levien, Cecil 20, 21
Lexington USS 83, 212
Lockheed Hudsons 28, 45–52, *51*, 77–8; Pratt & Whitney engines 49
Louisiade Archipelago 215–6
Luftwaffe 22
Lutz, Theron 180, 212–4, 238

M

McGrath, Daniel 86–7
McIntosh, Jack 136
McLauchlan, E. L. 237
McNicol, Sir Walter 32
Maeda, Yoshimitsu 205, 211
Manus Island 158
Mapos 173
Martin Marauder B-26 69
Mascot aerodrome 102
Masters, Peter 167–8, 177, 202, 203, 210, 211
Matson, Bill 129–31, 134–5, 208
Matsu Maru 216–20

media *see* press
Meng, Lewis 156–7
Menzies, Robert 98
Metzler, Mrs Kit 36, 137, 185, 233
Metzler, Paul 16–7, 35–6, 137, 233–5; prisoner of war 185, 235–6
Milne Bay 230
Mitaya, Commander 169
Mitsubishi F1M floatplanes 215
Mitsubishi Type 1 (Betty) bomber 81, 83, 97
Mitsubishi Type 86 (Nell) bomber 81
Mitsubishi Type 96 50
Mitsubishi Zeroes 15, 68, 73, 124–5; design of 145–9, 179–80; Maeda's wreck 205, *206–7*
Miyazaki, Gitaro 177, 224
Mizusaki, Captain 239
Moore, Alex 184
'Moresby Song, The' 227–8
Morrisey, Robert 87–9
Munro, Don 208

N

Nagatomo, Katsuaki 76–7
Neal, Ray 97, 98
Neosho 220
Netherlands East Indies 35
New Caledonia 66
New Guinea 12–4, 20, 222–4, 231
New Hebrides 231
New Zealand 66, 225
NGVR (New Guinea Volunteer Rifles) 26–7, 81–2, 129, 140–2, 173–4, 197; Lae reconnaissance 183–4
Nicolay, Arthur 78, 236–7
Nishizawa, Hiroyoshi 39–41, 88, 183, 188, 192, 193, 205, 225
Norman, Allan 214, *218–9*, 239, 240
Norton, Jim 110, 113

O

O'Connor, Ron 113, 143–5

O'Hea, Geoff 45
Oishi, Genkichi 89
Ok Tedi 22
Okabe, Nachei 169
Okada, Shigeaki 217
Ota, Toshio 225
Oyens, C. W. A. 235–6

P

Parer, Damien 205
Park, Bill 20
Parker, Bill 215
Parker, Bill senior 215, 238, 240
Pearce, Charles 42, 187, 200–1, 204
Pearl Harbour 83
Pedrina, Bill 48, 50, 52, 83, 201, 226
Pedrina, Jeff 48
Perrett, John ('Jackie') 79, 185
Pettett, John 99–*103*, 109, 122, 124–5, 127, 151, 152, 171, 220
Philippines 225
Phillips, Bob 184
Piper, John: 75 Squadron 116, 123, 126, 131, 139, 149, 192; enlistment 99, 103–4, 110, 111; John Jackson 183; Kokoda 163; Lae airbase attacks 167–8, 171–2; Milne Bay 230
Placer 22
Port Moresby: 75 Squadron arrives at 119–20; air battles over 69–70, 73–6, 119–20, 131–4, 139, 149, 156–8, 175–9, 182, 189–96, 203–5; Allied defence of 97–8; Americans in 156–8, 164, 208, 210–1; daisy cutters 175–9; garrison 67, 93–5, *100–1*, 139–40, 197–8; importance of 55–6; Japanese landing plans 216; Japanese plans for 65, 86; Japanese reconnaissance 97–8, 119–20, 139; observation posts 94–5, 139–42, *144*; Rouna Falls hospital 178–9; Seven Mile airbase 29

255

press 72, 90, 238
press propaganda 69–70

Q
QANTAS 11, 41, 42

R
RAAF (Royal Australian Air Force): 75 Squadron. *see* 75 Squadron; missing airmen 236–40
Rabaul: Allied bombing of 68–9, 70–1, 180–2; Japanese invasion of 17, 28–30, 34, 152; Simpson Harbour 38–41, *40*, 42, 45–6, 160; victims of Matupi 239–40
radar 94, 139
Radio Tokyo 136–7
RAF (Royal Air Force) 11, 49, 56, 139
Ramsay, Alan 132
Raynor, Garth 81–2
Red Cross Bureau 79, 137
Reed, Sanger 180, 212–4, 238
Rigby, Jack 32
Robertson, Norman 68
Rowe, Tom 8–10
Royal Flying Doctor Service 12
Royal Navy 14, 57
Rundle, Keith 236–7, 239
Russell, Jock 132–4

S
Sakai, Saburo 158–61, 166, 175, 177, 179–80, 188, 192, 193, 224
Sakai, Yoshimi 178
Salamaua 20, 23–6; aerial recognition photo *84–5*; evacuation of 31–4; Japanese attacks on 26–7, 30; Japanese landing at 81–3; observation posts 140–2
Sandford, Clarence 89–90
Sasai, Jun-ichi 180, 188, 224
Schwab, V. A. 183
Seymour, Robert 71
Sherman, Tom 91–2
Shoho 216, 220
Shokaku 220
Shortland Islands 154
Simpson, J. W. 237
Singapore 14, 57–8
Sloan, Lincoln 16
Smith, Ross and Keith 12
Solomon Islands 152, 158, 212
Soviet Union 66
Stock, Esther 31–4, *33*, 232
Sturdee, Vernon 64–5
Swann, Don 116
Sweeting, Bill 236
Sydney Eye Hospital 231
Sydney Harbour 57, 59

T
Thompson, Bob 16–7, 35–6, 233–5
Thursday Island 87, 90–1
Tiger Moth biplanes 102
Topping, Bill 183
Torres Strait 86–9, 90
Townshend, J. V. 154
Townsville airbase 67–8, 110, 115, 179, 213–4, *221*
Truk airbase 88
Tucker, Arthur 103, *176*, *221*; 75 Squadron 135, 178, 189–91, 200, 208; Ellerton 198–9; enlistment 98–9, 105–6, 109; flight to Evans Head 110–1; later career 231–2; returns to Australia 211
Turnbull, Peter 116, 122, 124, 125, 127, 132–3, 230

U
United States: aircraft industry 108; Australia 66–8, 179; bombing of 225–6; trans-Pacific routes 64–7
United States Navy 11
University of Sydney 231
Uto, Kazushi 224–5

V
Vandenberg, Richard 27
Vanuatu 231
Vial, Leigh 140–2, *144*, 149, 226

Volunteer Defence Corps 111–2

W
Wackett, Lawrence 119–20, 128, 232–3
Wackett, Wilbur 119, 124–9, 182, 232–3
Wau 20–1
Wauchope (NSW) 111–3
Whetters, Alan 106, 178, 192, 193, 196–7, 230
White, Osmar 55–6, 69–70, 73, 97, 202–4
Williams, Richard 12, 14–5, 48–9, 58
Wirraways 60, 87
Woods, Jeff 110, 143, 174, 220
Woods, John 167
World War I 12, 13
Wright, Orville and Wilbur 106

Y
Yamashita, Masao 203
Yeowart, Bob 28–31
Yirrkala Mission 90
Yokohama Maru 82, 83
Yorktown, USS 212, 220–1
Yoshida, Motosuna 68
Yoshii, Kyoichi 133–4
Yoshino, Satoshi 50, 52, 224

Z
Zeppelin airships 21
Zeroes *see* Mitsubishi Zeroes
Zuikaku 220